ZODIACAL COURSE

+

CURSO ZODIACAL

Bilingual - Bilingüe

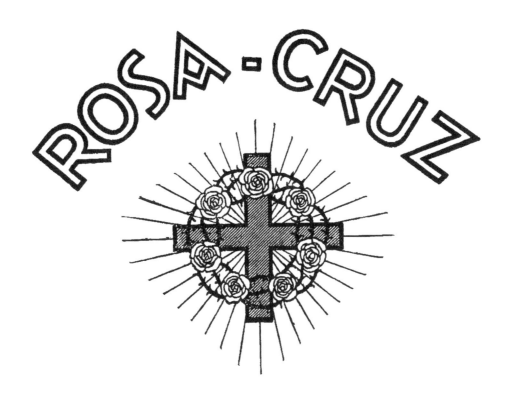

DR. ARNOLDO KRUMM-HELLER

"HUIRACOCHA"

1931

EDITOR'S NOTE:

The capitalization and punctuation have been duplicated (as much as possible) from the originals in order to preserve the Author's style. All pictures, footnotes, and the items in [brackets] have been added by the present Editor in order to help clarify and provide insight into this text's subject matter.

The materials from Arnoldo Krumm-Heller are from his *Revista Rosacruz* ["*Rose-Cross Magazine*"], which was published between 1927 - 1936. Some of the materials from Samael Aun Weor are transcriptions of recorded lectures (from *El Quinto Evangelio* ["*The Fifth Gospel*"]), published in 2000, as well as from his books.

Zodiacal Course = Curso Zodiacal

© 2018 by Daath Gnosis Publishing (A.S.P.M.)
ISBN 978-1-304-94405-4
All Rights Reserved. Printed in the United States of America.

Based on the writings of Arnoldo Krumm-Heller (Huiracocha).

First Edition December 2013 (Private printing)
Second Edition March 2014
Third Edition January 2016
Fourth Edition May 2017
Fifth Edition February 2018

ZODIACAL COURSE

DR. KRUMM-HELLER (HUIRACOCHA)

Archbishop of the Holy Gnostic Church.

1931[1]

---

[1] Editor's note: In March of 1929 Krumm-Heller began the distribution of his "Zodical Course", among the subscribers of his *Rose Cross Magazine* and this was completed in 1931.

Zodiacal Course by Arnoldo Krumm Heller (Huiracocha) **Curso Zodical** por Arnoldo Krumm Heller (Huiracocha)

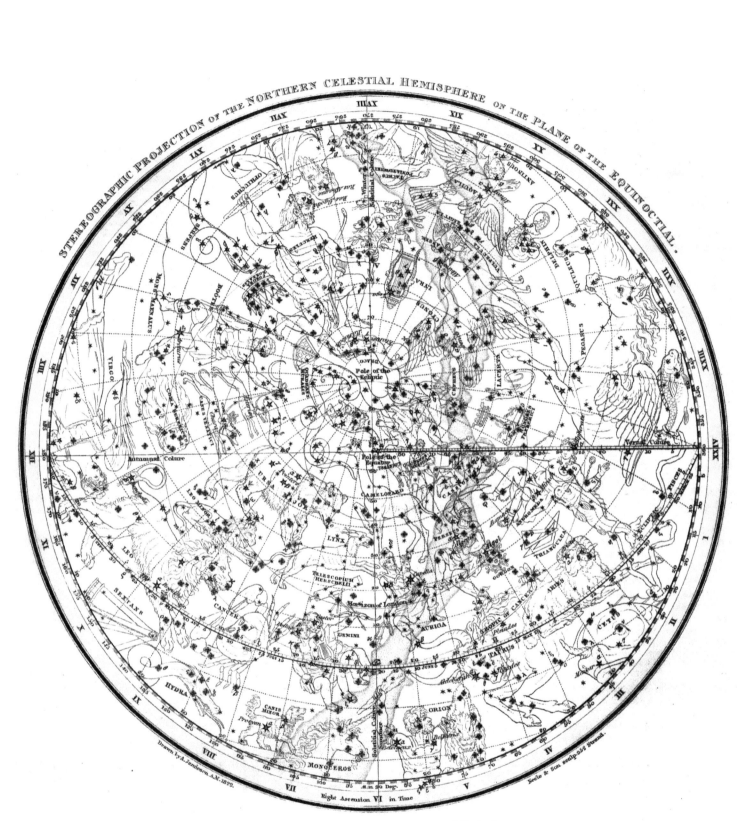

CONTENTS

Editor's Preface 7
   Extract from *The Rosecross Magazine*:
   Alchemy

Introduction 11

Daily Disciplines 20

   1) Aries 21
   2) Taurus 29
   3) Gemini 39
   4) Cancer 49
   5) Leo 57
   6) Virgo 67
   7) Libra 77
   8) Scorpio 85
   9) Sagittarius 97
   10) Capricorn 105
   11) Aquarius 117
   12) Pisces 125

Editor's Appendix 135

Extract from *El Quinto Evangelio* 137
   a) IN THE BEGINNING WAS THE VERB

Extracts from *The Magic of Silence* 141
   b) PERSONAL CONSECRATION
   c) CONSECRATION TO THE MASTER
   d) UNIVERSAL AND COSMIC FORCE
   e) INVOCATION TO THE LIGHT
   f) PRACTICE OF THE LIGHT

Extracts from *The Rosecross Magazine* 149
   g) LIGHT
   h) MORE LIGHT
   i) TANTRA
   j) TANTRA [Part 2]

Extract from *El Quinto Evangelio* 179
   k) [THE] POTENTIALITIES OF THE
      CREATIVE ENERGY

ÍNDICE

Prefacio del editor 7
   Extracto del *Revista Rosacruz*: Alquimia

Introducción 11

Disciplinas Diarias 20

   1) Aries 21
   2) Tauro 29
   3) Géminis 39
   4) Cáncer 49
   5) Leo 57
   6) Virgo 67
   7) Libra 77
   8) Escorpio 85
   9) Sagitario 97
   10) Capricornio 105
   11) Acuario 117
   12) Piscis 125

Apéndice del Editor 135

Extracto del *Quinto Evangelio* 137
   a) EN EL PRINCIPIO ERA EL VERBO

Extractos de *Magia del Silencio* 141
   b) CONSAGRACIÓN PERSONAL
   c) CONSAGRACIÓN AL MAESTRO
   d) FUERZA UNIVERSAL Y CÓSMICA
   e) INVOCACIÓN A LA LUZ
   f) PRACTICA DE LA LUZ

Extractos del *Revista Rosacruz* 149
   f) LUZ
   g) MAS LUZ
   h) TANTRA
   i) TANTRA [Parte 2]

Extract del *Quinto Evangelio* 179
   k) POTENCIALIDADES DE LA ENERGÍA
      CREADORA

Extracts from *The Rosecross Magazine* 185
  l) MAILBOX
  m) Alchemy [Part 2]
	Extractos del *Revista Rosacruz* 185
	  l) BUZÓN
	  m) Alquimia [Parte 2]

Extract from *El Quinto Evangelio* 191
  n) [THE] GNOSTIC VISION OF SEXUALITY
	Extract del *Quinto Evangelio* 191
	  n) VISIÓN GNÓSTICA DE LA SEXUALIDAD

Extracts from *The Rosecross Magazine* 199
  o) THE SECRET OF VOCALIZATION AND ITS ASTOLOGICAL CORRESPONDENCE IN THE HUMAN BODY (THE STARS AND THE ENDOCRINE GLANDS)
  p) EURYTHMOSOPHIA
	Extractos del *Revista Rosacruz* 199
	  o) EL SECRETO DE LA VOCALIZACIÓN Y SU CORRESPONDENCIA ASTROLÓGICA EN EL CUERPO HUMANO (LOS ASTROS Y LAS GLÁNDULAS ENDOCRINAS)
	  p) LA EURITMOSOFÍA

Kabalistic Supplement ....…............. 209
  q) Astral, Celestial and other Hebrew Alphabets
	Suplemento Kabalístico ....…............. 209
	  q) Astral, Celestial y otros Alfabetos Hebreo

Correspondence Courses

Of the Fraternitas Rosicruciana Antiqua, with [its] seat in Berlín-Keiligensee-Germany.

Dictated by its Commander for Hispanic-America

1st. **Esoteric Zodiacal Course.**—It makes available all the occult practices necessary to prepare the body so that the divine forces can penetrate into it. Its results are: physical Strength/Force and Health, Spiritual Power and Light. This Course constitute a revelation for oneself.

2nd. **Runic Course.**—What was yesterday [a] privilege of [the] initiated priests, especially in the application of the Magic of the Runes, is now in the hands of the sincere student. Its keys will permit one to reconstruct within oneself each of the characters of the **great Living Alphabet,** unfolding[3] the transcendental faculties and converting oneself into [an] arbitrator[4] of one's own destiny. With it one enters into possession of the most ancient dialect[5] of **Light.**

3rd. **Course of Ario-Egiptian Kabalah.**—[This] is the bridge that connects the previous courses. Enclosed [in it are] all the clues and Arcana of the practical Kabalah.

---

[3] Literally 'desenvolver' means "unfold, unwrap; unwind; disentangle, extricate; develop; expound, explain"
[4] Literally 'árbitro' means "arbiter, arbitrator; mediator; umpire, referee"
[5] Literally 'idioma' means "Language, tongue, idiom (mode of speaking peculiar to a dialect or language), lingo (the language peculiar to a nation or country), speech.", but we have translated this term as 'dialect' throughout this text for uniformity.

Zodiacal Course by Arnoldo Krumm Heller (Huiracocha)	Curso Zodical por Arnoldo Krumm Heller (Huiracocha)

Since[6] the key[7] for the **Kabalah** is the **Tarot** (deck[8] of 78 cards), the objective of this Course is to teach [the sincere student how] to read within each one of its 78 plates (which constitute the pages of the most ancient book of the world) wherein is contained all the mysteries of life: **Past, Present and Future,** which are in them; [afterwards you will] know enough to decipher it. The **Ario-Egyptian Tarot** is the perpetuator of our own western tradition.

Conditions—(previous promise of silence): ESOTERIC ZODIACAL COURSE (12 lessons) 3 dollars. RUNIC COURSE (18 lessons) 3 Dollars.

Course of Ario-Egiptian Kabalah, *free,* to all those who acquire a legitimate **Tarot** Deck, [the] cost of [which] is 5 Dollars; since these 78 colored cards are indispensable for study.[9] The only interest which is pursued in this Course is to divulge our own western tradition.

D o c t o r   K R U M M - H E L L E R
Berlin - Heiligensee - Jagerweg 10 - Germany.

Como la llave de la **Cábala** es el **Tarot** (naipe de 78 cartas), el objeto de este Curso es enseñar a leer en cada una de sus 78 láminas, que constituyen las páginas del más antiguo libro del mundo, donde se guardan todos los misterios de la vida: **Pasado, Presente y Futuro,** están en ellas; basta saberlo descifrar. El **Tarot Ario-Egipcio** es el perpetuador de nuestra propia tradición occidental.

Condiciones—(previa promesa de silencio): CURSO ESOTÉRICO ZODIACAL (12 lecciones) 3 dollars. CURSO RÚNICO (18 lecciones) 3 Dollars.

Curso de Cábala Ario-Egipcia, *gratis,* a todos los que adquieran un Naipe **Tarot** legítimo, cuyo precio es de 5 Dollars; pues sus 78 cartas en colores son indispensables para el estudio. El único interés que se persigue con este Curso es divulgar nuestra propia tradición occidental.

D o c t o r   K R U M M - H E L L E R
Berlín - Heiligensee - Jagerweg 10 - Alemania.

---

[6] Literally 'Como' means "as, like; by way of"
[7] Literally 'llave' means "brace; key; piston; lock; tap, faucet"
[8] Literally 'naipe' means "pasteboard, cardboard; playing card"
[9] Editor's note: This appears to be the 'Deutsches Original Tarot' or "Original German Tarot" first published by A. Frank Glahn (1865-1941) as a compliment to his book *Das Deutsche Tarotbuch* (1909) [*The German Tarotbook*]. This deck is also known under various other names including the 'Glahn Tarot', the 'Hermann Bauer Tarot' (from the name of a publisher of the deck, Hermann Bauer), and the 'Hans Schubert Tarot' (from the name of the apparent Designer and Artist who drew them according to Glahn's descriptions). Krumm-Heller refers to them as the 'Nordic Tarot' or 'Nordic Cards'.

[Inserted by the editor, not in the original]

Extract from
The Rosecross Magazine
Bogota, January 1937

Alchemy

Do not rely on the letter which kills but upon the spirit that gives Life.

The word "Alchemy" is derived etymologically from the egyptian [language] and signifies "prepare the black".[10]

The "black" refers to the universal substance.

The alchemists prepared a powder that some say was red. Cagliostro defined it thus. And others [defined it as] black.

What is certain is that what we make[11] today is blackish.

An alchemist who I see every day, makes an extract of tar[12] from[13] various vegetable substances and in this mixture is put a small quantity of [the] alchemical substance, of [the] philosophical stone; and then [the] result [is] a remedy that really cures all diseases.

It is called [the] **universal balsam**[14], and [one] takes[15] [a] few drops while fasting.

---

[10] Editor's note: Compare "In the Sacred Temples of the old Egypt of the Pharaohs, when the neophyte was at the point of suffering the ordeals of Initiation, a Master drew near to him and quietly murmured into his ear this mysterious phrase: "REMEMBER THAT OSIRIS IS A BLACK GOD"." from Ch.15 of *Tarot & Kabalah* (1978) by Samael Aun Weor.
[11] Literally 'hacemos' means "make; manufacture; create; construct, build; fashion, shape; compose; emit; wage, conduct (war, battle); prepare, do; cause; perform; effect; force; render; fabricate; behave, act in a particular manner; live through; be"
[12] Literally 'brea' means "tar, pitch"
[13] Literally 'y' means "and"
[14] Literally 'balsamo' means "balsam; balm, salve"
[15] Literally 'prescribe' means "prescribe, write an order form for medication; order remedies or treatment (about a doctor); recommend, advise"

Zodiacal Course by Arnoldo Krumm Heller (Huiracocha)	Curso Zodical por Arnoldo Krumm Heller (Huiracocha)

Consider my own experience.

I had suffered for years from [problems] with the intestines, such as diarrhea, with intervals of tenacious[17] constipation.

Neither my vegetarian diet[18], nor my hygienic exercises, nor anything [else], gave[19] me [any relief].

My belly was rebellious to everything [I ate] and [so] I lived with great care, because the slightest neglect[20] decomposed[21] me.

[When I] arrived in Germany, I took the first five drops and from that moment[22] [on] I have been as healthy as Twenty years ago.

Today, regarding the functioning of my belly, I am [like] a clock.

I saw another alchemist in Paris.

He had put lead in a retort and the mass was boiling.

He [then] took[23] the tip[24] of the blackish substance and instantly it converted the lead into gold.

This gold, which is made under certain constellations and formulas, attracts gold in general.

The universal substance is found everywhere and is the basis of everything.

Veamos mi propia experiencia.

Yo he sufrido durante anos de los intestinos, como diarreas, con intervalos de estrenimiento tenaz.

No me sirvieron ni mi regimen vegetariano, ni mis ejercicios higienicos, ni nada.

Mi vientre era rebelde a todo y vivia con sumo cuidado, porque el mas leve descuido me descomponia.

Llegue a Alemania, tome las primeras cinco gotas y desde ese instante estoy tan sano como Veinte anos atras.

Hoy dia, en cuanto al funcionamiento de mi vientre, soy un reloj.

Vi otro alquimista en París.

Había puesto plomo en un retorta y la masa estaba en ebullición.

Tomó la punta de la sustancia negrusca e instantáneamente se convirtió el plomo en oro.

Ese oro, que se hace bajo ciertas constelaciones y fórmulas, atrae el oro en general.

La sustancia universal se encuentra por todas partes y es la base de todo.

---

[17] Literally 'tenaz' means "tenacious, not easily loosened; stubborn, obstinate"
[18] Literally 'regimen' means "regime, government; diet, regimen"
[19] Literally 'sirvieron' means "serve, wait upon; attend; do; answer; help; issue"
[20] Literally 'descuido' means "omit; abandon; disregard, neglect"
[21] Literally 'descomponia' means "decompose, break down; disarrange; discompose; decompount; go bad"
[22] Literally 'instante' means "instant, moment; very short space of time"
[23] Literally 'Tomó' means " take, seize; accept; have; drink, eat; impound; touch; understand; draw; reduce; live on"
[24] Literally 'punta' means "bodkin; tip; end; extremity; peak; nib, pen nib; hustler"

It grows plants; [and] through its power we develop ourselves, and the transmutation of the stone[25] in the interior of the earth is due to the impulse of that substance which is diluted everywhere and that the alchemist unites, joins and preserves for their works.

"This substance is found everywhere, but if the occultist does not find it in himself [then he] will not find it anywhere [else]".

It is the raw material [or 'materia prima'], the origin of everything and is found everywhere, united with different substances.

The substance in which it is most easily isolated[26] is mercury, [and it is] for this [reason that] the ancients said that mercury was the source of everything.

The alchemists of the Middle Ages, had as [their] dogma: "Mercurius philophicum est nigredo perfecta".[27]

Then, as the alchemists observed the phenomena of nature, they found a significant relationship between their work and the formation of the fetus in the womb.

Forty days are required [for] the spermatozoa or spermatozoon to take human form.

Afterwards, the formation of the human being is achieved in seven divisions of [that] time[28] –in total 280 days–.

…

As it is above, so it is below; just as the cell is formed, man is [also] formed, and just as man is formed, the universe is [also] formed.

---

[25] Literally 'piedras' means "stone, rock; flint"
[26] Literally 'aísla' means "isolate, insulate; seclude, sequester, separate; cut off, shut off, maroon"
[27] Latin meaning something like: "[The] philosophical mercury is perfected blackness".
[28] Editor's note: 40 x 7 = 280

| Zodiacal Course by Arnoldo Krumm Heller (Huiracocha) | Curso Zodical por Arnoldo Krumm Heller (Huiracocha) |

The alchemists deduced a scientific cosmogony[29] from the whole human formation.

[What is] interesting, then, is the relationship of the human being to the planetary exterior; that is to say, the influence which the stars [and planets] exercise upon the growth, development and destiny of the human being.

For a long time astronomers were laughing when the alchemist-astrologer claimed[30] to find forces in the zodiac, since the astronomer was saying that this circle was imaginary and never real, until finally the advancement of spectral analysis[31] has shown that there are different rays in each one and [that there are also different rays] within the conjunction of the [zodical] signs which they believed to only be imaginary.

Huiracocha.

[End of editor's insert]

Los alquimistas dedujeron de la formación humana toda una cosmogonía científica.

Interesante es entonces la relacion del ser humano con el exterior planetario; es decir, la influencia que ejercen las estrellas sobre el crecimiento, desarrollo y destino del ser humano.

Por mucho tiempo los astronomos se reian cuando el alquimista astrologo pretendia encontrar fuerzas en el zodiaco, ya que el astronomo decia que aquel circulo era imaginario y jamas real, hasta que ultimamente el adelanto del analisis espectral ha comprobado que existen rayos diferentes en cada uno y entre el conjunto de los signos que se creian tan solo imaginarios.

Huiracocha.

[Fin de la inserción del editor]

---

[29] Literally 'cosmogonía' means "cosmogony, study of the origin and development of the universe"

[30] Literally 'pretendia' means "purport, pretend; profess, allege, claim"

[31] 'Spectral analysis' or 'Spectrum analysis' may refer to "Spectroscopy", a method of analyzing the properties of matter from their electromagnetic interactions. Spectroscopy is the study of the interaction between matter and radiated energy.

INTRODUCTION

Dear Disciple:

We invite you to think about [these] five words:

"LIGHT, LOVE, LIFE, KNOWLEDGE[32], TRIUMPH..."

Do not, dear brother, continue on until you have crystallized[33] the value of these five words in your mind.

The soul[34] of all matter is LIGHT.

The photon is the ultimate expression of the atom.

If you hit a flint with a piece of steel, [a] spark of light jumps[35] from both.

Rub two sticks [together] and a spark of light jumps [forth], rub your hands [together], you feel heat and although light jumps [forth], you don't see it.

When those who are in love [kiss and] are united [to one another at] the mouth, although you may not see it, they vibrate in light and life, the modification of their love attracts their opposing polarities for the generation of a new being...

Know that you can become like a God, knowing the science of Good and Evil, [and it] is then that[36] you will achieve your best triumphs.

---

[32] Literally 'Conocimiento' means "knowledge; privity; acquaintanceship; cognizance; fame; awareness, consciousness; conviction; shipping bill; expedition"
[33] Literally 'hecho carne' means "made [into] flesh"
[34] Literally 'alma' means "soul, spirit; heart; lifeblood"
[35] Literally 'salta' means "jump, leap; leapfrog; hop; dance; plunge; pounce"
[36] Literally 'cuando' means "when, at what time; at the hour which"

INTRODUCCIÓN

Querido Discípulo:

Empezaremos invitándote a pensar en cinco palabras:

"LUZ, AMOR, VIDA, CONOCIMIENTO, TRIUNFO..."

No pases adelante caro hermano sino has hecho carne en tu mente del valor de éstas cinco palabras.

El alma de la materia toda es LUZ.

El fotón es la última expresión del átomo.

Si golpeas un pedernal con un trozo de acero, de ambos salta una chispa de luz.

Frote dos palos y salta una chispa de luz, frota tus manos, sientes calor y aunque salta la luz, tú no la ves.

Besa a la amada y al unirse las bocas; aunque no le veas, vibran en luz y la vida, modificación del amor se atrae en sus polaridades opuestas para la generación de un nuevo ser...

Conociendo te vuelves como un Dios, sabes de la ciencia del Bien y del Mal, es entonces cuando haz alcanzado el mejor de tus triunfos.

But if these five words are the guardians of the arcanum[37] of the values of Knowledge, [then] before knowing [this arcanum] let us begin with the principle.

You have come to us and this proves[38] to us that [you] are not satisfied living with the religious teachings[39] that are professed [by so-called religious and esoteric groups], with the 'isms' that live [in many people's minds], and with your very own uncertain position within the environment[40] in which you find yourself[41].

Here is the reason for this ZODIACAL Course to reach your hands, it is a course that teaches you the "PAIN OF THINKING".

For the majority of the people, to think is to suffer the pains of childbirth[42].

Moreover, since childbirth establishes a relationship with conception and light is only given to that which has been conceived.

We beg you, therefore, to CONCEIVE in your mind of the hidden[43] foundation which connects[44] the five words that started the study of the present introductory lesson.

Knowing how to think is not repeating what others say.

Thinking is putting the mind in an edifying, constructive, and productive posture[45].

---

[37] Literally 'arcano' means "arcanum, arcane (known or understood by very few; mysterious; secret; obscure; esoteric)"
[38] Literally 'comprueba' means "check; test; test out; substantiate, prove"
[39] Literally 'principios' means "beginning, start, commencement; principle; element; entree, dish served as the main course of a meal"
[40] Literally 'medio' means "half; middle, center; means, method; environment; circle; midfielder"
[41] Literally 'desenvuelves' means "unfold, unwrap; unwind; disentangle, extricate; develop; expound, explain"
[42] Literally 'parto' means "childbirth, act of giving birth"
[43] Literally 'oculto' means "occult, hidden, covert"
[44] Literally 'entrañan' means "involve, entail; pose; carry"
[45] Literally 'actitud' means "attitude; posture; position, outlook, policy"

Zodiacal Course by Arnoldo Krumm Heller (Huiracocha)	**Curso Zodical** por Arnoldo Krumm Heller (Huiracocha)
It is to connect the MIND with the reality of things in themselves, their values, their foundations[46], their laws and their relations in the Cosmos.	Es conectar la MENTE con la realidad de las cosas en sí, sus valores, sus fundamentos, sus leyes y sus relaciones en el Cosmos.
Thinking is knowing for ourselves what exists in the Universe.	Pensar es conocer por nosotros mismos lo que existe en el Universo.
In order to think we need a set of tools which are the SENSES and the FACULTIES.	Para pensar precisamos de un conjunto de herramientas que son los SENTIDOS y las FACULTADES.
The SENSES are located in our physical body and require respective organs for their functioning.	Los SENTIDOS se encuentran ubicados en nuestro cuerpo físico y para sus funciones precisan de órganos respectivos.
As you know, there are five [of them]; you know their corresponding organs.	Ya lo sabéis, son cinco; conocéis ya sus órganos correspondientes.
The FACULTIES are many, but your RELIGION has taught you that they are limited to three: MEMORY, UNDERSTANDING[47] and WILLPOWER.	Las FACULTADES son muchas, aunque tu RELIGIÓN te ha enseñado que se limitan a tres: MEMORIA, ENTENDIMIENTO y VOLUNTAD.
The faculties are different from the senses in that their expression does not require certain organs.	Las facultades se diferencian de los sentidos en que para su manifestación no precisan de órganos determinados.
They live in a world apart and we can enumerate some of them [here]: MEMORY, UNDERSTANDING, WILLPOWER, IMAGINATION, FANTASY, INSPIRATION, CONCENTRATION, MEDITATION, REASONING, DISCERNMENT, INTUITION, AESTHETIC SENSE OF BEAUTY, etc., etc.	Viven en un mundo aparte y podemos enumerar algunas de ellas: MEMORIA, ENTENDIMIENTO, VOLUNTAD, IMAGINACIÓN, FANTASÍA, INSPIRACIÓN, CONCENTRACIÓN, MEDITACIÓN, RAZONAMIENTO, DISCERNIMIENTO, INTUICIÓN, SENTIDO ESTÉTICO DE LA BELEZA, etc., etc.
The hindustani teach in their philosophy about more than 26 faculties including clairaudience, clairvoyance, astral[48] unfolding[49], levitation and some others that we will gradually teach you.	Los indostánicos enseñan en su filosofía más de 26 facultades entre las que incluyen clariaudiencia, clarividencia, desdoblamiento consciente, levitación y algunas otras que poco a poco te iremos enseñando.

---

[46] Literally 'fundamentos' means "foundation; fundament, basis, base; reason, grounds; basic principles"
[47] Literally 'entendimiento' means "understanding, comprehension; mind, intellect; wit"
[48] Literally 'consciente' means "conscious, aware; alive", but this seems to be refering to astral projection
[49] Literally 'desdoblamiento' means "widening; splitting; unfolding"

| Zodiacal Course by Arnoldo Krumm Heller (Huiracocha) | Curso Zodical por Arnoldo Krumm Heller (Huiracocha) |

Think for YOURSELF [and] comprehend that the body you have, is not the same as the body that you feed, dress and love.

There is something within that body, even if you do not see it, [or] feel it.

It is not your body that desires, that yearns, no, THE CORPSE CAN NEITHER DESIRE NOR YEARN.

When SOMETHING has escaped from your body, your body does not vibrate in Love, nor [does it vibrate] in hate, nor [does it vibrate] in any desire.

We must name[50] this thing [that] escapes [from the physical body] somehow.

[Therefore] in order to understand this THING between YOU and ourselves, [and] because of its resemblance to the constitution and the appearance of the stars, we call it: [the] ASTRAL BODY[51].

For the functions that is performs [we call it]: [the] BODY OF DESIRES.

The Body of Desires or Astral Body, is perfectly rendered[52] in the Physical Body[53], which transmits the vibrations necessary [for it] to blindly obey the impulse of its desires, but between the Astral Body and the Physical Body there is an intermediary which we call: [the] VITAL BODY[54].

Piensa en TI comprende que tienes cuerpo, que no eres el cuerpo mismo, que lo alimentas, lo vistes y lo amas.

Hay algo dentro de ese cuerpo que aún cuando tú no lo ves, lo sientes.

No es tu cuerpo quien desea, el que anhela, no, EL CADÁVER NI PUEDE DESEAR NI ANHELAR.

Cuando ALGO se ha escapado de tu cuerpo, tu cuerpo no vibra en Amor, ni en odio, ni en deseo alguno.

Ese algo escapado vamos a denominarlo de alguna manera.

Para entendernos entre TI y nosotros a ese ALGO, por su semejanza a la constitución misma y al aspecto de los astros lo denominaremos: CUERPO ASTRAL.

Por las funciones que desempeña: CUERPO DE DESEOS.

Este Cuerpo de Deseos o Cuerpo Astral, se interpreta perfectamente en el Cuerpo Físico, al que transmite las vibraciones necesarias para que obedezca ciegamente al impulso de sus deseos, pero entre el Cuerpo Astral y el Cuerpo Físico, existe un intermediario al que denominaremos: CUERPO VITAL.

---

[50] Literally 'denominarlo' means "name, denominate; term; designate"
[51] The Astral Body (or Body of Desires) corresponds to #3 on the diagram.
[52] Literally 'interpreta' means "interpret; translate; perform, play; read"
[53] The Physical Body corresponds to #1 on the diagram.
[54] The Vital Body corresponds to #2 on the diagram.

It is precisely the Vital Body that provides[55] the corresponding energy for the physical and astral bodies, which is transformed into the Energy of the nervous system[56], as [an] intermediary for the respiratory functions and its secret correspondences, [the Vital Body] loads up[57] the two bodies [the Physical and Astral] with forces (in their two polarities) for the realization of the phenomenon known as: LIFE.

The objective of the present Course is to acquaint[58] you with a group of Natural laws [and] with their corresponding secrets for the development of these three Bodies.

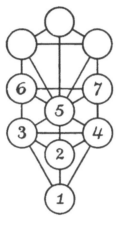

We have not spoken about other bodies, but as you can imagine, there is one for thinking with abstract concepts, one for thinking with the boundaries of the absolute, and finally there are other bodies that are directly related to the Divine Planes.

Matter and Energy are two inseparable terms.

Matter is condensed energy; Energy is subtle[59] [or refined] matter.

Modern Science has dismissed the absurd division between the two.

Nuclear physics has shown that matter is a constant carrier of energy and it is a force that can not live without form.

So Matter-Energy; Life-Form; Intelligence-Willpower, are three points which we invite you to think [about], as they are found manifest [in] Nature.

---

[55] Literally 'suministra' means "provide, supply; accommodate; furnish"
[56] Literally 'Energía nerviosa' means "nervous Energy"
[57] Literally 'cargan' means "load; burden; encumber; charge; stoke"
[58] Literally 'conocer' means "know, become acquainted, meet; learn; recognize; see; taste"
[59] Literally 'sutilizada' means "subtilized"

Es precisamente el Cuerpo Vital que suministra la energía correspondiente a los cuerpos físico y astral, que transformada en Energía nerviosa, por intermedio de las funciones de la respiración y sus secretos correspondientes, cargan a los dos cuerpos de fuerzas en sus dos polaridades para la realización del fenómeno conocido con el nombre de: VIDA.

El presente Curso tiene por objeto hacerte conocer un grupo de leyes de la Naturaleza con sus correspondientes secretos para el desarrollo de estos tres Cuerpos.

No te hemos hablado de otros cuerpos, pero ya puedes imaginarte, que hay uno para pensar dentro del concepto abstracto, otro para pensar dentro de los lindes de lo absoluto y por fin existen otros cuerpos que corresponden directamente a los Planos Divinos.

Energía y Materia son dos términos inseparables.

Materia es la energía condensada; Energía la materia sutilizada.

La Ciencia moderna ha despojado la división absurda entre la una y la otra.

La física nuclear nos ha comprobado que la materia es una constante carga de energía y que ésta es una fuerza que no puede vivir sin la forma.

Así pues Materia-Energía; Forma-Vida; Inteligencia-Voluntad, son tres aspectos que te invitamos a pensar, en como se encuentra manifestada la Naturaleza.

Zodiacal Course by Arnoldo Krumm Heller (Huiracocha)	Curso Zodical por Arnoldo Krumm Heller (Huiracocha)

The Law of evolution executes[60] the essential[61] changes [in nature] and in man [his] thinking creates what his body of desires longs for[62].

In four different worlds these three aspects unfold[63] [so as] to manifest the Work of Creation from the rock [or mineral], plant, animal, man and [even] God himself.

We also have two aspects according to Creation [which] are found in front of your senses, but you can not perceive them.

The first is the unmanifested world, [and] the second is the manifested [world]; this is the Visible World and the Invisible World.

To penetrate into the Invisible World and its mysteries is to acquire the Knowledge that neither the Religions, nor the Universities are concerned[64] with providing[65].

[From] your general knowledge of Science you are taught the division of our planet into two HEMISPHERES or perfectly equal halves.

The Northern or Boreal Hemisphere and the Southern or Austral Hemisphere.

The climatic conditions, geology and life[66] in general [are not the same and] consequently develop[67] differently in the two Hemispheres.

La Ley de la evolución efectúa los cambios indispensables y en el hombre el pensamiento crea lo que su cuerpo de deseos anhela.

En cuatro mundos diferentes estos tres aspectos se desenvuelven para manifestar la Obra de la Creación desde la roca, el vegetal, el animal, el hombre y Dios mismo.

Dos aspectos también tenemos según la Creación se halle delante de tus sentidos o no la puedes percibir con ellos.

El primero es el mundo de lo inmanifestado, de lo manifestado el segundo; esto es, el Mundo Visible y el Mundo Invisible.

Penetrar en el Mundo Invisible y en sus misterios es adquirir el Conocimiento que ni las Religiones, ni las Universidades se han preocupado de dárnoslo.

Tus conocimientos generales de la Ciencia te enseñan la división de nuestro planeta en Dos HEMISFERIOS o mitades perfectamente iguales.

El Hemisferio Norte o Boreal y el Hemisferio Sur o Austral.

Las condiciones climáticas, geológicas y vitales en general se desarrollan, por consiguiente de diferente manera en los dos Hemisferios.

---

[60] Literally 'efectúa' means "effect, execute; bring about, effectuate; prosecute"
[61] Literally 'indispensables' means "indispensable, requisite, essential, necessary"
[62] Literally 'anhela' means "yearn for, long for; aspire; covet"
[63] Literally 'desenvuelven' means "unfold, unwrap; unwind; disentangle, extricate; develop; expound, explain"
[64] Literally 'preocupado' means "preoccupied; worried, concerned; troubled, disquiet; qualmish"
[65] Literally 'dárnoslo' means "give; present; deal; produce, yield; cause; perform; say; take; teach; lecture; start, begin; overlook; surrender"
[66] Literally 'vitales' means "life, vital"
[67] Literally 'se desarrollan' means "grow; burgeon; proceed; develop"

Being [that] the earth constitutes a part of the immense organism called the Cosmos, it is logical to assume that there exists a relationship between our planet and the sun, the moon, and the other planets (its brothers).

Through a little observation [one can] deduce that there are four seasons[68] in the Northern Hemisphere, but only two in the Southern Hemisphere, [although only] as long as we are within the corresponding geographical zones [in the Southern Hemisphere], since, in this hemisphere there are the four seasons but precisely [at the] opposite time of [their] appearance [in the Northern Hemisphere].

For example, while in Argentina the 21st of september [is the] Beginning of spring.

When summer begins in Argentina [it is] on the 21st of December, [while] in Europe Winter begins.

In the rest of [South] America we have only two seasons: the dry [season] and the rainy [season].

Thus, there is one way to follow a Zodiacal Course that we must apply for South America [and the Southern Hemisphere, and another for the Northern Hemisphere].

In Europe the white caucasian race is predominant; in the South American Continent [it is] the [Native] Indian, so we are forced to conclude by saying that if the psychosomatic values are peculiar in each ethnic group, then the methods to awaken the sleeping faculties have to be in intimate relation with them and [with] the anatomic-psycho-physiological possibilities.

We do not care if your skin is white, your eyes are blue and you hair is blonde or if one parent, or both, are of south american descent.

---

[68] Literally 'estaciones' means "station; season; time"

For you these lessons have been precisely adapted, [just] as for your brothers with black hair, cinnamon skin and jet-black eyes

Our glorious predecessors[69] divided South America into four distinct parts which assembled [together] we designate [as] TAHUANTINSUYO.

Sages, like those from other Continents, knew how to orient themselves and caused their world to be divided by an immense and luminous imaginary cross, and engraved the four cardinal points, North, South, East and West, which they called in their dialect[70]: CHINCHASUYU, COLLASUYU, ANTISUYU and CUNTISUYU.

It should be Noted that our predecessors established the East as the main point of orientation; for the Europeans, according to the signaling of the magnetic compass it is the North, just as the sunrise was the primordial point for the aboriginal astronomers.

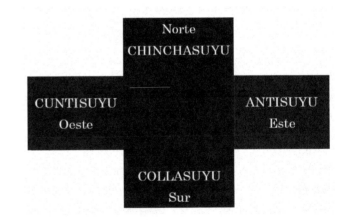

The astronomical year began in TAHUANTISUYO when CHONTARURO began to flourish, precisely when entering the 21st of september, [with] the sun in the cardinal sign of Libra.

---

[69] Literally 'antepasados' means "forefathers, ascendants, antecedents, ancestor, predecessor, progenitor"
[70] Literally 'idioma' means "Language, tongue, idiom (mode of speaking peculiar to a dialect or language), lingo (the language peculiar to a nation or country), speech.", but we have translated this term as 'dialect' throughout this text for uniformity.

We have already said that this course has as its objective[71] to develop the faculties and senses and to establish a Real harmony between the physical Body, the Vital [Body] and the Astral [Body].

It is, therefore, the hour[72] to communicate these[73] secrets to you one by one in the [appropriate] time on one's [cosmic] journey, which will begin with the next lesson.

Dr. A. Krumm Heller.

Hemos dicho ya que este curso tiene por objeto desarrollar las facultades y sentidos y establecer una Real armonía entre el Cuerpo físico, el Vital y el Astral.

Ha llegado, pues, la hora de comunicarte sus secretos uno a uno en el tiempo de su recorrido que iniciaremos en la próxima lección.

Dr. A. Krumm Heller.

---

[71] Literally 'objeto' means "object, thing; goal, purpose; exhibit; single"
[72] Literally 'hora' means "hour; certain time of day; term; tour"
[73] Literally 'sus' means "its; her; his; their; your"

DAILY DISCIPLINES:[74]

- Personal Hygiene.
- Sign of the Cross.
- Prayer: from "Personal Consecration".
- Prayer: "Consecration to the Master".
- Prayer: "Solar Logos".
- Relaxation Exercises.
- "Exercise of the Light".
- "Zodiacal Exercise".
- "Retrospective Exercise".

DISCIPLINAS DIARIAS:

- Higiene Personal.
- Señal de la Cruz.
- Oración: de "Personal Consagración".
- Oración: "Consagración al Maestro".
- Oración al: "Logos Solar".
- Ejercicio de Relajación.
- "Ejercicio de la Luz".
- "Ejercicio Zodiacal".
- "Ejercicio Retrospectivo".

---

[74] Some of these Prayers and Exercises are given in *The Magic of Silence* and can be found in the Editor's Appendix

ARIES

Dear Disciple:

You've spent years studying the Rose Cross Magazine[75], and have probably been in correspondence with me and [so there has been] enough time in order [for you] to form your own concepts and a clear judgement[76] of what our Philosophy is, which we have always said that is practiced in distinguished[77] degrees.

Similarly[78], if you know our Ritual, observe that we repeat three times that "Our Law is LIGHT, LOVE, LIFE, LIBERTY AND TRIUMPH…"

Just meditate for an instant upon the meaning of these five words so as to deduce that everything that we could [ever] want is contained within them.

But if I give you a Course, if I put you at the beginning of a practical and straight path, it will not be possible to start at the highest [point], without the word that is at the center and which makes us swing[79] into balance[80].

This is the word pronounced by the Second Vigilant.

Then we will go[81] to what the First Vigilant expresses, and finally to what the Master says…

---

[75] Editor's note: This was a magazine put out by the Author about Rosicrucianism from 1927 until his death in 1949.
[76] Literally 'juicio' means "judgment, act of judging; forming of an opinion; ability to judge, good sense; trial"
[77] Literally 'eminente' means "eminent (high in station, rank, or repute; prominent; distinguished)"
[78] Literally 'asimismo' means "similarly, in the same manner, likewise"
[79] Literally 'oscilar' means "oscillate, vary regularly between two positions"
[80] Literally 'oscilar la balanza' means "oscillate [on] the scales"
[81] Literally 'ascendiendo' means "ascend, rise; promote, advance; elevate; prefer; total"

ARIES

Querido Discípulo:

Ya llevas años estudiando la Revista Rosa Cruz, y probablemente habrás tenido correspondencia conmigo y tiempo sobrado para formar tu propio concepto y un claro juicio de cuanto es nuestra Filosofía, de la que siempre dije que es práctica en grado eminente.

Si conoces asimismo nuestro Ritual, observarás que por tres veces se repite que "Nuestra Ley es LUZ, AMOR, VIDA, LIBERTAD Y TRIUNFO"…

Basta meditar un instante sobre el significado de estas cinco palabras para deducir que todo cuanto podemos desear se encuentra encerrado en ellas.

Pero si he de darte un Curso, si he de colocarte en el comienzo de un sendero práctico y rectilíneo, no va a ser posible comenzar por lo más elevado, sino por la palabra que está en el centro y que hace oscilar la balanza.

Es la palabra que pronuncia el Segundo Vigilante.

Luego iremos ascendiendo a lo que expresa el Primer Vigilante, y por último a lo que dice el Maestro…

Zodiacal Course by Arnoldo Krumm Heller (Huiracocha)	Curso Zodical por Arnoldo Krumm Heller (Huiracocha)

In the beginning, Life brought about[82] the genesis of matter.

Life was created[83] from itself.

Life is the Light that blooms from the same Vital Fire that separates itself into its particles.

But as these particles were already Light in their formation and Life at the same time, and had their origin in the First Cause, [it is a] consequence, then, that the Light in itself is God[84]...

Nonetheless, let's cut out this preamble to enter into the real practice.

Our Life we know is not just that we are a Superior Animal whose sole purpose is to eat, to travel through the world, to systematically procreate and to operate businesses for our welfare.

You have to think furthur; you must realize that we are Angels, that we are shackled Gods, subjects in the bottom of a cloister[85], and that the purpose of our Life is to liberate ourselves, to free ourselves[86] from those bonds and to awaken within ourselves all the potential that we [have] enclosed[87] [within].

Archimedes said: "Give me a point of support and I will move the world."

Well, then, this point of support is what I can offer you, good Disciple, if we can agree on our assessments[88].

En un principio, al operarse el génesis de las cosas, fue la Vida.

La Vida creóse de si misma.

La Vida es Luz que brotó del mismo Fuego Vital al separarse sus partículas.

Pero como estas partículas fueron ya Luz en su formación y Vida al mismo tiempo, y tuvieron su origen en la Causa Primera, resulta, pues, que la Luz en sí es Dios mismo...

Sin embargo, cortemos aquí este preámbulo para internarnos en la verdadera práctica.

Nuestra Vida nos hace conocer que no somos solamente un Animal Superior cuyo exclusivo objeto sea comer, transitar por el mundo, procrear por sistema y operar negocios para nuestro bienestar.

Hay que pensar más; es forzoso darse cuenta de que somos Ángeles, de que somos Dioses encadenados, sujetos en el fondo de un claustro, y que el objeto de nuestra Vida es liberarnos, desasirnos de esas ligaduras y lograr el despertar en nosotros de todas las potencialidades que encerramos.

Arquímedes decía: "Dadme un punto de apoyo y moveré a mi voluntad el mundo".

Pues, bien, ese punto de apoyo yo te lo puedo ofrecer, buen Discípulo, si nos ponemos de acuerdo en nuestras apreciaciones.

---

[82] Literally 'operarse' means "operate, run, work; operate on; bring about, effect"
[83] Literally 'creóse' means "create, make; invent, originate; develop; launch; found, establish"
[84] Literally 'Dios mismo' means "God himself"
[85] Literally 'claustro' means "cloister (a place of religious seclusion, as a monastery or convent; any quiet, secluded place)"
[86] Literally 'desasirnos' means "to disengage ourselves"
[87] Literally 'encerramos' means "enclosed, shut in; imprisoned, locked up/in, jailed; confine; encase, box up; include"
[88] Literally 'apreciaciones' means "appreciation; appraisal, assessment; estimate, appraisement"

For example, if for you a thing is blue, while I see [it as] green, [then] it will not be possible for us to agree if [we] are trading goods[89], but if we start from the same point of view, recognizing that everything we are doing is infinitely more serious than comparing goods, then we can begin.

Look, each machine has its lever[90], its rudder[91], from where it is managed, and our organism (which is a really complicated machine) also has its [own lever].

Here is the point of Archimedes where we can support[92] [ourselves].

Then, if we are a duality of Soul and Body, and [if] it is precisely in the Soul where our conduct[93] resides, [then] we need to find the point of contact between them, and this is only found in the Grand Sympathetic Nervous System.

The Fluidic Body, we could say, lives in the subconscious, and the conscious vital part is only its reflection.

This subconsciousness, is a kind of lens[94] through which man can see his deeds[95] that, in general, escape from his consciousness.

That is to say, the Fluidic Body does not have willpower, on the contrary, [it] reacts upon all the impressions that are sufficiently strong, [and] they can either be started by ourselves or by [someone else's] suggestion, or even by self-suggestion.

---

[89] Literally 'adquirir géneros se trata' means "acquire goods to trade"
[90] Literally 'palanca' means "lever; crowbar; handle; stockade; springboard; pull, influence; toggle"
[91] Literally 'timón' means "rudder; helm"
[92] Literally 'apoyar' means "lean, rest against; recline; hold up, prop up; support, prop; sustain; underwrite"
[93] Literally 'actuación' means "action, conduct, behavior; performance, operation; showing; proceedings"
[94] Literally 'objetivo' means "target, objective, aim, goal"
[95] Literally 'actuaciones' means "performance, show, presentation; execution; act, deed; act of presenting an artistic work to an audience"

Por ejemplo, si para ti una cosa es azul, mientras yo la veo verde, no será posible que acordemos si de adquirir géneros se trata; pero si partimos del mismo punto de vista reconociendo que todo lo que nos ocupa es infinitamente más serio que comparar géneros, entonces podemos comenzar.

Mira, cada máquina tiene su palanca, su timón, desde donde se le maneja, y nuestro organismo, que es una verdadera maquina complicada, tiene también el suyo.

He aquí el punto de Arquímedes donde nos podemos apoyar.

Luego, si somos una dualidad de Alma y Cuerpo, y es precisamente en el Alma donde reside nuestra actuación, hay que buscar el punto de contacto entre ambos, y este sólo lo hallamos en el Sistema Nervioso del Gran Simpático.

El Cuerpo Fluídico, llamémosle así, vive en el subconsciente, y la parte vital consciente es solamente su reflejo.

Esa subsciencia, es a modo de un objetivo mediante el cual puede el hombre ver las actuaciones de si mismo que, por lo general, escapan de su consciencia.

Es decir, el Cuerpo Fluídico no tiene voluntad, todo lo contrario, reacciona sobre todas las impresiones que sean lo suficientemente fuertes, bien sea que éstas partan de sí mismo o de la sugestión, o por la autosugestión misma.

We have a kind of Mechanical[96] Willpower and [we also have] a Conscious Willpower.

The first we call the subconscious [willpower], and we seek to establish a bridge where the two connect.

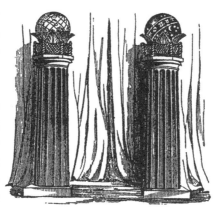

Two very strong manifestations [that are] like two great columns in our lives are HUNGER AND SEXUAL DESIRE, [these are] factors which end up[97] governing[98] the elemental man.

The desire to nourish oneself and to cohabitate reside in every atom, because cohesion[99] and sustenance[100], are nothing but the result of hunger and love.

What is our Life in itself? this has not yet been defined.

One could say that our personal life is [a] constituent[101] part of the Universal Life and that this manifests itself through Light and Heat, although[102] at first[103], this is [only perceived as] the Light [that] flows[104] from a Spiritual Sun.

From that Light or Spiritual Sun everything, the entire Creation, is made.

Tenemos una especie de Voluntad Motriz y una Voluntad Consciente.

La primera la podemos llamar subconsciente, y hemos de buscar establecer un puente donde ambas conecten.

Dos manifestaciones muy fuertes como dos grandes columnas en nuestra vida, son EL HAMBRE Y EL DESEO SEXUAL, cuyos factores vienen a regir, al hombre elemental.

El deseo de alimentarse y cohabitar reside en cada átomo, porque la cohesión y el sostenimiento, no son más que una resultante de hambre y amor.

Lo que es nuestra Vida en si, aún no se ha podido definir.

Solo diríamos que nuestra vida personal, es parte integrante de la Vida Universal y que ésta se manifiesta mediante la Luz y el Calor, aunque en primer término, está la Luz como dimanación de un Sol Espiritual.

De esa Luz o Sol Espiritual se ha hecho todo, la Creación entera.

---

[96] Literally 'Motriz' means "motive, moving; motor; driving"
[97] Literally 'vienen' means "come; reach; arrive; result from; happen, occur; infiltrate; settle; land"
[98] Literally 'regir' means "govern, rule; manage; determine"
[99] Literally 'cohesión' means "cohesion (the act or state of cohering, uniting, or sticking together)"
[100] Literally 'sostenimiento' means "sustenance (means of sustaining life; nourishment)"
[101] Literally 'integrante' means "integrant (making up or being a part of a whole; constituent)"
[102] Literally 'aunque' means "though; although, even though; while; as"
[103] Literally 'en primer término' means "firstly, primarily, first of all, in the first"
[104] Literally 'dimanación' means "Act of springing or issuing from, origin; flow, move along smoothly, stream"

When we eat, we create new particles in our blood and in our tissues, and when we cohabitate[105], we convert ourselves into creators, even when this creation is not conscious because we are drawn[106] by a desire.

Nonetheless, we suspect[107] that, behind those desires or impulses, there are divine forces[108].

We therefore need everything to become conscious, that is to say, [if] everything that is in us is [either] unconscious or subconscious, then, if our personal lives and our subconsciousness form a part of the Cosmic Life and the [Cosmic] Subconsciousness, then our consciousness is also [a] part of the Cosmic Consciousness which is the Spiritual Light, and, consequently, perfectly conscious.

There is a Law that says: "Only the same or similar will comprehend."

This is the reason why the material part of our brain can never comprehend spiritual things.

For this the Disciple needs to know themselves and sense their spirit, that is to say, [they need to sense themselves] living in a body and not [as] the body itself.

First of all the occultist [should] reveal[109] to themselves all their defects, without lies[110] and with true honesty.

---

[105] Literally 'cohabitamos' means "coexist; cohabit (live together and have a sexual relationship without being married)"
[106] Literally 'arrastrados' means "drag, pull along; carry away; win over, sway;"
[107] Literally 'sospechamos' means "suspect, imagine to be so, believe to be true"
[108] Literally 'existen fuerzas divinas' means "divine forces exist"
[109] Literally 'dijera' means "say, utter; tell; call; mention; recite"
[110] Literally 'engaños' means "deceit, double cross, betrayal; spoofing"

Here is the first practice as well: To occupy[111] oneself every night, for least five minutes, with one's own defects, thinking of them and making the most fervent promise to amend[112] them.

There is a Judge within[113] ourselves, but [we] do not hear its voice.

We are deaf and do not hear the excitement[114] of our own nerves.

We need to begin by sitting comfortably with the eyes fixed on a specific[115] point, without making a single movement or blinking, in order to achieve a complete relaxation of our muscles.

To achieve [this], even [if it is just] for a few minutes, we [should] transform[116] ourselves into this point itself, which is complete peace and tranquility.

[This] is the first step in order to get[117] to Shamadi[118] or sleep which is provoked [by] the Initiate, through which one reaches, in five minutes, superior forces [which are] greater than ten hours of regular sleep.

He aquí la primera práctica también: Ocuparse cada noche, al menos durante cinco minutos, en los propios defectos, pensando en ellos y haciendo la más ferviente promesa de enmendarse.

Hay dentro de nosotros un Juez, pero no escuchamos su voz.

Estamos sordos y no le oímos por la excitación de nuestros nervios.

Es preciso que comencemos por sentarnos cómodamente con la vista fija en un punto determinado, sin hacer un sólo movimiento ni pestañear, como para lograr un relajamiento completo de nuestros músculos.

Así lograremos, siquiera durante algunos minutos, convertirnos en ese punto mismo que es todo paz y tranquilidad.

Es el primer escalón para llegar al Shamadí o sueño que se provoca el Iniciado, mediante el cual se alcanza, en cinco minutos, fuerzas superiores a diez horas de sueño ordinario.

---

[111] Literally 'Ocuparse' means "occupy, live in; take up, go about, undertake, set about, deal with"
[112] Literally 'enmendarse' means "reform, amend; go straight"
[113] Literally 'de' means "of; about; from; by; at; with"
[114] Literally 'excitación' means "exciting, thrilling, stirring, provoking, causing excitement"
[115] Literally 'determinado' means "resolute, determined; specific, particular; appointed"
[116] Literally 'convertirnos' means "transform, convert; proselytize"
[117] Literally 'llegar' means "arrive, come; reach; roll along; land; immigrate; invade; get; travel; vaporize"
[118] Literally 'Shamadí' means "Shamadi (Samādhi in Hinduism, Buddhism, Jainism, Sikhism and yogic schools is a higher level of concentrated meditation, or dhyāna, which transcends the realms of body, intellect and emotions, and where the mind becomes silent.)"

With this practice we also get charged[119] with strength[120] and power, but it is necessary that in our subconsciousness we carry this intention[121], however slight: to fill[122] ourselves with Spiritual Light.

Then, immediately, we should go to the opposite pole, that is to say, to educate and dominate our willpower suggesting [to] ourselves the idea: I AM, I WANT/WILL[123].

The Great All, the Cosmos, is a perennial[124] rhythm and breathes in a special rhythm.

Let us, therefore, breath deep seven [times] always thinking of the penetration of the air through the nose, [and that] entering with[125] it [is] all the life, all the Light, and [that it is] charging us as if we were an accumulator.

Then, and in order for it to proceed[126] within ourselves, we raise our hand[127], but not in a state of laxity rather [in a state] of tension, moving the head forward seven times, backward seven times, seven times to the right, seven times to the left, rotating[128] the neck [and head] seven [times] to the left side and seven [times] to the right.

Con esta práctica llegamos también a cargarnos de fuerza y poder, pero es necesario que en nuestro subconsciente llevemos el deseo, aunque sea leve, de llenarnos de Luz Espiritual.

Luego, inmediatamente, debemos acudir al polo opuesto, es decir, a educar y dominar nuestra voluntad sugiriéndonos la idea de: YO SOY, YO QUIERO.

El Gran Todo, el Cosmos, es un ritmo perenne y respira dentro de un ritmo especial.

Hagamos nosotros, pues, siete respiraciones profundas pensando siempre que, al penetrar el aire por la nariz, entra por ella toda la vida, toda la Luz, y nos carga como si fuéramos un acumulador.

Luego, y para que actúe en nosotros, levantemos la mano, pero ya no en estado de laxitud sino de tensión, moviendo la cabeza siete veces hacia delante, siete hacia atrás, siete hacia la derecha, siete hacia la izquierda, siete dando vueltas al cuello por el lado izquierdo y siete por el derecho.

---

[119] Literally 'cargarnos' means "load; burden; encumber; charge; stoke; oppress; carry; plow; attack, assault; lean, incline; pester, annoy; veer, change direction; crowd together"
[120] Literally 'fuerza' means "strength, quality of being strong, might; durability; determination, resolve; effectiveness; intensity"
[121] Literally 'deseo' means "desire, wish; want; will; yearning"
[122] Literally 'llenarnos' means "fill; cover; pack; stuff; crowd; occupy; equate"
[123] Literally 'QUIERO' means "want, will; wish; like; feel like"
[124] Literally 'perenne' means "perennial; enduring; perpetual; everlasting; continuing; recurrent"
[125] Literally 'por' means "for, in order to; on behalf of; because of; by; via, by way of; to; at; after; around; along"
[126] Literally 'actúe' means "act, perform; play; appear; operate; proceed; sit"
[127] Editor's note: It is unclear which hand is indicated, but if we can choose, then let's pick the right.
[128] Literally 'vueltas' means "walking; detour; round; turn; spin; change; revolution"

Let's do these practices with the intention of this Light first acting upon our head, upon the part of Aries, the first Constellation of the Zodiac, [and] then doing a concentration in which we bring the mind to the front [of the head] thinking that [there] exists a Gland there ENTIRELY[129] [MADE OF] LIGHT.

Let's continue with the mind moving[130] to the Eyes, the Nose, the Mouth –center of language– and [next] we concentrate[131] intensely upon the structure[132] of our Throat, then [we] direct[133] this mental current[134] to the Ears.

So we meditate on the five senses, all together in the head.

These practices which correspond to Aries, must be constantly done within [the] four weeks during which [you] should keep [them] up[135].

Hagamos estas prácticas con la intención de que esa Luz actúe primero sobre nuestra cabeza, sobre la parte de Aries, la primera Constelación del Zodíaco, haciendo luego una concentración en que llevemos la mente a la frente pensando que existe allí una Glándula TODA LUZ.

Sigamos con esa mente plástica a los Ojos, a la Nariz, a la Boca –centro del lenguaje– y pensemos intensamente sobre la construcción de nuestra Garganta, encaminando luego esta corriente mental hacia los Oídos.

Así meditaremos en los cinco sentidos, todos reunidos en plena cabeza.

Estas prácticas que corresponden a Aries, deberán hacerse constantemente hasta dentro de cuatro semanas en que debes seguir.

---

[129] Literally 'TODA' means "all; whole, entire; every, each; indiscreet; any"
[130] Literally 'plástica' means "plastic, flexible, pliant; expressive;"
[131] Literally 'pensemos' means "think, deliberate, conceive in the mind; believe; contemplate, consider; ponder, reflect"
[132] Literally 'construcción' means "construction; erection, building, structure"
[133] Literally 'encaminando' means "guide, direct; route"
[134] Literally 'corriente' means "current, flow (of water, electricity, etc.); tendency, drift; tide; swim; rain"
[135] Literally 'seguir' means "follow, keep track of; chase; pursue; continue; shadow; keep; run"

TAURUS

Dear Disciple:

Impatiently have you longed [for] the second part [of this Course], but it was good that you had more time in order to [do] the first preparatory exercises.

Ancient Astrology says that the life within us is nothing more than a struggle[136] between Venus and Mars.

[These are the] two polarities that try[137] to equilibrate themselves, and if we observe the location of our Endocrine Glands [then] we will see that there are always two that are near[138] each other, and this happens even in the head, in which [the] Epiphysis [or Pineal gland] and [the] Hypophysis [or Pituitary gland] are very close to each other.

Then we will see the same thing in the neck with the Thyroid and Epithelial Bodies[139] [or Parathyroid Glands] and [the same is true] throughout the rest of the body; [these] two poles [are] in eternal action and reaction.

The Planet Mars is the one that acts in Aries, the head, and Venus with Taurus follows in the neck. There exists, then, a struggle between the head and neck.

One could say that Venus has closed the way to Mars, and that Mars, in its turn, defends itself in the neck against the influences that rises from below.

---

[136] Literally 'lucha' means "fight, battle, combat; wrestle; quarrel"
[137] Literally 'tratan' means "treat, behave towards; attend; process; like; carry; doctor"
[138] Literally 'avecinan' means "approach, come near, come nearer, come close, come closer"
[139] 'Epithelial bodies' are also know as "Hassall's bodies" or "Hassall's corpuscles" (bodies of epithelial cells found in the medulla of the thymus), but the singular term 'Epithelial body' refers to the parathyroid gland (the four small endocrine glands lying close or embedded in the posterior surface of the thyroid gland).

But Venus has its vanguard[140] in the head, then, while Mars dominates the Pineal gland with its martian forces, the struggle with Venus has already begun in the Pituitary.

Physically it looks like one animates growth[141] while the other demands[142] for Mars to moderate itself.

Where the two forces meet[143] a spark of light bursts forth[144] and [therefore] we directed the first [of our] practices [to the area] above it.

One of these Glands produces sleep, the other demands the vigil [state]; while Venus wants to sleep, Mars wants to continue fighting.

Secondary glands throughout the head, brain, ears, nose and mouth, are also animated by these astral influences [which are] in eternal struggle; for example, while some provide saliva, others dry it [up], and so [the] result [is] the manifestation of life in an eternal struggle.

This fight has already begun in the divine plane between Mercury and Jupiter, the first [fights] with the tatwic forces of Anupadaka and the second with [the tatwic forces of] Adi.[145]

---

[140] Literally 'vanguardia' means "advance guard, vanguard (the forefront in any movement, field, activity, or the like)"
[141] Literally 'crecimiento' means "growth; evolution; cultivation; increase; inflation"
[142] Literally 'exige' means "exact, demand, require; levy; need, necessitate; beg"
[143] Literally 'encuentran' means "find, locate; espy; meet, encounter"
[144] Literally 'brota' means "sprout, burst forth; grow quickly; cause to sprout"
[145] Editor's note: According to Krumm-Heller's book *Tattwameter* (1927), "...the Anupadaka and Adi Tattvas ...are the eternal principles of the divine world... in them the state of ecstasy or Shamadi is achieved." And Samael Aun Weor says in Ch. 9 of *The Mystery of the Golden Blossom* (1971), "...the gnostic Esotericist, in full ecstasy during coitus, victoriously enters the region of the Monads in the splendid world of the Anupadaka Tattwa. In the level preceding that world of Anupadaka lies the extraordinary principle of power which is the domain of space, time and causality, and is called Akash Tattwa. (The dwelling of Atman-Buddhi-Manas)."

[Inserted by the editor, not in the original[147]]

...Our understanding begins with Prana. Prana then works, [and] modifies itself into Akash, and [then] Akash works, modifying itself into ether, and [then] ether modifies itself, [and] breaks itself down into a series of Tatwas, which it gives rise to.

...Pranic influence brings a division of Akash into other modifications. These five modalities or states of the Tatwa are called:
Akash, the ethereal principle.
Vayu, the aerial principle.
Tejas, the principle of heat and of light.
Prithvi, the principle of earth.
Apas, the principle of water or liquid.

...Nature is a great living organism, in final synthesis this great machine is controlled by Elemental Forces...

TATWAS	ELEMENTS
AKASH	PRINCIPLE OF ETHER
VAYU	PRINCIPLE OF AIR
TEJAS	PRINCIPLE OF FIRE
PRITHVI	PRINCIPLE OF EARTH
APAS	PRINCIPLE OF WATER

This first order which is mentioned is in accordance with Rama Prasat [and Krumm-Heller]; the TRUE order is:

TATWAS	ELEMENTS
AKASH	PRINCIPLE OF ETHER
TEJAS	PRINCIPLE OF FIRE
VAYU	PRINCIPLE OF AIR
APAS	PRINCIPLE OF WATER
PRITHVI	PRINCIPLE OF EARTH

[End of editor's insert]

---

[147] The first part of this insert is from Krumm-Heller's book *Tattwameter* (1927); the second part is from Ch. 29 of *Tarot & Kabalah* (1978) by Samael Aun Weor.

[Insertada por el editor, no en el original[148]]

...Nuestro entendimiento principia con Prana. Prana entonces obra, modificándose como Akash, y Akash, modificándose, obra como éter, y el éter, modificándose, se desintegra en una serie de Tatwas, a los que da origen.

...La influencia pránica ocasiona una división del Akash en otras modificaciones. Estas cinco modalidades o estados del Tatwa se llaman:
Akash, el principio etéreo.
Vayu, el principio aéreo.
Tejas, el principio del calor y de la luz.
Prithvi, el principio de tierra.
Apas, el principio del agua o líquido.

...La Naturaleza es un gran organismo viviente, en última síntesis esta gran máquina está dirigida por Fuerzas Elementales...

TATWAS	ELEMENTOS
AKASH	PRINCIPIO DEL ÉTER
VAYÚ	PRINCIPIO DEL AIRE
TEJAS	PRINCIPIO DEL FUEGO
PRITVI	PRINCIPIO DE LA TIERRA
APAS	PRINCIPIO DEL AGUA

Este primer orden que se menciona es de acuerdo con Ramá Prasat [y Krumm-Heller]; el orden VERDADERO es:

TATWAS	ELEMENTOS
AKASH	PRINCIPIO DEL ÉTER
TEJAS	PRINCIPIO DEL FUEGO
VAYÚ	PRINCIPIO DEL AIRE
APAS	PRINCIPIO DEL AGUA
PRITVI	PRINCIPIO DE LA TIERRA

[Fin de la inserción del editor]

---

[148] La primera parte de este inserto es del libro *El Tattwametro* (1927) por Krumm-Heller; la segunda parte es del Cap. 29 de *Tarot y Kábala* (1978) por Samael Aun Weor.

At the moment when the Sun comes out to fight Apas (the liquid principle) with Akash (the ethereal principle) then since the ethereal is more mobile[149] [it] wins, and the Sun comes to act on the head [of the physical body] in that Tatwa with Mercury, because Mercury, let us notice, has the effect [both] of Mars and Venus united in a descriptive sign.

Shortly after taking command, Mars, then, is the lord or dominant in the head with Aries.

The Tatwas as a whole are like a balancing[150] [act], we have the upward [moving] air and ethereal [principles], and we have the solid and liquid downward [moving principles]; in the middle is Tejas maintaining the balance with the principle of heat and light.[151]

The Disciple will see in this a key and will see the error of the T. S.[152] who wrongly place Prithvi first holding, then, that it is liquid then solid before turning into[153] ethereal.

In the first letter[154] [for the Lesson for Aries] we said LIGHT, [and] LOVE.

Light reminds us of Lucifer[155], Mars; which is followed by Venus, Love.

---

[149] Literally 'movible' means "movable, mobile; fickle; loose"
[150] Literally 'balanza' means "scales; balance; judgement, assessment"
[151] Editor's note: If we take the 7 Tatwas (including the two Superior ones) in the following rectified order:
   1) Anupadaka
   2) Adi
   3) Akash
   4) Tejas
   5) Vayu
   6) Apas
   7) Prithvi
Then we can see that Tejas, "the principle of heat and light", is still in the middle, "maintaining the balance".
[152] Editor's note: 'T. S.' appears to refer to the "Theosophical Society."
[153] Literally 'a ser' means "to be"
[154] Literally 'carta' means "letter; document; charter; epistle; map; card"
[155] The word Lucifer is derived from the Latin words *lucem ferre* and means "light-bearer".

Let's look at the [astrological] symbols with [a] circle.

The Sun or the Universal Spirit, goes out[158] [and] makes[159] an arrow or cross going up and then this is the [sign of] Mars; if the arrow or cross goes down, [then] it is [the sign of] Venus.

There are two moons in Aries, in Taurus [there is] a Moon over [a] circle, [and] in Gemini then[160] with Mercury these symbols are joined, until separating the moon in Cancer.

All these symbols or ways of making astrological signs make us think.

We [also] said in the first letter that the key is in the Grand Sympathetic Nervous System, but the nervous fluid before being fluid has to be liquid, and so we began with the liquid nervous system or the Endocrine Glands.

Sun = Sol

Mars = Marte

Venus = Venus

Aries = Aries

Moon = Luna

Taurus = Taurus

Gemini = Géminis

Mercury = Mercurio

Cancer = Cáncer

Fijémonos en los símbolos del círculo.

El Sol o el Espíritu Universal, hace salir una flecha o cruz para arriba y entonces es Marte; si la flecha o cruz va abajo, es Venus.

En Aries son dos lunas, en Taurus una Luna sobre el círculo, en Géminis después con Mercurio se unen esos símbolos, hasta separarse la luna en Cáncer.

Todos esos símbolos o formas de hacer los signos astrológicos nos hacen pensar.

Hemos dicho en la primera carta que la clave esté en el Sistema Nervioso Gran Simpático, pero el fluido nervioso antes de ser fluido tiene que haber sido líquido, y por eso hemos de principiar con el sistema nervioso líquido o sea con las Glándulas Endocrinas.

This acts upon the mechanical[161] willpower and then upon the conscious willpower.

Hunger and love are two forces that are battling[162] [each other], and nonetheless they need each other.

We must act first [of all] on the liquid system, in order to then dominate the fluidic [system].

Este actúa sobre la voluntad motriz y después resulta la voluntad consciente.

Hambre y amor son dos fuerzas que se combaten, y sin embargo se necesitan entre sí.

Hemos de actuar primero sobre el sistema líquido, para luego poder dominar el fluídico.

---

[158] Literally 'salir' means "exit, leave, go out; appear, come into view; escape; enter; hatch, emerge from an egg; defray, pay, cover the expenses of; project; quit; lead; win"
[159] Literally 'hace' means "make; manufacture; create; construct, build; fashion, shape; compose; emit; wage, conduct (war, battle); prepare, do; cause; perform; effect; force; render; fabricate; behave, act in a particular manner; live through; be"
[160] Literally 'después' means "then, afterwards, later, subsequently, after"
[161] Literally 'Motriz' means "motive, moving; motor; driving"
[162] Literally 'combaten' means "fight, combat, battle"

With the practices of the previous letter, we have acted upon the foundation[163], the Light.

This was necessary, because the Light is what is paramount[164].

In the space between the Pineal and the Pituitary Glands, between the center of feeling[165] and the nervous center; there is something invisible, an astral gland, ENTIRELY[166] [MADE OF] LIGHT, as [was] indicated in the first practice.

We have indicated [this] abstractly, now we are becoming[167] [more] concrete.

We would get[168] nothing (for the time being) by acting upon the Pineal [Gland], unless we open the way through the neck.

Now in the neck, [in the] region of Taurus-Venus, there is the Thyroid [Gland], which is a second Pineal [Gland].

As we shall see later, in the Epithelial Bodies[169] [or Parathyroid Glands] the Pituitary repeats itself.

Con las prácticas de la carta anterior hemos actuado sobre la base, la Luz.

Fue necesario así, porque la Luz es lo primordial.

En el espacio entre las dos Glándulas Epífisis e Hipófisis, entre el centro del sentir y el centro nervioso; hay algo invisible, una glándula astral, TODA LUZ, ya indicada en la primera práctica.

Lo hemos indicado en abstracto, ahora vamos a lo concreto.

Nada sacaríamos por de pronto con actuar sobre la Epífisis, si no abriéramos el camino por el cuello.

Ahora en el cuello, región de Taurus-Venus, está la Tiroides, que es una segunda Epífisis.

Como veremos después, en los Cuerpos Epitelares se repite la Hipófisis.

---

[163] Literally 'base' means "ase, foundation; bottom layer; principal element, fundamental part"
[164] Literally 'primordial' means "primordial; overriding; capital; fundamental, primary, essential, of primary importance"
[165] Literally 'sentir' means "feeling, sensation; perception; emotion; pity, compassion"
[166] Literally 'TODA' means "all; whole, entire; every, each; indiscreet; any"
[167] Literally 'vamos' means "go, proceed, move; travel; walk; suit; lead; drive; ride"
[168] Literally 'sacaríamos' means "take out, remove; bring out; draw out, extract; get; take; bring up; let; produce; educe, deduce; protract"
[169] 'Epithelial bodies' are also know as "Hassall's bodies" or "Hassall's corpuscles" (bodies of epithelial cells found in the medulla of the thymus), but the singular term 'Epithelial body' refers to the parathyroid gland (the four small endocrine glands lying close or embedded in the posterior surface of the thyroid gland).

[Inserted by the editor, not in the original]   [Insertada por el editor, no en el original]

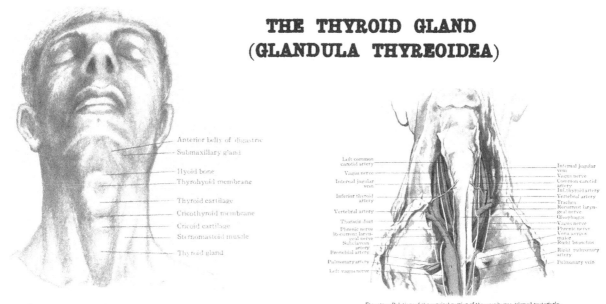

THE THYROID GLAND
(GLANDULA THYREOIDEA)

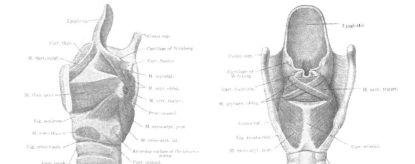

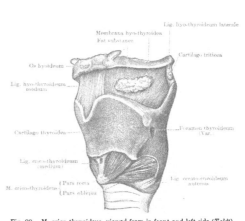

[End of editor's insert]   [Fin de la inserción del editor]

The Thyroid produces iodine, and iodine destroys everything bad. With it we will open up [a] passageway[170] through the neck.	La Tiroides produce yodo, y el yodo destruye todo lo malo. Con él vamos a abrirnos paso por el cuello.
Venus dominates the ears, the nose, the tongue, the sexual organs and the kidneys.	Venus domina las orejas, la nariz, la lengua, los órganos sexuales y los riñones.
In Alchemy [Venus is] represented [by] sulfur and in the metals [it is represented by] copper.	En Alquimia representa el azufre y en los metales el cobre.
This metal resides in the milk of women and in certain milky secretions of all bodies, both masculine and feminine.	Este metal reside en la leche de la mujer y en ciertas secreciones lechosas de todos los cuerpos, tanto masculino como femenino.
Venus acts in Taurus and Libra, and with the [corresponding] exercises we act in order to encourage[171] the production of this secretion.	Venus actúa en Taurus y Libra, y con los ejercicios actuamos para fomentar la producción de esa secreción.
Taurus is receptive, [it] represents the place[172] where one can sow, and the neck is a kind of nursery[173] for the whole organism.	Taurus es receptivo, representa el terreno donde se puede sembrar, y en el cuello hay una especie de semillero para todo el organismo.

In many secret societies, there are signs that are made upon the neck because the neck holds a kind of spiritual uterus, since in it is also the cradle[174] of manifested language.	En muchas sociedades secretas hay signos que se hacen sobre el cuello, porque el cuello encierra una especie de útero espiritual, pues, en él está también la cuna del lenguaje manifestado.
In the previous practice we concentrated on the eyes, the nose and the mouth, and finally on the center of language.	En la práctica anterior nos concentramos sobre los ojos, la nariz y la boca, y a lo último sobre el centro del lenguaje.
Today we use language to open the passageway.	Hoy nos valemos del lenguaje para abrirnos paso.

---

[170] Literally 'paso' means "passage, way, route, course; passing, going by; transition, change; migration, seasonal relocation of birds or other animals in groups; passageway, corridor; pass, narrow road between mountains; strait"
[171] Literally 'fomentar' means "foment; promote; foster, encourage; advance, develop; nourish; patronize, sponsor"
[172] Literally 'terreno' means "terrain; land, ground; park; location"
[173] Literally 'semillero' means "seedbed; seed box; breeding ground; nursery, place for growing and selling plants; hotbed, area of covered and heated ground in which plants are grown in and out of season"
[174] Literally 'cuna' means "cradle; cribe, cot; bassinet"

Let us say "Aaaaaaaaaa" but quickly, inspiring; not as it is generally done [by] exhaling, and let's think:

> "Come outer[175] Light of the cosmos and unite with what[176] we have[177] in the brain, proceeding[178] to the neck"

and then, with "Uuuuuuuuuu", the light that purifies [and] burns[179] [the impurities as it is] leaving[180].

Let us close with the "Mmmmmmmmm" and let us think about our mantram AMEN, "so be it", to produce things with the word AUM.

Let us do all this without exerting ourselves, more with the mind than anything else, and in the next letter we will proceed[181] down the [rest] of the body.

Digamos Aaaaaaaaaa pero muy corto, inspirando; no como lo hacemos generalmente expirando, y pensemos:

> Venga la Luz de fuera, del cosmos y unida con la que tenemos en el cerebro vaya al cuello

y luego con la Uuuuuuuuuu salgan por la luz que purificó quemando.

Cerremos con la Mmmmmmmmm y pensemos en nuestro mantram AMEN, "así sea", al producir las cosas con la palabra AUM.

Hagamos todo esto sin esforzarnos, más con la mente que con otra cosa, y en la otra carta iremos bajando al cuerpo.

---

[175] Literally 'fuera' means "abroad, outside; without; away; out"
[176] Literally 'la que' means "the [thing] that"
[177] Literally 'tenemos' means "have, possess; hold; bear; carry; wear; experience; practice; meet with; travel; show"
[178] Literally 'vaya' means "go, proceed, move; travel; walk; suit; lead; drive; ride"
[179] Literally 'quemando' means "burn, incinerate; scorch; shrivel; frost"
[180] Literally 'salgan' means "exit, leave, go out; appear, come into view; escape; enter; hatch, emerge from an egg; defray, pay, cover the expenses of; project; quit; lead; win"
[181] Literally 'iremos' means "go, proceed, move; travel; walk; suit; lead; drive; ride"

GEMINI

Dear Disciple:

Clairvoyants[182] observe that the Chakras ([the] circles, discs, [or] wheels of the magnetic centers) are immobile[183] in the majority of human beings and that only when occult practices are done and [when] the Disciple becomes [a] Rose Cross [Adept], do the wheels begin to spin, which Gichtel[184] describes to us as such and that Leadbeater offers us in the Theosophical form[185].

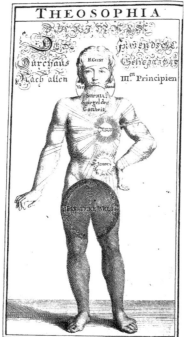

Gichtel sees these wheels as [different] kinds[186] of roses and lotus flowers and notes that [they] correspond [to] and are derived from our own Glands.

[It was] no more than twenty years [ago] that we knew one more extension of the importance of the Endocrine Glands.

Previously, man knew less of anatomy and this was the cause of the confusion [of] the Heart in its tatwaic effects ([the] central impulse that sustains[187] matter in [a] certain vibratory state), with [the tatwaic effects of] the Parathyroid Glands.

---

[182] Literally 'videntes' means "seers, clairvoyants"
[183] Literally 'inmóviles' means "immobile, stationary; immovable, motionless, still"
[184] Editor's note: This refers to *Theosophia practica* (1779) by Johann Georg Gichtel
[185] Editor's note: This refers to *The Chakras: A Monograph* (1927) by C.W. Leadbeater
[186] Literally 'especies' means "species, subdivision of a genus; sort, kind; description; idea, notion; remark"
[187] Literally 'mantiene' means "maintain, keep in existence, sustain; keep in good condition, preserve; support, provide for"

[Inserted by the editor, not in the original]   [Insertada por el editor, no en el original]

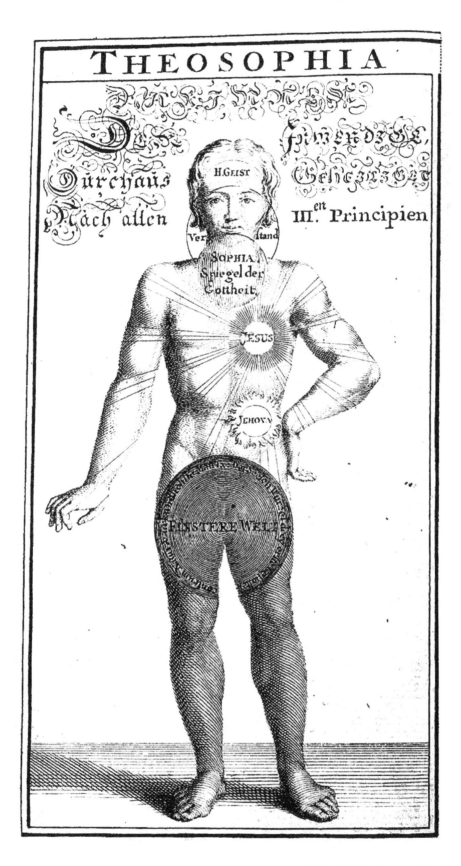

[End of editor's insert]   [Fin de la inserción del editor]

As the majority of our Disciples know the oriental theosophical terminology, we will say that after having awakened[191] [the] Sahasrara [chakra], we pass [on] to [the] Ajna and Vishudda [chakras], and now, in the Parathyroid Glands, we arrive at [the] Anahata [chakra].

We head down the neck, and continue to descend [down the body], we are [going to] meet[192] with that ultimate and enigmatic center of emotions.

Steiner was the first who drew attention to the Heart and its great importance as [a] plexus, but [we] do not admit the effect of [the] chakras as Leadbeater presents them, who probably ignored the occult anatomy [of the] Rose Cross [Fraternity] because of[193] his inability to read the works of the epoch of Gichtel, written in a hodgepodge[194] of medieval german and latin.

We drew this conclusion when we talked with him.

The Heart is not a pump[195], as it has been described, but it is a body moved by the sanguineous[196] impulse and we shall see its occult role later.

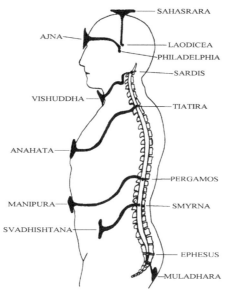

Como la mayor parte de los Discípulos conocen la terminología teosófica oriental, diremos que después de haber despertado Sahasrara pasamos a Ajna y Vishuddi, y ahora, en los Cuerpos Epitelares, llegamos a Anahata.

De la cabeza hemos bajado al cuello, y al seguir descendiendo, nos hallamos con este último y enigmático centro de emociones.

Steiner, fue el primero que nos llamó la atención sobre el Corazón y su grandiosa importancia como plexo, pero no admitía el efecto de chacras como lo presenta Leadbeater, quien probablemente ignora la anatomía oculta Rosa Cruz por su incapacidad para leer esas obras de la época de Gichtel, escritas en una mezcolanza de alemán y latín medieval.

Esa conclusión sacamos cuando hablamos con él.

El Corazón no es una bomba, tal como se ha descrito, sino que es un cuerpo movido por el impulso sanguíneo y su papel oculto hemos de ver más tarde.

---

[191] Literally 'despertado' means "awaken, wake up, arouse (i.e. from sleep); enthuse, rouse"
[192] Literally 'hallamos' means "find; discover; locate; meet with"
[193] Literally 'por' means "for, in order to; on behalf of; because of; by; via, by way of; to; at; after; around; along"
[194] Literally 'mezcolanza' means "hotchpotch, hodgepodge, mixture"
[195] Literally 'bomba' means "bomb, explosive device; bombshell, something shocking; pump; shade; bubble; balloon; drum"
[196] Literally 'sanguíneo' means "sanguineous, bloody"

Today we continue with our [overview of the] occult magnetic centers, which are intimately related to the Glands of Internal Secretion, even if it is sensible[197] to make amends with Leadbeater, but we know that many of the occult practices of the Esoteric Section of the T. S.[198] are wrongly specified[199] and are [even] harmful[200].

In order for the Disciple to comprehend the importance of the Epithelial Bodies or Parathyroid Glands as they have also been called, we need to necessarily[201] transfer ourselves [over] to the field of pathology and study something of a disease that is deeply related to these Glands.

Knowing, then, the diseased aspect, we can more easily comprehend the need for a healthy[202] body and the action exercised by the Glands.

This disease, to which we refer ourselves, is tetany[203] (convulsive tension of the muscles subject to the rule of the will) that we know firstly through an insufficiency of nutrition and which manifests itself with accentual[204] spasms of the extremities.

These patients suffer from a type of cramps or regular[205] convulsive movements, either in the eyelids, in the hands, in the face, in the belly or in the extremities.

---

[197] Literally 'sensible' means "feeling, sensitive, perceptible; noticeable; regrettable; amenable; appreciative"
[198] Editor's note: 'T. S.' appears to refer to the "Theosophical Society."
[199] Literally 'concretadas' means "concretized, made specific"
[200] Literally 'perjudiciales' means "damaging, harmful, injurious"
[201] Literally 'forzosamente' means "necessarily, needs, perforce"
[202] Literally 'sano' means "healthy, well, not sick, in good health; sane, pure minded"
[203] Tetany or tetany seizure is a medical sign consisting of the involuntary contraction of muscles
[204] Literally 'tónicos' means "tonic; accentual (of or pertaining to accent or stress)"
[205] Literally 'habituales' means "habitual, regular; featureless; hardened; crude; tame"

There are people who manifest [a] certain nervous tic that has not yet [been] explained by [modern] medicine, and has its origin in these Glands.

We give as [an] example the Dance of Saint Vitus[206].

Of course, all [these diseases are the] exteriorization of [a] diseased character[207] affecting[208] a number of motor movements [that happen] in parts [which] should act only [when there is] the will [to do so, meaning they are involuntary].

Here we can see the point: an invasion of one nervous system by another.

The symptomatological table of diseases caused by defects in the Parathyroid Glands is enormous in its variety, and many known diseases, such as those of the nerves of the Heart, of the Intestines and of the Stomach, can be explained and cured if we direct the therapeutic action to[209] the Glands in question.

It is very curious that tetany is observed more in men than in women, appearing in all parts, especially in the spring months.

That is to say, at the time that ARIES and TAURUS deliver their power [over] to GEMINI, [which] is the entrance of the lungs into the neck and arms, where the latter Sign has its dominion.

Hay personas que manifiestan cierto tic nervioso que aún no se ha explicado la medicina, y que tiene su origen en dichas Glándulas.

Daremos como ejemplo el Baile de San Vito.

Desde luego, todos ellos exteriorizan una cantidad de movimientos motores de carácter enfermizo en partes donde solamente debía actuar la voluntad.

Aquí vemos al punto una invasión de un sistema nervioso a otro.

El cuadro sintomatológico de las enfermedades originadas por defectos de los Cuerpos Epitelares es enorme en su variedad, y muchas enfermedades conocidas, como las de los nervios del Corazón, de los Intestinos y del Estómago, pueden ser explicadas y curadas si dirigimos la acción terapéutica sobre las Glándulas en cuestión.

Es bien curioso que la tetania se observe más en los hombres que en las mujeres, apareciendo en todas partes, sobre todo en los meses de primavera.

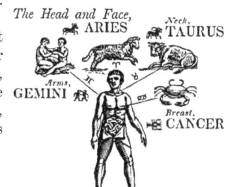

Es decir, en el tiempo en que ARIES y TAURO entregan su poder a GÉMINIS, es la entrada del cuello a los pulmones y a los brazos, donde tiene su dominio este último Signo.

---

[206] Saint Vitus' dance may refer to Chorea disease or Sydenham's chorea, which is an abnormal involuntary movement disorder, one of a group of neurological disorders called 'dyskinesias'.
[207] Literally 'carácter' means "print; character, nature, disposition; figure, personage"
[208] Literally 'de' means "of; about; from; by; at; with; out; off"
[209] Literally 'sobre' means "concerning, about; on, atop; onto, upon; super, above; in"

We have already told[210] [you about] the struggle between Venus and Mars.	Ya hemos advertido la lucha entre Venus y Marte.
We have said in the previous lesson[211], that there is a struggle between the Pituitary [gland] and the Pineal [gland], now the same phenomenon is repeated between the Thyroid and Parathyroid [Glands], whose effect can be seen[212], of course, [by] the medical official.	Hemos dicho en la instrucción anterior, que así como hay una lucha entre la Hipófisis y la Epífisis, ahora se repite ese mismo fenómeno entre la Tiroides y las Paratiroides, cuyo efecto puede constatar, desde luego, la medicina oficial.
Venus, again, faces[213] Mars; and, just like in war, barbed wire fences are put up, that is to say barriers and obstacles for the enemy, Mars (who also dominates in Scorpio) seeks[214] this element in order to launch[215] its venom, which Venus (in the Thyroid) tries[216] to stop.	Venus, de nuevo, se enfrenta a Marte; y así como en la guerra se colocan alambradas, es decir trabas y obstáculos al enemigo, Marte, que domina también en Escorpión, busca ese elemento para lanzar sus venenos que Venus en la Tiroides trata de detener.
It is repeated another time, as in the performance[217] of the Pituitary and the Pineal [Glands], one of which is drowsy[218], [and] cunning[219], while the other, Mars, is activity.	Otra vez se repite, como en la actuación de la Hipófisis y la Epífisis, que el uno es dormilón, solapado, mientras que el otro, Marte, es la actividad.
Here we see[220], for the first time, the dual[221] aspect of the Planet Mars in the Signs of Aries and Scorpio.	Aquí observamos, por la primera vez, el doble aspecto del Planeta Marte en los Signos de Aries y Escorpión.

---

[210] Literally 'advertido' means "warn, caution; forewarn; point out; notice; admonish"
[211] Literally 'instrucción' means "instruction, teaching, education, training; direction, guidance"
[212] Literally 'constatar' means "confirm, verify; prove; observe, note"
[213] Literally 'enfrenta' means "face, stand opposite; stand face to face"
[214] Literally 'busca' means "search for, seek, look for; scout for; forage; call for, ask for"
[215] Literally 'lanzar' means "throw, cast; send; sling; aim; shoot; pitch; release; launch; dart, dash"
[216] Literally 'trata' means "treat, behave towards; attend; process; like; carry; doctor"
[217] Literally 'actuación' means "performance, show, presentation; execution; act, deed; act of presenting an artistic work to an audience"
[218] Literally 'dormilón' means "drowsy, sleepy, tired; restful, soporific"
[219] Literally 'solapado' means "crafty, cunning, underhand"
[220] Literally 'observamos' means "observe, watch, study; monitor, supervise; discern; keep, honour; fulfill religious commandments; follow, abide by; remark, comment"
[221] Literally 'doble' means "double; twofold; ambidextrous; disingenuous"

Let us now enter into the terrain[222] of the Twins [or Gemini].

We have said that all life is a constant struggle between Venus and Mars, but in this region (which[223] we are now penetrating with the magnetic forces awakened) corresponds to Mercury in Gemini.

In the ancient Initiations, the Mystic[224] (origin of the word mystery) was locked in an obscure chamber[225].

This chamber represented Chaos.

They had to pass through a narrow corridor which represented the neck and then they gave[226] him the emblems of Mercury as [the] organizer of this same Chaos.

On the Rosebush[227], we have followed the sprouting of the leaves, the formation of the petals, [and which are] now entering the epoch of materializing[228] themselves [into] the flower.

Mercury is the Spirit that comes from Heaven down to earth.

The head is Heaven; the neck [is] space (the Chaos), and now we are in front of our own earth.

In Egypt they gave the symbol of the Ankh (the symbol of life) to the neophytes.

Let us remember the famous painting of Amenhotep III.

Entremos ahora en el terreno de los Gemelos.

Hemos dicho que toda la vida es una lucha constante entre Venus y Marte, pero en esa región donde penetramos ahora con las fuerzas magnéticas despertadas, corresponde a Mercurio en Géminis.

En las Iniciaciones antiguas, el Mysto (origen de la palabra misterio) era encerrado en una cámara obscura.

Esta cámara representaba el Caos.

Tenía que pasar por un corredor estrecho que representaba el cuello y entonces le entregaban los emblemas de Mercurio como organizador de este mismo Caos.

En el Rosal, hemos seguido el brote de las hojas, la formación de los pétalos, entrando ahora la época de concretarse la flor.

Mercurio es el Espíritu que baja del Cielo a la tierra.

La cabeza, es el Cielo; el cuello el espacio, el Caos, y ahora estamos ante la puerta de nuestra propia tierra.

A los neófitos en Egipto les daban el símbolo de Ankh, el símbolo de vida.

Recordemos el famoso cuadro de Amenofis III.

---

[222] Literally 'terreno' means "terrain; land, ground; park; location"
[223] Literally 'donde' means "where; whereabouts; how"
[224] Mystic from the Latin *mysticus*, from the Ancient Greek μυστικός (mystikos, "secret, mystic"), from μύστης (mystēs, "one who has been initiated").
[225] Literally 'cámara' means "hall; chamber; vault; lieu; tire"
[226] Literally 'entregaban' means "deliver, convey; give over; consign; submit; surrender; address; serve"
[227] Literally 'Rosal' means "rosebush, shrub from the genus Rosa which produces roses"
[228] Literally 'concretarse' means "materialize, take shape, become definite"

Zodiacal Course by Arnoldo Krumm Heller (Huiracocha)	Curso Zodical por Arnoldo Krumm Heller (Huiracocha)

The Papyrus of Leyden treats[229] this symbol as [a] neck[230], that is to say, life passes as breath[231] through the neck.

Enclosed[232] within this [symbol is] a secret of the Runes, that we will also know through these practices, but much later.[233]

Mercury, in the Sign of Virgo, is the representation of the day, while the Twins [or Gemini] still remains[234] at night.

One can see that the current[235] of Light which we have brought from above is now obscured by the action of Venus, but nonetheless, this same Light is what[236] opens the path [to us].

It appears that the very Sign of the Twins represents a path flanked by two walls.

Gemini = Géminis

Now in Mercury, everything is done with movement[237].

As the word indicates, Mercury brings[238] all movement, and before reaching the Lungs, we need to prepare the air at the superior part [of the chest or in the neck] in order to achieve[239] the next[240] action.

El Papiro de Leyden trae ese símbolo como cuello, es decir, la vida pasa como aliento por el cuello.

Encierra eso un secreto de las Runas, que conoceremos también en estas prácticas, pero más tarde.

Mercurio es, en el Signo de Virgo, la representación del día, mientras que los Gemelos aún permanecen en la noche.

Se ve que la corriente de Luz que hemos traído desde arriba se oscurece ahora por la acción de Venus, pero, no obstante, esta misma Luz trata de abrirse camino.

Parece que hasta el mismo Signo de los Gemelos representa un camino flanqueado por dos murallas.

Ahora en Mercurio todo se hace móvil.

Como la palabra lo indica, Mercurio trae todo movimiento y antes de llegar a los Pulmones, necesitamos preparar el aire en la parte superior para lograr luego la acción.

---

[229] Literally 'trae' means "bring; carry; cover up; wear; get"
[230] Literally 'cuello' means "neck; collar"
[231] Literally 'aliento' means "breath; wind; encouragement"
[232] Literally 'Encierra' means "shut in, imprisoned; close in on; surrounded, jailed; confine, include"
[233] Editor's note: In 1931, when the 12 lessons of the Zodiacal Course were completed, Krumm-Heller immediately began distributing the lessons of the "Course of Rune Magic".
[234] Literally 'permanecen' means "remain, stay, abide"
[235] Literally 'corriente' means "current, flow (of water, electricity, etc.); tendency, drift; tide; swim; rain"
[236] Literally 'trata' means "treat, behave towards; attend; process; like; carry; doctor"
[237] Literally 'móvil' means "movable, mobile; fickle"
[238] Literally 'trae' means "bring; carry; cover up; wear; get"
[239] Literally 'lograr' means "get, obtain; achieve, attain; reach; win"
[240] Literally 'luego' means "then, afterwards, next; in the next place; later on; soon, presently; now, anon; later"

The Hindus speak of awakening the Kundalini (The Serpent of Fire) through breathing exercises, and Rama Prasad[241] offers practices in this respect, impressive for the indians who have for centuries had a very simple[242] nourishment[243] and have far fewer [dietary] elements than us.

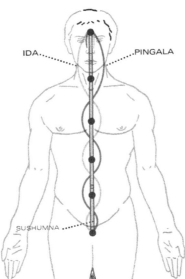

These same elements, if we do these same practices, are closing the doors of [the] Brahmarandhra[244], and we need to start with softer and lighter exercises for the Ida and Pingala (the two positive-negative columns that link[245] [the] Kundalini).

The darkness[246], that we have mentioned, is what produces dreams[247].

That is to say, [it produces] the transition[248] from the vigil [state] to the [state of] sleep and from the [state of] sleep to the vigil [state].

---

[241] This refers to the book *The Science of Breath and the Philosophy of the Tattvas*, also known as *Nature's Finer Forces*, by Rama Prasad an English translation of which was published in 1894 by the Theosophical Publishing Society.
[242] Literally 'sencilla' means "simple, easy; straightforward; informal; naive; primitive"
[243] Literally 'alimentación' means "feeding; nutrition, nourishment; alimentation"
[244] "'Brahmarandhra' means the hole of Brahman. It is the dwelling house of the human soul. This is also known as 'Dasamadvara', the tenth opening or the tenth door. The hollow place in the crown of the head known as anterior fontanelle in the new-born child is the Brahmarandhra." from the section called 'Kundalini Yoga – Theory' of *Kundalini Yoga* (1935) by Swami Sivananda.
[245] Literally 'enlazan' means "link, connect; tie, bind; knit together"
[246] Literally 'obscuridad' means "obscurity, blackness, darkness, gloom;"
[247] Literally 'ensueños' means "dream; fantasy; reverie, day dream"
[248] Literally 'paso' means "passage, way, route, course; passing, going by; transition, change; migration, seasonal relocation of birds or other animals in groups; passageway, corridor; pass, narrow road between mountains; strait"

Los Hindúes hablan de despertar a Kundalini (La Serpiente del Fuego) por medio de ejercicios respiratorios, y Rama Prasad[249] ofrece unas prácticas a este respecto, admirables para los indios que durante siglos han llevado una alimentación muy sencilla y tienen muchos menos elementos morbosos que nosotros.

Estos mismos elementos, si hacemos nosotros esas mismas prácticas, nos cierran las puertas para Brahmarandra[250], y por eso necesitamos comenzar por ejercicios más suaves y ligeros sobre el Ida y el Pingalá (las dos columnas positivo-negativas que enlazan a Kundalini).

La obscuridad que hemos mencionado, es la que produce los ensueños.

Es decir, el paso de la vigilia al sueño y del sueño a la vigilia.

---

[249] Esto se refiere al libro *La Ciencia de la Respiración y la Filosofía de los Tattvas*, también conocidas *Fuerzas Sutiles de la Naturaleza*, por Rama Prasad una traducción al Inglés de los cuales fue publicado en 1894 por la Sociedad Editora Teosófica y en Español en 1920.
[250] "«Brahmarandhra» significa «el hueco de Brahman». Es la morada del alma humana. También se lo conoce como «Dasamadwara», la décima abertura o la décima puerta. El Brahmarandhra es el sitio hueco, existente en la coronilla, conocido como fontanela anterior en los recién nacidos. Se halla entre los dos huesos parietales y occipitales." de la sección llamada "Kundalini Yoga - Teoría" de *Kundalini Yoga* (1953) por Swami Sivananda.

The Disciple should take note[251] (during these practices in [the period of] Gemini) of their own dreams.

All dreams have their symbolic value, and the Masters observe the Disciple while [he or she is] going through[252] them.

Generally we dream of what we have been thinking [about] very intensely before we [go to] sleep, and this is the cause of why (during this practice) the disciple should fall asleep after having concentrated on something that relates to our studies.

That is to say, of an eagerness[253], for example, to see our Temple, to think of a Master or, perhaps, of a Tree, the Tree of Life...

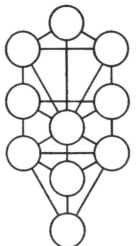

In short, any concentration or exercise of the imagination, making[254] the five respirations through the nose, opening the arms and the legs, then expelling the air through your mouth while closing [the] legs and arms.

These practices can be done in bed or sitting comfortably.

It is also very effective to meditate on the phenomenon of birth, because, let's remember, that NOW SOMETHING IS GOING TO BE BORN WITHIN US.

---

[251] Literally 'fijarse' means "set; lodge; latch on to; become fixed; take notice"
[252] Literally 'duran' means "endure, continue on in spite of difficulty; continue, keep doing something; hold out"
[253] Literally 'afán' means "industry; eagerness; hard work, toil"
[254] Literally 'haciendo' means "make; manufacture; create; construct, build; fashion, shape; compose; emit; wage, conduct (war, battle); prepare, do; cause; perform; effect; force; render; fabricate; behave, act in a particular manner; live through; be"

CANCER

Dear Disciple:

The Septenary[255] described in the occult anatomy of the medieval Rosicrucians and confirmed by the theosophists, [is what] we represent [as the] seven different bodies, the first made from crude[256] matter and the last from [a] divine substance, all together in a single individual, [which are] like an upright dividing line with another line crossing the material and the spiritual, and so we have with the three higher bodies and the four lower [bodies], our sacred symbol of the Cross.

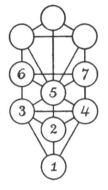

At the center, where the lines converge, we place[257] the Rose, because, it is the Sun that travels with its magnetic current[258] passing through the Parathyroid [Glands] to the centers dominated by the Sign of Cancer [related to the chest].

The Sun reaches Cancer [on] the 21st of June; this is [when] the king star [is] in [its] highest ascension, and then we celebrate the Summer Solstice.

On the feast of the Rose of Saint John[259], we also celebrate the Sun at its peak of activity in our heart or corporal[260] Sun.

CÁNCER

Querido Discípulo:

El Septenario descrito en la anatomía oculta de los Rosacruces medievales y confirmado por los teósofos, nos representa siete cuerpos diferentes, hecho el primero de materia grosera y el último de substancia divina, todos aglomerados en un solo individuo, como una línea recta dividiendo con otra línea transversal lo material de lo espiritual, y así tenemos con los tres cuerpos de arriba y los cuatro de abajo, nuestro símbolo sagrado de la Cruz.

En el centro donde convergen las líneas, nos figuramos la Rosa, pues, ella es el Sol que, caminando con su corriente magnética, pasa por los Cuerpos Epitelares a los centros dominados por el Signo de Cáncer [relacionarse con el pecho].

El Sol llega a Cáncer el 21 de Junio; es el astro rey en el máximo de ascensión, y entonces celebramos el Solsticio de Verano.

En la fiesta de la Rosa, de San Juan, celebramos también al Sol en su máximo de actividad sobre nuestro corazón o Sol corporal.

---

[255] Literally 'Septenario' means "Septenary (of or pertaining to the number seven or forming a group of seven)"
[256] Literally 'grosera' means "gross; coarse, crude, vulgar; disgusting, offensive"
[257] Literally 'figuramos' means "figure, think; rank"
[258] Literally 'corriente' means "current, flow (of water, electricity, etc.); tendency, drift; tide; swim; rain"
[259] Editor's note: It is unclear when the 'feast of the Rose...' is, but the 'feast of St. John' is on June 24th, sometimes even celebrated on the night before (on the 23rd) as St. John's Eve.
[260] Literally 'corporal' means "corporal, bodily"

Zodiacal Course by Arnoldo Krumm Heller (Huiracocha)	**Curso Zodical** por Arnoldo Krumm Heller (Huiracocha)

The Mysteries present us [with] two great luminaries; the Sun and the Moon.	Los Misterios nos presentan dos grandes luminarias; el Sol y la Luna.
The Moon is the Planet of Cancer, Cancer is the Sign of artists, [and] of thinkers; therefore, [it] encourages the Imagination, and we know from our occult studies that we need to first prepare the Imagination in order to achieve Inspiration.[261]	La Luna es el Planeta de Cáncer, Cáncer es el Signo de los artistas, de los pensadores; pues, anima la Imaginación, y sabemos por nuestros estudios ocultos, que necesitamos preparar primero la Imaginación para lograr la Inspiración.[265]
Matter is nothing but Crystallized Spirit, and since all Matter radiates[262], [then] that radiation is the Cosmic Force.	La Materia, no es más que Espíritu Cristalizado, y como toda Materia irradia, esa irradiación es la Fuerza Cósmica.

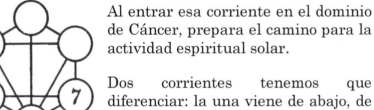

Upon entering this current[263] [or stream of Cosmic Forces] in the domain of Cancer, [we are] preparing the way for solar spiritual activity.	Al entrar esa corriente en el dominio de Cáncer, prepara el camino para la actividad espiritual solar.
We have to differentiate [between the] two currents: one from below, from the Earth, from the three inferior bodies, [and] the other from the heights of the Cosmos.	Dos corrientes tenemos que diferenciar: la una viene de abajo, de la Tierra, de los tres cuerpos inferiores, la otra de lo alto del Cosmos.
The currents emanating from the three superior bodies merge in the center, in the fourth body, in the mental [body][264].	Las corrientes emanadas de los tres cuerpos superiores se confunden en el centro, en el cuarto cuerpo, en el mental[266].
Mercury, as a symbol, teaches us this; below is the Cross of Matter, above [is] the Moon (the soul) and in the center [is] the Sun ([the] spirit) and thus [we] comprehend our Heart as the central Sun of our organism.	Mercurio, como símbolo, nos enseña eso; abajo tiene la Cruz de la Materia, arriba la Luna, el alma, y en el centro el Sol, espíritu, y así se comprende nuestro Corazón como el Sol central de nuestro organismo.
All the Glands of Internal Secretion grow and develop from birth, but are [also] headed, little by little, towards death.	Todas las Glándulas de Secreción Interna van creciendo y desarrollándose desde el nacimiento, pero se van acabando poco a poco hasta la muerte.

---

[261] Editor's note: See Ch.85 of *Tarot & Kabalah* (1978) by Samael Aun Weor for more information about this topic.
[262] Literally 'irradia' means "emit radiation, radiate; irradiate, give off, pour out, eradiate; emenate, pour out, shower;"
[263] Literally 'corriente' means "current, flow (of water, electricity, etc.); tendency, drift; tide; swim; rain"
[264] Editor's note: The Mental Body corresponds to #4 on the diagram.

[265] Nota del editor: Ver Ch.85 de *Tarot y Cábala* (1978) por Samael Aun Weor para obtener más información acerca de este tema.
[266] Nota del editor: El cuerpo mental se corresponde con el n° 4 en el diagrama.

| Zodiacal Course by Arnoldo Krumm Heller (Huiracocha) | Curso Zodical por Arnoldo Krumm Heller (Huiracocha) |

Except [for] one, which is to say, [the one that] dies on its own, separate[267] [from the rest of the body]; [which] is the Thymus gland.

It forms a notable exception, since, [it] only grows and acts on our growth during childhood.

We know that during the intra-uterine[268] life we develop at the mercy of the planetary influence [of the moon] and during [those] nine months we receive the influence of the seven stars [or planets], repeated two [times], and those two are what forever characterize us.

At the moment of birth, the stars [and planets] imprint [upon] us, one might say, a mark, [or] an itinerary on the forehead and on the hands, which we have to live; [this] is our horoscope, and the art of Astrology is nothing more than copying this itinerary.

We see how enormous the growth of a child is in the first days of life, and if we followed in that [same] proportion[269] we would become giants.

Full of pleasure[270] parents weigh the children and are happy to see increases[271] gram by gram, [and] pound by pound.

But soon [the children] will restrain[272] [themselves], [and] will stop this development, until finishing at about 21 years [of age].

Menos una, esa se puede decir, muere por su cuenta, aparte; es la glándula Timo.

Ella forma una excepción notable, pues, sólo crece y actúa en nuestro crecimiento durante la infancia.

Sabemos que durante la vida intrauterina nos desarrollamos a merced de la influencia planetaria y durante los nueve meses recibimos la influencia de los siete astros, repitiéndose dos, y esos dos son los que nos caracterizan para siempre.

En el momento de nacer, los astros nos imprimen, se podría decir, una marca, un itinerario en la frente y en las manos, el cual tenemos que vivir; es nuestro horóscopo, y el arte de la Astrología no es nada más que copiar ese itinerario.

Vemos cómo es de enorme el crecimiento de un niño en los primeros días de vida, y si siguiéramos a ese compás llegaríamos a ser gigantes.

Llenos de placer pesan los padres a los niños y se alegran al ver cómo aumentan de gramo en gramo, de libra en libra.

Pero al poco va refrenándose, va deteniéndose ese desarrollo, hasta terminar más o menos a los 21 años.

---

[267] Literally 'aparte' means "aside, to the side; on the side; except, besides"
[268] Literally 'intrauterina' means "intrauterine, located within the uterus, occurring within the uterus"
[269] Literally 'compás' means "compass; measure; timing; beat; pulse"
[270] Literally 'placer' means "pleasure, delight, enjoyment"
[271] Literally 'aumentan' means "increase, enlarge, add to, augment; multiply; raise, heighten, intensify"
[272] Literally 'refrenándose' means "rein, restrain, control; refrain, restrain oneself"

| Zodiacal Course by Arnoldo Krumm Heller (Huiracocha) | Curso Zodical por Arnoldo Krumm Heller (Huiracocha) |

We will not grow any more, reaching a period of stagnation and then we go back down towards decline[273], and all of this is caused [by] the Thymus gland, which weighs 15 grams at birth and goes [on] to weigh 30 grams during puberty and then disappears.

It does not disappear entirely, but it remains, and these remains are of paramount[274] importance for us, the occultists.

Growing up is not only a phenomenon of the material body, but also has its spiritual application, since, if the material part of the gland grows [and develops] the material body, [then] its spiritual exponents [also] grow [and develop] us spiritually.

The practice of the present lesson[275] has as [its] objective to not let the rest of the gland disappear, but on the contrary, to retain it and force[276] it to work [once] again[277] towards our wishes[278].

We know the action of the Moon in making the water increase in the high tides and then to decrease them [in the low tides]; so too does the Moon make the Thymus gland grow, which now goes down [in order to] receive a repulsion[279] [of energy] in its destructive action from [the energy of] the Sun.

The Moon operates[280] upon all liquids and [that includes] the liquid that comes out of the Thymus and lymph glands.

Ya no crecemos más, viene un periodo de estancamiento y luego volvemos para abajo a decrecer, y todo eso lo causa la glándula Timo, que al nacer pesa 15 gramos y llega en la pubertad a 30 gramos para luego desaparecer.

No desaparece del todo, sino que quedan restos y estos restos son de suma importancia para nosotros los ocultistas.

Crecer no es un fenómeno sólo del cuerpo material, sino que tiene también su aplicación espiritual, pues, si la parte material de la glándula hace crecer el cuerpo material, sus exponentes espirituales nos hacen crecer espiritualmente.

La práctica de la presente circular tiene por objeto no dejar desaparecer el resto de la glándula, sino al contrario, retenerla y obligarla a trabajar de nuevo a nuestro deseo.

Conocemos la acción de la Luna en hacer crecer las aguas en las mareas altas y bajarlas después; así también la Luna fue la que hizo crecer la glándula Timo, que ahora al bajar recibe un rechazo en su acción destructora por el Sol.

La Luna actúa sobre todos los líquidos y el líquido que sale de la Timo es la linfa.

---

[273] Literally 'decrecer' means "decrease, abate, ease off"
[274] Literally 'suma' means "top; ultimate"
[275] Literally 'circular' means "circular, paper or leaflet intended for public distribution"
[276] Literally 'obligarla' means "oblige, compel; coerce, compel to do something; push; bind"
[277] Literally 'de nuevo' means "again, back, anew, afresh"
[278] Literally 'deseo' means "desire, wish; want; will; yearning"
[279] Literally 'rechazo' means "repulse, rebuff, rejection; disavowal; rebound"
[280] Literally 'actúa' means "act, perform; play; appear; operate; proceed; sit"

Lymph fluid is known as the basis of nutrition, and thus allows us occultists a glimpse [into] the wonderful phenomenon of metabolism.	El fluido de la linfa es como sabemos la base de la nutrición, y así podemos entrever los ocultistas el maravilloso fenómeno del metabolismo.
Lymph is a fluid liquid, transparent, opaline[281] [substance], with [a] salty flavor; it contains many leukocytes[282] and especially lymphocytes[283].	La linfa es un líquido fluido, transparente, opalino, de sabor salado; en ella encontramos muchos leucocitos y sobre todo linfocitos.
The lymphatic plasma has the same principles as blood [plasma], but in other proportions, and here we catch a glimpse [of] the relationship between [the] Sun and [the] Moon, thus, the Moon prepares the path for the Sun, and the lymph is the great preparer[284] for the formation of blood, therefore, the lymphatic liquid collects[285] the nutritive elements from the blood and sends out the waste[286] left behind[287] by the action of metabolism.	El plasma linfático tiene los mismos principios que el sanguíneo, sólo que en otras proporciones, y aquí entrevemos la relación entre Luna y Sol, pues, la Luna prepara el camino al Sol, y la linfa es el gran preparador para la formación de la sangre, pues, el líquido linfático recoge los elementos nutritivos de la sangre y envía para fuera los desechos dejados por la acción del metabolismo.
Without the Thymus gland this action of the lymph would not be possible, thus, its arteries come from the mammary[288] [glands] and the Thyroid.	Sin la glándula Timo no sería posible esa acción de la linfa, pues, sus arterias vienen de la mamaria y de la Tiroides.

---

[281] Literally 'opalino' means "opaline (an opaque or semiopaque whitish glass)"
[282] Leukocytes or white blood cells are cells of the immune system involved in defending the body against both infectious disease and foreign materials.
[283] A lymphocyte is a kind of white blood cell and a landmark of the adaptive immune system. The adaptive immune system, also known as acquired immunity, creates immunological memory after an initial response to a specific pathogen, leading to an enhanced response to subsequent encounters with that same pathogen.
[284] Literally 'preparador' means " preparer; trainer, coach"
[285] Literally 'recoge' means "collect, gather; bring in; harvest; fold; scavenge; lift; reclaim; secure"
[286] Literally 'desechos' means "waste, rubbish"
[287] Literally 'dejados' means "untidy, slovenly; lost; abandoned"
[288] Literally 'mamaria' means "mammary, breast"

It is sufficient[289] to have experienced a removal[290] of the Thymus [gland] in order to observe a lesser[291] development and a decrease[292] in lymphocytes, making[293] us fat[294] and anemic[295].

Now let us imagine all of these effects on our spiritual exponents.

In our spiritual life there are also periods of rapid growth, we have periods [of] infancy and [periods] of maturity; we have times when we feel encouraged, predisposed, more capable of producing, and in those periods we constantly grow intellectually and spiritually.

What one has not essentially learned, as a foundation by 21 years [of age], one never learns.

Men who do not form their home[296] and their fortune before [reaching] 35 years [of age], will never [do so].

While this is the general [rule], an exception is formed [when] the occultists do the Rosicrucian practices, [because] at all times they can cause[297] a reactivation of their intellectual faculties and form [a] fortune even after 50 years [of age], [by] applying our keys, but always [by] giving movement [to] the magnetic centers, or (that is) making the chakras rotate.

---

[289] Literally 'basta' means "be enough, be sufficient, suffice"
[290] Literally 'ablación' means "ablation, surgical removal, excision"
[291] Literally 'menor' means "minor, smaller; lesser; least; younger, junior; young; under age"
[292] Literally 'disminución' means "diminution, reduction, decrease"
[293] Literally 'poniéndonos' means "put, place; lay; insert; impose; mark; adjust; send; contribute; subscribe; perform; translate"
[294] Literally 'adiposos' means "adipose, of or consisting of fat, fatty"
[295] Literally 'anémicos' means "anaemic, lacking red blood cells, lacking blood (Medicine); suffering from anemia"
[296] Literally 'hogar' means "home; fireplace, section of a chimney which opens into a room in which a fire can be lit; hearth, floor of a fireplace; interior; menage"
[297] Literally 'lograr' means "get, obtain; achieve, attain; reach; win"

Se ha experimentado que basta una ablación de la Timo para observar un menor desarrollo y una disminución de linfocitos, poniéndonos adiposos y anémicos.

Ahora imaginemos todos esos efectos en nuestros exponentes espirituales.

En nuestra vida espiritual hay también periodos de crecimiento rápido, tenemos época infantil y de madurez; tenemos tiempos en que nos sentimos animados, predispuestos, más capases de producir, y en esas épocas crecemos constantemente intelectual y espiritualmente.

Lo que no se aprende como esencia, como base hasta los 21 años, no se aprende nunca.

Los hombres que no forman su hogar y su fortuna hasta los 35 años, no lo harán nunca.

Si bien eso es lo general, forman una excepción los ocultistas que hacen prácticas Rosacruces, pues, ellos en todo tiempo pueden lograr una reactivación de sus facultades intelectuales y formar fortuna aún después de los 50 años, aplicando nuestras claves, pero siempre que pongan en movimiento los centros magnéticos, o sea que hagan rotar los chacras.

Mexican Initiation taught the significance of the OLIN symbol or [the symbol of] movement.

Therein are shaped[298] the Cosmic Forces that come from above and the Terrestrial Forces [that come] from below, and in the center is the Sun.

The growth and development of the Glands are a repetition of the growth and development of humanity in its different races, of the shock[299] between them and [of] their mutual relations.

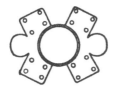

Our dreams are particuliar to our race.

Ask a black or an oriental stranger to our race who [talks of their] dreams, and we are surprised that their dreams are different.

We generally continue in the dreams that we've been preoccupied[300] with before falling asleep.

Let us, therefore, take advantage [of] this circumstance and, before remaining dormant to the descent of the Cosmic Forces from above, let us think [of, or concentrate] on the form of a Triangle with the point down, and the other Triangle of the Earth [pointing] up, forming the Seal of Solomon or the mexican Sign of OLIN.

La Iniciación mexicana enseñaba el significado del símbolo OLIN o movimiento.

En él están señaladas las Fuerzas Cósmicas que vienen de lo alto y las Fuerzas Terrestres de lo bajo, y en el centro está el Sol.

El crecimiento y desarrollo de las Glándulas son una repetición del crecimiento y desarrollo de la humanidad en sus diferentes razas, del choque entre ellas y sus relaciones mutuas.

Nuestros ensueños son peculiares a nuestra raza.

Preguntemos a un negro o a un oriental ajeno a nuestra raza lo que sueña, y nos sorprenderemos de que sus ensueños sean diferentes.

Nosotros generalmente continuamos en los ensueños lo que nos ha preocupado antes de quedarnos dormidos.

Aprovechemos, pues, esa circunstancia y pensemos antes de quedarnos dormidos en el descenso de las Fuerzas Cósmicas de arriba, en forma de Triángulo con la punta hacia abajo, y subiendo el otro Triángulo de la Tierra, formándose el Sello de Salomón o el Signo mexicano de OLIN.

---

[298] Literally 'señaladas' means "form, shape, fashion, create; design; constitute; arrange; take shape; educate, teach, train; form up"
[299] Literally 'choque' means "shock; crash, collision; conflict"
[300] Literally 'preocupado' means "preoccupied; worried, concerned; troubled, disquiet; qualmish"

In the previous letter[301] [the Lesson for Gemini] we spoke [about the] recommendation of the exercise for Imagination, but now let us pass on to the realm of Inspiration, thus we will feel inspired for the approaching day, and utilizing[302] the following practices with the Sun, we will open the center of Intuition, which corresponds to the heart.

We do the same breathing exercises [as in the previous lessons], but we mentally send the air to these centers so as to awaken Inspiration.

We need [to do] something [in order] to activate the blood circulation, and for this we moisten[303] the chest with cold water upon waking or when getting up in the morning.

The hindus go to the Ganges in order to wash themselves when doing this exercise.

Our mental body reflects [our] Imagination, and so during this whole month we [should] think about this action, attracting to ourselves the Cosmic Forces from above and then the Terrestrial [Forces] from below, in order to amalgamate[304] [them] into the centers that correspond to the Sign of Cancer.

En la carta anterior hablamos recomendado ya el ejercicio de la Imaginación, pero ahora la pasamos al terreno de la Inspiración, pues, nos sentiremos inspirados al día siguiente, y con las próximas prácticas con el Sol nos abriremos el centro de la Intuición, que corresponde al corazón.

Hacemos los mismos ejercicios de respiración, pero mandándonos mentalmente que el aire vaya a esos centros a despertar la Inspiración.

Necesitamos activar algo la circulación sanguínea, y por eso nos mojamos al levantarnos por la mañana o al despertar, el pecho con agua fría.

Los hindú van al Ganges, para hacerse lavados, cuando hacen este ejercicio.

Nuestro cuerpo mental obedece a la Imaginación, y por eso durante todo el mes pensemos en esa acción, atrayéndonos las Fuerzas Cósmicas de arriba y enseguida las Terrestres de abajo, para que se amalgamen en los centros que corresponden al Signo de Cáncer.

---

[301] Literally 'carta' means "letter; document; charter; epistle; map; card"
[302] Literally 'con' means "with; by, to, in"
[303] Literally 'mojamos' means "wet, soak in water; moisten; drench, soak, saturate"
[304] Literally 'amalgamen' means "amalgamate (to mix or merge so as to make a combination; blend; unite; combine)"

LEO

Dear Disciple:

In the ancient initiations one had to suffer the ordeal of Water under the Sign of Cancer; the ordeal of Fire under Leo. That of the Earth under Taurus and that of Air under Gemini.

The Disciple lived and lives in Leo, redemption… It is [for this reason that] the redeemer is always THE SON OF THE SUN.

If the radiant star principle awakened the fire with Aries, now it verifies the transmutation [of that fire] in all that exists, [by] maturing the seeds[305] in Leo.

It is the same in us, but for this purpose[306], it is necessary for the mirages[307] of the imagination and [the] pictures[308] of fantasy to be burned and to be destroyed so as to awaken the true personality of our INNER BEING so that we can intuitively create.

In this Sign of Leo, the Sun is encountered at its center, projecting its influence with all [its] vigor[309], and it is the cause of what would not be possible to do, by suddenly exposing man (in [his] physical life) to the energy of the fiery star.

LEO

Querido Discípulo:

En las iniciaciones antiguas hacían sufrir la prueba del Agua bajo el Signo de Cáncer; la prueba del Fuego bajo el de Leo. La de la Tierra bajo Tauro y la del Aire bajo Géminis.

El Discípulo vivía y vive siempre en Leo la redención… Por eso el redentor es siempre EL HIJO DEL SOL.

Si el radiante astro principió con Aries despertando el fuego, ahora en Leo verifica la transmutación en todo lo existente, madurando los granos.

Así mismo es en nosotros, pero es necesario, para ese efecto, que los espejismos de la imaginación y cuadros de la fantasía se vayan quemando y se destruyan a fin de que se despierte la verdadera personalidad de nuestro SER INTERNO[310] para que podamos crear intuitivamente.

En este Signo de Leo, se encuentra el Sol en su centro, proyectando su influencia con todo vigor, y es la causa de que en la vida física no sea posible exponer al hombre, de súbito, bajo la energía del ardiente astro.

---

[305] Literally 'granos' means "grain, kernel; berry; particle, speck; pimple; carbuncle"
[306] Literally 'efecto' means "bill; effect, result; backspin"
[307] Literally 'espejismos' means "mirage; illusion, delusion"
[308] Literally 'cuadros' means "square; stable, structure in which horses and other animals are housed; picture; painting; plot; table; chart"
[309] Literally 'vigor' means "vigor, physical strength; ability to survive; energy, vitality"

[310] Originalmente "nuestro YO"

The Cosmic Forces, the current[311] of Light, increases[312], little by little, with Aries. Followed by Taurus, Gemini and Cancer, until reaching Leo where the great work is realized.

Up to this point, all the elements have been brought [together] in order for this astral combustion (to which we are referring) to occur[313], and from then on, [it] begins[314] going downwards, [and] the work of discarding the useless, [of] cleaning the underworld[315] and [of] spewing[316] [out] the slag[317].

In Arcanum 11 (the bound[318] lion) a smiling woman opens the jaws of a lion with gentle hands, that is to say, effort is not required for an extraordinary power, as if it were the symbol of omnipotence in the conquest of the animal nature.

Consciously, then, the Disciple should approach this moment [by] looking for Initiation within themselves, because it is the Sun, within ourselves, in one's energetic[319] current[320], that offers it to us.

La Fuerza Cósmica, la corriente de Luz, va entrando poco a poco con Aries. Sigue con Tauro, Géminis y Cáncer, hasta llegar a Leo donde la obra magna se realiza.

Hasta este punto, se han traído todos los elementos para que se efectúe esa combustión astral a que nos referimos, y a partir de él, yendo hacia abajo, viene la labor de desechar lo inútil, limpiando los bajos fondos y escupiendo las escorias.

En el Arcano 11 (el león amordazado) una mujer sonriente abre las fauces de un león con mano suave, es decir, por un poder extraordinario que no exige esfuerzo, como si fuera el símbolo de la omnipotencia en la conquista de la naturaleza animal.

Conscientemente, pues, debe el Discípulo acercarse a este momento buscando dentro de sí la Iniciación, porque es el Sol, dentro de nosotros, en su corriente activa, quien nos la ofrece.

---

[311] Literally 'corriente' means "current, flow (of water, electricity, etc.); tendency, drift; tide; swim; rain"
[312] Literally 'entrando' means "enter, go in; approach, come near to; access, gain entrance to; introduce; tackle; attack; rise; input"
[313] Literally 'se efectúe' means "take place, happen, occur; take effect"
[314] Literally 'viene' means "come; reach; arrive; result from; happen, occur; infiltrate; settle; land"
[315] Literally 'bajos fondos' means "underworld; lower depths; gutter, lowlife, slums"
[316] Literally 'escupiendo' means "spit; spew; cough up; bleed"
[317] Literally 'escorias' means "slag, scoria, waster material that remains after smelting metal"
[318] Literally 'amordazado' means "bounded, gagged, muzzled, clamped"
[319] Literally 'activa' means "active, energetic; alert, brisk; deedful"
[320] Literally 'corriente' means "current, flow (of water, electricity, etc.); tendency, drift; tide; swim; rain"

The different colored rays, that we speak of [in] the Rosicrucian [doctrine], may penetrate into us, all flowing towards a center where it seems to nourish itself, starting from there only one [color, that of] orange-gold, from [where] it passes through our vertebral column and finally comes to concentrate itself in the Heart, [the] center of all Light.

During the winter the Sun is closer to the Earth and we know that its influence is less pronounced, [even though] it should be the opposite.

It changes in the summer, [when] it is furthest away from us, when it is most active and when more impulses also [come to us] from the other Planets.

Everything breathes.

[This is] what puts[321] the Earth into its constant rhythm like a recumbent[322] lady[323], and we not only breathe through the Lungs, but every pore is [also] an airway in constant activity with which we inhale[324] Oxygen and we exhale[325] Carbon.

The Sun in its turn inspirates Spiritual Force, while exhaling Light and Heat.

We will see, much later, that the Solar Plexus breathes this same Light and Heat, while expelling Magnetism.

We have already passed from Imagination to Inspiration and [so now] let us assume that the practices and meditations of the previous letters[326] have awakened these faculties.

---

[321] Literally 'hace' means "make; manufacture; create; construct, build; fashion, shape; compose; emit; prepare, do; cause; perform; effect; force; render; fabricate; behave, act in a particular manner; live through; be"
[322] Literally 'yaciente' means "recumbent (lying down, reclining, leaning; inactive; idle)"
[323] Literally 'dama' means "king; queen; lady, gentlewoman; dame"
[324] Literally 'inspiramos' means "inspire; embolden; prompt; upload; inhale, breathe in"
[325] Literally 'espiramos' means "breathe out, exhale, expire"
[326] Literally 'cartas' means "letter; document; charter; epistle; map; card"

The Sun now has INTUITION.

IN, INTU, in almost all dialects, these radicals indicate something within, something interior, [and for us it indicates] concentration.

When men through their calculations and wisdom can no longer progress[327], the final Key, Intuition, is presented to them, which is the spiritual center of instinct, then, just like how in the material impulse in all animals gives[328] legitimate[329] direction, Intuition is the only [way that] the right way[330] can be indicated to us.

Intuition extracts its forces from the Body, Soul and Spirit, and like everything in nature [which] is intuitively conscious, man is put into contact with the Great All through his breathing, [so] breath in its turn [is] luck[331], [what gives us our] fortune.

Rama Prasad[332] has said: "HE WHO BREATHES, HAS LUCK."

We have said many times that it is not the Planets themselves nor the Zodiacal Signs which are important, but the forces that radiate from the Planets and transform themselves into the Signs of the Zodiac.

---

[327] Literally 'avanzan' means "advance, move forward; come forward; proceed; develop; encroach; thrust forward; toil"
[328] Literally 'en' means "in, into; for, to; on, at; by; about"
[329] Literally 'justa' means "just, fair, equitable; righteous; correct; legitimate"
[330] Literally 'camino del bien' means "way of good, path of good, way of good, right path"
[331] Literally 'suerte' means "destiny, fate, fortune, something which is to happen to a person; future course of events; luck, chance; condition, situation; sort, type, kind; stage"
[332] This refers to the author of *The Science of Breath and the Philosophy of the Tattvas*, also known as *Nature's Finer Forces*, mentioned in the Lesson of Gemini.

El Sol trae ahora la INTUICIÓN.

IN, INTU, en casi todos los idiomas, son radicales que indican algo adentro, algo interior, la concentración.

Cuando los hombres mediante sus cálculos y sabiduría ya no avanzan más, se les presenta la última Clave, la Intuición, que es el polo espiritual del instinto, pues, así como en lo material impulsa a todos los animales en justa dirección, la Intuición es la única que nos puede indicar el camino del bien.

La Intuición extrae sus fuerzas del Cuerpo, Alma y Espíritu, y como todo en la naturaleza es intuitivamente consciente, al ponerse el hombre en contacto con el Gran Todo mediante su respiración, respira a su vez suerte, fortuna.

Rama Prasad[333] lo ha dicho: "AQUEL QUE RESPIRA, TIENE SUERTE".

Ya hemos dicho muchas veces que no son los Planetas mismos ni los Signos Zodiacales los que tienen importancia, sino las fuerzas que radican en los Planetas y vienen a transformarse en los Signos del Zodiaco.

---

[333] Esto se refiere al autor de *La Ciencia de la Respiración y la Filosofía de los Tattvas*, también conocido como *Fuerzas Sutiles de la Naturaleza*, que se menciona en la lección de Géminis.

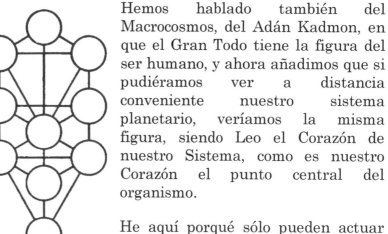

We have also spoken of the Macrocosmos, of Adam Kadmon, in whom the Great All has the figure of the human being, and now we add that if we look from [a] suitable distance [at] our planetary system, we will see the same figure [of Adam Kadmon], [with] the Heart of our System being Leo, [just] as it is our Heart [which] is the central point of the organism.

This is why only the forces of the Sun can act here precisely in LEO.

The Evangelists[334] are represented by four Kabalistic figures, Mark preserves the figure of Leo.

Mark, according to legend, was a painter, and the painter is the artist who, having imagined a picture gives way to Inspiration, but this picture was already latent in the soul through Intuition.

From here [we can see] that they are [all] in direct relation [to each other] Leo, Mark and Intuition.

In Leo we touch[335] the solar sphere of the Cosmic Christ, this being the Sign opposite to Aquarius.

For this [reason] Mark proposed that Baptism, be [done] with Fire instead of being done with Water, and this Fire is none other than what can be seen in the central Sun acting in Leo.

This same Sign [understood] as [the] Heart of the Cosmic Rhythm, is what leads the Sun to boil[336] the juice[337] of plants, and converts the Water into Wine, symbolized at the Wedding of Canaan.

---

[334] Literally 'Evangelistas' means "evangelist, gospeller, one who preaches the Christian gospel"
[335] Literally 'tocamos' means "blow; feel, touch; play; handle; beat, fall upon; press; ground; perform; sound"
[336] Literally 'hervir' means "boil; seethe; poach; surge"
[337] Literally 'zumo' means "squash, juice"

Hemos hablado también del Macrocosmos, del Adán Kadmon, en que el Gran Todo tiene la figura del ser humano, y ahora añadimos que si pudiéramos ver a distancia conveniente nuestro sistema planetario, veríamos la misma figura, siendo Leo el Corazón de nuestro Sistema, como es nuestro Corazón el punto central del organismo.

He aquí porqué sólo pueden actuar ahí las fuerzas del Sol precisamente en LEO.

Los Evangelistas son representados por cuatro figuras Cabalísticas, conservando Marcos la figura de Leo.

Marcos, según la leyenda, fue pintor, y el pintor es el artista que, después de haber imaginado un cuadro le da forma por la Inspiración, pero ese cuadro ya estaba latente en el alma por la Intuición.

De aquí que estén en relación directa Leo, Marcos y la Intuición.

En Leo tocamos ya la esfera solar del Cristo Cósmico, siendo este Signo la oposición de Acuario.

Por eso Marcos propone que el Bautizo, en lugar de ser con Agua sea con Fuego, y ese Fuego no es otro que el que se desprende del Sol central actuando en Leo.

Este mismo Signo como Corazón del Ritmo Cósmico, es el que impulsa al Sol para hacer hervir el zumo de las plantas y hace convertir el Agua en Vino, simbolizado así en las Bodas de Canaan.

| Zodiacal Course by Arnoldo Krumm Heller (Huiracocha) | Curso Zodical por Arnoldo Krumm Heller (Huiracocha) |

The Gnostic Church teaches the Mystery of the Bread and the Wine.

The grains contained in Bread, were grown and matured through the solar force; and Wine, made [from] Grapes [that grew] on the Vine, were developed and transformed in order to be consumed together in the Holy Eucharistic Unction.

"This is my Body (the Bread); [and] this is my Blood (the Wine)", is said [in] the Sacred Rites of all Religions, and [they] are taken together.

In [a] similar way our solid part and the liquid that we carry [within], have been transformed through the lymph [system], through the organic Sun, that is to say, the Heart Chakra, which forms and transforms everything within our organism.

At the core[338] of each seed there is some Sun, and therefore we call this life, because life comes from the Sun, but not the Planet rather the radiant, Living Light, which manifests itself and expresses itself through the Sun.

Gnostics know this force as [the] CHRISTONIC FORCE, because the word Christ (from the greek[339]) means not only Messiah, but Light, Redeemer, and it is the christic or christonic force that redeems us from within, [that] we save and we sublimate when the vibrations of Leo are connected in our Heart with those of the Leo-heart of our planetary system, that is to say, the Central Sun, the Father.

La Iglesia Gnóstica enseña el Misterio del Pan y del Vino.

Pan que contenido en los granos, creció y maduró por la fuerza solar; y Vino que, hecho Uvas en la Vid, se desarrollo y transformó para consumirse reunidos en la Santa Unción Eucarística.

Este es mi Cuerpo (el Pan); esta es mi Sangre (el Vino), dicen los Ritos Sagrados de todas las Religiones, y juntos se toman.

De igual manera nuestra parte sólida y la que llevamos liquida, se han transformado por medio de la linfa, mediante el Sol orgánico, es decir, el Chacra del Corazón, que forma y transforma todo dentro de nuestro organismo.

En el núcleo de cada semilla hay algo de Sol, y a eso llamamos vida, puesto que la vida viene del Sol, pero no del Planeta sino de la Luz Viva, radiosa, que se manifiesta y expresa por medio del Sol.

Los Gnósticos conocen esta fuerza como FUERZA CRISTONICA, porque la palabra Cristo (del griego) no sólo significa Ungido, sino Luz, Redentor, y es la fuerza crística o cristónica que dentro de nosotros nos redime, nos salva y nos sublima cuando se conectan las vibraciones de Leo en nuestro Corazón con las de Leo-corazón de nuestro sistema planetario, es decir, con el Sol Central, el Padre.

---

[338] Literally 'núcleo' means "nucleus, kernel; center, core"
[339] Christ comes from the Greek Χριστός (Khristós) which literally means "the anointed one".

The polarity established in the Cosmos is already made manifest[340] through the Solar and Lunar forces, [the] left and right sides[341], and it is curious that the Optic Nerve is formed in [a] Cross.	La polaridad establecida en el Cosmos es ya manifestada por las fuerzas Lunares y las Solares, parte izquierda y derecha, y es curioso que el Nervio Óptico esté formado en Cruz.
The right side of the body obeys[342] the left side of the brain and vice versa, so it is not unusual that while the heart is located to the left side [of the body], the Pranic Force of Leo penetrates through the right nostril[343] of the nose.	La parte derecha del cuerpo obedece a la parte izquierda del cerebro y viceversa, por esto no es raro que, si bien el corazón está situado al lado izquierdo, la Fuerza Pránica de Leo penetre por la ventanilla derecha de la nariz.
When the permutation[344] of Gold is done[345], the Angel accompanies us to the magic figure of Leo, and then we feel that the Sun is [a] living creature, [a] Spirit that radiates from the Primeval[346] Force from which we live, gestate, flower, fruit, enrich, enable, brighten, succeed, [and] refresh[347] [ourselves].	Cuando se hace la permutación del Oro, el Ángel que nos acompaña toma la figura mágica de Leo y entonces sentimos que el Sol es vida creadora, Espíritu que irradia de la Fuerza Primitiva de que vivimos, gestación, florecimiento, fruto, riqueza, poderlo, brillo, éxito, lozanía.
All these concepts are exponents[348] of the Sun, and when this consciously thinking energy penetrates through the right nostril with the Christonic Forces, [then] we can capture the REALIZATION of all these exponents within ourselves.	Todos estos conceptos son exponentes del Sol, y al hacer penetrar por la ventanilla derecha esta energía pensando conscientemente en las Fuerzas Cristónicas, nos podemos captar la REALIZACIÓN de todos esos exponentes dentro de nosotros.

---

[340] Literally 'manifestada' means "displayed, manifested, expressed, revealed, made manifest"
[341] Literally 'parte' means "part; message; report; dispatch; news bulletin; portion; section, segment; share; side; role; contender; spare part"
[342] Literally 'obedece' means "obey, take orders; mind; answer"
[343] Literally 'ventanilla' means "small window"
[344] Literally 'permutación' means "permutation (the act of permuting, alteration, transformation; the act of changing the order of elements arranged in a particular order)"
[345] Literally 'hace' means "make; manufacture; create; construct, build; fashion, shape; compose; emit; prepare, do; cause; perform; effect; force; render; fabricate; behave, act in a particular manner; live through; be"
[346] Literally 'Primitiva' means "primitive, primeval; original; early"
[347] Literally 'lozanía' means "lushness; rankness; freshness"
[348] Literally 'exponentes' means "exponent (a person or thing that expounds, explains, or interprets; a person or thing that is a representative, advocate, type, or symbol of something)"

It is, however, indispensable that the exercises be [done] with consciousness, before the universal force acts[349] in us with the final practice in the lymph [system], and then transforms into blood, thanks to the contact of the solar force, like how chlorophyll is formed in plants.

Our personality resides[350] in the Sun, and to catch this instant we must leave all our Glands [behind and] concentrate ourselves only upon the Heart, so that this force, which we have descended from the Epiphysis [or Pineal gland], Hypophysis [or Pituitary gland], Thyroid, Epithelial Bodies [or Parathyroid Glands] and Thymus [Gland] reaches the formation [of] a septenary, since there exists an immense secret (that we can not disclose) in the seven Planets and seven Glands culminating in the Sun.

Now when we pass on to the Runes and to its practices, we will be able to comprehend this mystery.

In the heart [one] can not act with gymnastic exercises, but [instead] with prayer and breathing every morning, [one can] try to cover the left nostril and fill the chest with air.

We have to think that this air is not going to the lungs, but mentally we are sending it to the heart, so that it acts there for transformation, [for] spiritual combustion, which physically becomes[351] the blood in the lungs.

---

[349] Literally 'actúa' means "act, perform; play; appear; operate; proceed; sit"
[350] Literally 'radica' means "resides, lies, locate"
[351] Literally 'se hace' means "become, be; turn into; get; turn around; form; go through"

We [should] also think, while doing this exercise, [that] we are [being] inundated by [the] Sun with Psalm 39, Verses 4, 8 and 20[352] when it says: "God, convert[353] us, show us your Face and we will be saved."

The Face of God is the Spiritual Sun and its force is the only [thing] that can save us from obstacles in order to give us Initiation.

---

[352] This appears to be a typo for Psalm 80: 3,7 and 19 (79: 4,8 and 20 in the Latin Vulgate), which says "Convert us, O God [אלהים]: and show us thy face, and we shall be saved." (80:3); "O God of hosts [אלהים צבאות], convert us: and show thy face, and we shall be saved." (80:7); "O Lord God of hosts [יהוה אלהים צבאות], convert us and show thy face, and we shall be saved." (80:19); these verses are from the Douay-Rheims Bible, published in 1899.

[353] Literally 'conviértenos' means "transform, convert; proselytize"

VIRGO

Dear Disciple:

In every Human Being there are two currents[354] [or streams of energy] which influence them.

[These] two currents which oppose one another [also] encounter [each other] in our organism [which is] its most perfect laboratory for transmutation.

This laboratory is the Heart, which we discussed in our previous letter[355] [the Lesson for Leo].

One of these currents comes from on high, from heaven, from the invisible world. The other [comes] from below, from the earth, from what is solid.

They are like two ocean currents one [of] which comes from cold regions and the other comes from the tropics until colliding[356] and confusing itself within that of its opposition, producing extravagant[357] and beneficial rains.

We have followed step by step, the first of these currents brought from on high, penetrating into us under Aries in the head, and we have carried through the Epiphysis [or Pineal Gland], Hypophysis [or Pituitary Gland], Thyroid, Epithelial Bodies[358] [or Parathyroid Glands] and Thymus [Gland] until reaching the Heart, [which is the] vital center and energetic Sun of our entire organism.

VIRGO

Querido Discípulo:

Dos corrientes son las que influyen en todo Ser Humano.

Dos corrientes opuestas entre si que encuentran en nuestro organismo su más perfecto laboratorio de transmutación.

Este laboratorio es el Corazón, de que hemos tratado en nuestra carta anterior.

Una de esas corrientes viene de lo alto, del cielo, del mundo invisible. La otra de abajo, de la tierra, de cuanto es sólido.

Son como dos corrientes marítimas que la una viniera de regiones frías y la otra partiera de los trópicos hasta chocar y confundirse dentro de su oposición, produciendo lluvias pródigas y bienhechoras.

Hemos seguido paso a paso la primera de esas corrientes traída desde lo alto, penetrando en nosotros bajo la ayuda de Aries por la cabeza, y la hemos llevado pasando por la Epífisis, Hipófisis, Tiroides, Cuerpos Epitelares y Timo, hasta llegar al Corazón, centro vital y Sol energético de todo nuestro organismo.

---

[354] Literally 'corriente' means "current, flow (of water, electricity, etc.); tendency, drift; tide; swim; rain"
[355] Literally 'carta' means "letter; document; charter; epistle; map; card"
[356] Literally 'chocar' means "shock; smash; crash, collide"
[357] Literally 'pródigas' means "prodigal; wasteful, extravagant, profligate"
[358] 'Epithelial bodies' are also know as "Hassall's bodies" or "Hassall's corpuscles" (bodies of epithelial cells found in the medulla of the thymus), but the singular term 'Epithelial body' refers to the parathyroid gland.

We have seen [that] each one of these Glands corresponds to a Zodiacal Sign and a Planet, and now let us penetrate into the domains of the terrestrial currents, that is to say, of the Square [which is] inverted [and opposed] to the Compass in the Masonic symbol.

We have already explained the mystery of the Clavicle of Solomon and of the Mexican Olin Sign, which is, as if we were saying, the involution [is descending] from above, and now we come to the inferior terrain[359], from below, that of evolution.

Remember that sign of the masonic emblem to which we have referred, in which there appears [an] inverted Square and Compass and, in the center, the letter "G" [which is the] initial of Generation, [and] which is obtained only when we reach the center of the two triangles, [which are] also inverted, that [we] will form said Square and Compass.

The Spirit is indicated by the Triangle with its apex upwards and now we have to examine the Triangle with its apex downwards representing Matter that stretches[360] [in order] to spiritualize itself.

From above we have reached[361] the subtle spiritual [force or current coming] from infinity in order to redeem [it] in its progress within Matter, and now it leaves its encounter in order to collide[362] and to be reunited in the Heart.

---

[359] Literally 'terreno' means "terrain; land, ground; park; location"
[360] Literally 'tiende' means "spread, extend; lay; tend; draw"
[361] Literally 'llegó' means "arrive, come; reach; roll along; land; immigrate; invade; get; travel; vaporize"
[362] Literally 'chocar' means "shock; smash; crash, collide"

| Zodiacal Course by Arnoldo Krumm Heller (Huiracocha) | Curso Zodical por Arnoldo Krumm Heller (Huiracocha) |

The Sign of Virgo, which is the one with which we work[363], covers the whole belly[364] and, while the Kidneys correspond to the Sign of Libra, the Adrenal[365] Glands or "Supplementary Kidneys" are[366] in Virgo.

This Sign has Mercury as its Planet and in it is the key because (remembering the symbol that represents it) we see that [it] brings up the Moon (the astral current [or stream of energy]), in the center is the Circle or Sun (Heart) and below the Cross (matter).

Mercury = Mercurio

It is so wisely hidden [in] Nature, that the Adrenal Glands not only have as [their] sign the Moon and the Triangle, but in fact they are really and materially constructed in this way (see page 64 [of] Esoteric Rose[367]).

These Glands are located[368] in the superior pole of the kidneys and are of [a] flat form and of [a] yellow color, the right gland preserves[369] [a] triangular figure and the left [gland is] semi-lunar [in shape], according to [what] the treaties[370] of anatomy textually state.

These Glands have or secrete a substance very [well] known in Medicine, which is given the name of Adrenaline[371] [or Epinephrine].

El Signo de Virgo, que es con el que avanzamos, abarca todo el vientre y, aunque los Riñones corresponden al Signo de Libra, las Glándulas Suprarrenales o Riñones Suplementarios encarnan en Virgo.

Este Signo tiene como Planeta a Mercurio y en él se ve la clave porgue, recordando el símbolo que le representa, vemos que lleva arriba la Luna (la corriente astral), en el centro el Circulo o Sol (Corazón) y abajo la Cruz (la materia).

Es tan sabiamente oculta la Naturaleza, que las Glándulas Suprarrenales no sólo tienen como signo a la Luna y al Triángulo, sino que real y materialmente están construidas en esta forma (véase Rosa Esotérica, página 64[372]).

Estas Glándulas se encuentran situadas en el polo superior de los riñones y son de forma aplanada y de color amarillo, conservando la glándula derecha figura triangular y la izquierda semilunar, según dicen textualmente los tratados de anatomía.

Estas Glándulas tienen o segregan una substancia muy conocida en Medicina, a la que se da el nombre de Adrenalina.

---

[363] Literally 'avanzamos' means "advance, move forward; come forward; proceed; develop; encroach; thrust forward; toil"
[364] Literally 'vientre' means "abdomen, stomach, belly"
[365] Literally 'Suprarrenales' means "suprarenal, situated above the kidney"
[366] Literally 'encarnan' means "incarnadine; incarnate, embody; blood"
[367] Editor's note: It is unclear what Section of *Esoteric Rose* (1931) this page is referring to. But there is an image in the Section entitled 'THE ROSE AND OUR OWN PHYSIOLOGY' which is shown on the following page, and it is the only image in the book...
[368] Literally 'se encuentran situadas' means "[which] is encountered situated"
[369] Literally 'conservando' means "preserve, conserve; keep, retain"
[370] Literally 'tratados' means "treaty, tractate, agreement; discourse"
[371] Literally 'Adrenalina' means "adrenaline, epinephrine (hormone which causes blood pressure to rise)"

---

[372] Nota del Editor: No está claro lo que la Sección de *Rosa Esotérica* (1931) esta página se refiere. Pero hay una imagen en la Sección titulada 'LA ROSA Y NUESTRA PROPIA FISIOLOGÍA' que se muestra en la siguiente página, y es la única imagen en el libro ...

[Inserted by the editor, not in the original]   [Insertada por el editor, no en el original]

1) La Epífisis – 2) La Hipófisis – 3) El Tiroides
4) Los Cuerpos Epitelares – 5) El Timo – 6) Los Riñones Suplementarios
7) Las Glándulas Sexuales

1) The Epiphysis [or Pineal Gland]
2) The Hypophysis [or Pituitary Gland]
3) The Thyroid – 4) The Epithelial Bodies [or Parathyroid Glands]
5) The Thymus – 6) The "Supplementary Kidneys" [or Adrenal Glands]
7) The Sexual Glands

[End of editor's insert]   [Fin de la inserción del editor]

This substance is a powerful agent for surgerical operations because it is the most powerful[373] haemostatic[374] which is [presently] known, and its action is wonderful for the eyes, since the illnesses of these organs are cured instantly with the hormones of the referenced Glands.

[Our] Disciples must remember [all] that we have explained [about what] inherently[375] [exists] in the effects of the hormones situated in the head above the organ of Light.

Adrenaline is astringent and closes the doors where the [energetic] current that comes from below gathers[376] in order to evolve so that it arrives[377] prepared and sublimated[378] at the heart and can withstand[379] the transmutation that operates in this organ before converting itself into something superior and spiritual.

Virgo, as we have said, covers the whole Belly.

Firmicus[380] said that those born under this Sign have to suffer from flatulence[381], from cramping in the belly, from stomach inflammation and from difficult digestion.

---

[373] Literally 'enérgico' means "energetic, vigorous; vital, lively; forceful, forcible; forthright, emphatic; determined; positive"
[374] Literally 'hemostático' means "haemostatic (retarding or stopping bleeding, or the flow of blood within the blood vessels)"
[375] Literally 'inherente' means "inherent, intrinsic, existing as a natural and integral part, natural, inborn"
[376] Literally 'agolpa' means "throng, crowd, gather"
[377] Literally 'llegue' means "arrive, come; reach; roll along; land; immigrate; invade; get; travel; vaporize"
[378] Literally 'sutilizada' means "subtilized (to elevate in character, sublimate; to introduce subtleties into or argue subtly about)"
[379] Literally 'soportar' means "hold up; put up with, endure; outstay"
[380] Julius Firmicus Maternus was a Latin writer and notable astrologer, who received a pagan classical education that made him conversant with Greek; he lived in the reign of Constantine I and his successors. His triple career made him a public advocate, an astrologer and finally a Christian polemicist.
[381] Literally 'flatulencia' means "flatulence, accumulation of gas in the stomach"

Zodiacal Course by Arnoldo Krumm Heller (Huiracocha)	Curso Zodical por Arnoldo Krumm Heller (Huiracocha)
It seems, then, that in the 6th house, life is prepared in Virgo.	Se ve, pues, en la 6a. casa, que en Virgo se prepara la vida.
This affirmation of the famous Initiate Astrologer, should make us think.	Esta afirmación del célebre Astrólogo Iniciado, debe hacernos pensar.
Let us look at [the fact] that, upon receipt of the current from above, everything was prepared in the chest.	Fijémonos en que, al recibir la corriente de arriba, todo era preparación en el pecho.
Now this preparation is realized in the belly.	Ahora esta preparación se realiza en el vientre.
Previously the action[382] of the chest ascended to the eyes and now everything [is] performed in the belly and then ascends to the eyes.	Anteriormente la actuación del pecho ascendía a los ojos y ahora todo actúa en el vientre y también asciende a los ojos.
The difference is that the most spiritual organs are those that are located in the chest and brain, and the most material [organs are located] in the belly and the extremities.	La diferencia consiste en que los órganos más espirituales son los que radican en el pecho y cerebro, y los más materiales en el vientre y las extremidades.
The current [or stream of energy] that comes from below, from the earth, can not suddenly[383] go[384] to the regenerating, purifying and transforming organ –the Heart– and necessarily[385] needs to start[386] its[387] preparation in the belly under the Sign of Virgo, [by] receiving the hormones from the Adrenal Glands which are those that are kept[388] and suspended for the moment in order to [later] saturate it.	La corriente que viene de abajo, desde la tierra, no puede arribar bruscamente al órgano regenerador, purificador y transformador - el Corazón - y necesita forzosamente atravesar esa preparación en el vientre bajo el Signo de Virgo, recibiendo las hormonas de las Glándulas Suprarrenales que son las que detienen y suspenden de momento para saturarla.
Let us return again to the Sign of Virgo. Which is represented by an M and an arrow through it.	Volvamos otra vez al Signo de Virgo. Este está representado por una M y una flecha que la atraviesa.

---

[382] Literally 'actuación' means "performance, show, presentation; execution; act, deed; act of presenting an artistic work to an audience"
[383] Literally 'bruscamente' means "sharply, suddenly, brusquely, short, abrupt"
[384] Literally 'arribar' means "arrive, reach"
[385] Literally 'forzosamente' means "necessarily, needs, perforce"
[386] Literally 'atravesar' means "cross, traverse, pass over; outstep; break through; pierce"
[387] Literally 'esa' means "that; that one"
[388] Literally 'detienen' means "detain, arrest; delay; confine; keep, hold onto"

Now with [the Sign of] Scorpio, we notice that arrow [which is aimed slightly] upwards as [if] symbolizing the sexual forces.

This fact is truly eloquent.

Upon completion [of] the present secret course, we will go into something much deeper which will be given to the world for the first time and it is still unknown in Spain and America.

This is the Magic of the Runes, that is to say, [the Magic] of the Nordic Wisdom or Theosophy, which includes the SIG Rune, that of the conqueror[389], represented by an arrow in the oblique and downward form of [a] lightning [bolt], upon which could one put the phrase:

IN HOC SIGNO VINCIT.[390]

Only with this sign can one conquer.

Or what is the same: the terrestrial magnetic current which has risen through the legs and has received its first impulse in the sexual organs, will reach its goal (the Heart) under the direction of Virgo, holding the arrow of the conqueror and of triumph in order to arrive at the fire of the Heart and redeem itself.

Let us look well. So far we have come across the current from below, and [now] is the moment for us to encounter it.

In an ancient manuscript that we have seen when visiting a Rose Cross Master, to prepare for this Zodiacal Course, [the manuscript] began with Pisces followed by Leo, [and] finished with Libra.

---

[389] Literally 'vencedor' means "vanquisher, conqueror"
[390] Latin meaning "In this sign you will conquer"

One can comprehend this procedure in an epoch when it was still accepted that Heaven was above and the World was below us, but today we know that all [these] words are able to explain that, in reality, there is no up or down in the Cosmos.

For our part, we have our occult reasons for doing[391] this Course in the way we have [done it], following the Signs of the Zodiac as the ancient peoples have communicated them to us.

However, the [various] Yogas have for their part true exercises, since we are [now] entering their domain[392].

Yoga is, therefore, materialistic, it is something from below, it is Lunar, and not Solar like the Rose Cross [exercises].

Therefore [almost] all positions in Yoga are with bent legs or squatting.

We, however, stand upright [in our exercises], although there exists a point [of] similarity in practices for the exercises of the belly.

The practices of Virgo have been unmistakably[393] well preserved in the dances of the orientals, especially in Belly Dancing, which was also implemented in ancient Initiatic Temples, but the Key to all this has been lost.

All the previous practices, from the Head to the Heart, were in the first line and had [a] Psychic effect.

The practices that ascend from below have the opposite physical effect and [it] is precisely in the Fire of the Heart, where the amalgam[394] of the Physical and the Psychological are achieved.

---

[391] Literally 'llevar' means "carry, transport; take; convey; wear; win; lead; bear; spend; hunch, hump; heave; carry off; deliver; live through; encroach on"
[392] Literally 'el dominio de ellos' means "the domain of them"
[393] Literally 'manifiestamente' means "manifestly, evidently, clearly, obviously, unmistakably"
[394] Literally 'amalgama' means "amalgam, alloy, mixture of metals"

However, in part of the chest[395] we also have Physical exponents[396], [just] like in the belly[397] we have [a] Psychic [exponent] of the Solar Plexus.

The practices of the belly consist of [a] little bounce with the musculature of this organ while we are lying [down], and can be done in the morning or at night once [one is] laying[398] in bed.

We have to make the belly jump[399] or bounce[400], impelling[401] it, with the intention of putting it into motion[402] or agitating[403] the Adrenal Glands within it.

A German Doctor obtained[404] this secret years ago —we do not know [from] where— and published a book on this subject of abdominal gymnastics with which prodigious cures are achieved, advising[405] the bouncing[406] or plunging[407] of the belly, which reminds us [of similar results] obtained, many times unconsciously, by Azuero[408].

---

[395] Literally 'en la parte del pecho' means "in the part of the chest"
[396] Literally 'exponentes' means "index; exponent (a person or thing that expounds, explains, or interprets)"
[397] Literally 'en la parte del vientre' means "in the part of the belly/abdomen"
[398] Literally 'metidos' means "tucked, stuffed"
[399] Literally 'saltar' means "jump, leap; leapfrog; hop; dance; plunge; pounce"
[400] Literally 'brincar' means "bounce, jump; skip; hop; make jump; dance, skip or bounce about in a dance-like manner"
[401] Literally 'impulsándolo' means "impulse; act, operate; impel, propel; thrust; boost"
[402] Literally 'muevan' means "move, be in motion; put in motion; act on, take action; transfer from one place to another; change residence; excite, cause emotion; motivate, spur to action; suggest, propose"
[403] Literally 'agiten' means "wave, flutter; excite, agitate"
[404] Literally 'obtuvo' means "obtain, acquire, come by; procure, secure; earn, achieve"
[405] Literally 'aconsejando' means "advise, counsel; suggest; admonish"
[406] Literally 'brinco' means "bounce, jump; skip; hop; make jump; dance, skip or bounce about in a dance-like manner"
[407] Literally 'salto' means "jump, leap; leapfrog; hop; dance; plunge; pounce"
[408] Dr. Fernando Asuero (also known as Don Fernando) was a well-known Spanish physician (1886-1942), who practiced in San Sebastian and was famous for his ability to cure many "incurable" disease, sometimes simply by touching the patient's trigeminal nerve.

Sin embargo, en la parte del pecho tenemos también exponentes Físicos, como en la parte del vientre los tenemos Psíquicos hacia el Plexo Solar.

Las prácticas del vientre consisten en dar pequeños brincos con la musculatura de este órgano mientras estamos acostados, y pueden hacerse por la mañana o bien por la noche una vez metidos en el lecho.

Hay que hacer saltar o brincar el vientre, impulsándolo, con la intención de que dentro de él se muevan o agiten las Glándulas Suprarrenales.

Un Médico Alemán obtuvo ese secreto hace años - no sabemos de donde - y publicó un libro sobre esta cuestión de gimnasia abdominal con la que logró curaciones prodigiosas, aconsejando el brinco o salto del vientre, que nos recuerdan las obtenidas, muchas veces inconscientemente, por Azuero.

We are confident[409] that, by doing these practices, many chronic diseases (that some of our bretheren suffer from) will cease.

So, then, [sometimes] we have to suspend all the [other types of spiritual] practices before and during a month [and this] is unavoidable [in order] to verify the practices of Virgo that we have explained[410], making the abdominal organ jump, making the upwards and downwards movement, so that the terrestrial magnetic current is well prepared so it can reach[411] the Heart normally[412].

Tenemos la seguridad de que, al hacer estas prácticas, cesarán muchas enfermedades crónicas que pudieran padecer algunos de nuestros hermanos.

Así, pues, hemos de suspender todas las prácticas anteriores y durante un mes es forzoso verificar las prácticas de Virgo que dejamos expuestas, haciendo brincar el órgano abdominal, haciendo el movimiento hacia arriba y hacia abajo, a fin de que la corriente magnética terrestre sea bien preparada para que pueda llegar normalmente al Corazón.

---

[409] Literally 'seguridad' means "security, safety; reliability, assuredness; confirmation; irradiation"
[410] Literally 'expuestas' means "exposed; displayed"
[411] Literally 'llegar' means "arrive, come; reach; roll along; land; immigrate; invade; get; travel; vaporize"
[412] Literally 'llegar normalmente al Corazón' means "arrive at the Heart normally"

LIBRA

Dear Disciple:

The Disciples have observed how we have gone down the sidereal current –from above– until reaching the Heart and how we have begun to intercept[413] the current –from below– that goes (we could say) through successive screens[414] or filters in order to fulfill its objective in [the] superior planes.

That inferior current [which was] activated[415] in our last practice in the Belly, where the principle influence [of] Virgo is [to be found], since, according to the ancient Astrologers that Sign is related to the assimilation and disassimilation[416] of food, that is to say, with the phenomenon we call Metabolism.

Specifically, acting on the left side of the Liver, on the Spleen and on the whole Grand Sympathetic [Nervous] System and most especially on those mysterious Glands, the Islets of Langerhans[417], which play an important role in diabetes and from which Insulin is extracted.

Simply reading a book about the modern application of Insulin [allows one] to see how the substance acts on the digestion and Liver function, and the importance that modern Medicine gives to it [by] employing it in all diseases of the organs located in the Belly.

Consequently there is no Clinic –that follows the new procedures– which does not cure with Insulin or other products out of the Pancreas of animals.

---

[413] Literally 'atajar' means "intercept; tackle, head off"
[414] Literally 'cedazos' means "sieve, sifter"
[415] Literally 'actuó' means "act, perform; play; appear; operate; proceed; sit"
[416] Literally 'desasimilación' means "dissimilation, degradability, disassimilation"
[417] The islets of Langerhans are the regions of the pancreas that contain its endocrine (i.e., hormone-producing) cells.

Intimately and energetically, all the work of the Metabolism is realized under the action of the fluidic current that comes from the earth and is closely related (in this case) with the constellation of Virgo.

Now we hold[418] that this current (before doing[419] its work with nutrition and with [the] elimination of the morbid[420] elements) requires a prior preparation which [is] received in the organs that operate under the direct action of LIBRA.

Libra is the great equalizer[421], it is the Scales.

First of all, [it] weighs substances that are purported[422] to develop[423] [the body], and then [it] measures the receptive organs for the slag[424] and waste[425] [accumulating within them], an operation that occurs in [the] middle of the body, at the waist[426].

Therefore, the waist falls under the action of Libra, and in this location [we have] the Kidneys, the Bladder, the whole Vasomotor[427] System and Plexuses, [which] are [all] ruled by this Sign.

Libra also acts upon the thick[428] liquids such as Bile and upon everything that has [a] disinfecting action within our organism.

---

[418] Literally 'tenemos' means "have, possess; hold; bear; carry; wear; experience; practice; meet with; travel; show"
[419] Literally 'efectuar' means "effect, execute; bring about, effectuate; prosecute"
[420] Literally 'morbosos' means "unhealthy, morbid, sick"
[421] Literally 'equilibrador' means "equilibrator, balancer, equalizer"
[422] Literally 'pretenden' means "purport, pretend; profess, allege, claim"
[423] Literally 'elaborar' means "elaborate, provide additional details; process; work out, think out; develop"
[424] Literally 'escorias' means "slag, scoria, waster material that remains after smelting metal"
[425] Literally 'desechos' means "waste, refuse, rubbish; dross; rejected article"
[426] Literally 'cintura' means "waist, waistline, middle"
[427] Literally 'Vasomotor' means "vasomotor, altering the diameter of vessels (especially blood vessels)"
[428] Literally 'espesos' means "thick, dense; deep; stiff; heavy; dirty, untidy"

Libra is the great preparer, the great agent that measures things that have to penetrate into the body.

Therefore, it has its influence on all that which is Skin[429], from the head to the toes[430].

Bile is what gives the purity to the complexion[431] or is what blemishes[432] our face with its pigments.

Accordingly, women who want to have good skin or men who do not want to lose the fresh aspect [of their skin], must not forget this work of Libra [by] using only those plants that were cultivated under the influence of this Sign as cosmetics.

When we examine the figures of the Zodiacal Signs, we see that, beginning with Aries, it is also Libra [being] a kind of Scale with two plates as [a] symbol of equality, from here it has a downward [aimed] arrow.

In this way, if we count the Signs above and below, we have Libra in the center, that is to say, [it is] the sixth constellation, whereas it is also the sixth constellation if we count from [the] bottom up, starting from Pisces.

There is a perfect balance where the Macrocosm and Microcosm are equilibrated, the body from above and [the body] from below, the sidereal and the terrestrial.

We know that each Zodiacal Sign is ruled by a Planet, and the one that corresponds to Libra is Venus.

In letter[433] number 2 [which was the Lesson for Taurus], we spoke about the action of Venus in general.

---

[429] Literally 'Piel' means "skin, dermis; hide, pelt; rind, peel"
[430] Literally 'desde los pies a la cabeza' means "from the feet to the head"
[431] Literally 'cutis' means "skin, cuticle; complexion"
[432] Literally 'mancha' means "spot, mark; soil, dirty; smear, smudge"
[433] Literally 'carta' means "letter; document; charter; epistle; map; card"

Zodiacal Course by Arnoldo Krumm Heller (Huiracocha)	Curso Zodical por Arnoldo Krumm Heller (Huiracocha)
We said that it acts first upon the liquid system in order to dominate the fluidic [system], and while the liquid [itself] fell under the influence of Venus in Taurus, it is now in Libra [that] the thick, gelatinous part [of the fluidic system] dominates the secretions of the Ears, Nose and Tongue, Sexual Organs and Kidneys, which can be transmuted through vocalization.

This is why we say the "A" vowel.

We are, therefore, [when] in Libra, in the low tone of Venus, and on the other side [we are] in the high[434] [tone of Venus] in Taurus.

Astrology teaches that all the liquid aspects[435] correspond to the Moon, from the seas with their high and low tides, to the tears that flow[436] when we feel sorrow or joy.

The rise or fall of the sap of plants within their trunks [stems, or stalks] is subject to the Moon, but this action of the Moon is always associated with that of Venus since these two Planets are very [much] related to one another, [and thus, it] is curious that the Moon and Venus are the only two feminine Planets compared to[437] all the others that have masculine actions.

If we could squeeze[438] the body in order to separate all the solid aspects from the liquid [aspects, then] we would see a column of water, that is to say a double column that on one side is formed with solids and on the other with liquids, united within them both [would be] the fluidic [aspect] yielding[439] the action of the work upon these two exponents. | Dijimos que habla que actuar primero sobre el sistema liquido para poder dominar el fluídico, y mientras el liquido cayó bajo la acción de Venus en Tauro, ahora en Libra es la parte espesa, la gelatinosa, dominando las secreciones de las Orejas, Nariz y Lengua, Órganos Sexuales y Riñones, la que puede transmutarse por medio de la vocalización.

Por eso dimos la vocal A.

Estamos, pues, en Libra, en el tono bajo de Venus, y frente por frente a la misma altura de Tauro.

La astrología enseña que es a la Luna a la que corresponde toda la parte liquida, desde las aguas del mar con sus mareas altas y bajas, hasta la lágrima que se vierte cuando sentimos pena o alegría.

A la Luna está sometida la savia de las plantas cuando sube o desciende por los troncos, pero esa acción de la Luna va siempre asociada con la de Venus por tratarse de dos Planetas muy relacionados entre si, siendo curioso que la Luna y Venus sean los dos únicos Planetas femeninos frente a todos los demás que tienen acción masculina.

Si pudiéramos exprimir el cuerpo para separar toda la parte sólida de la liquida, veríamos que somos una columna de agua, es decir una columna doble que por un lado se forma con los sólidos y por otro con los líquidos, uniéndose en ambas lo fluídico que arroja la acción del trabajo sobre esos dos exponentes. |

---

[434] Literally 'altura' means "height, altitude; elevation; tallness; highness, loftiness"
[435] Literally 'parte' means "part; message; report; dispatch; news bulletin; portion; section, segment; share; side; role; contender; spare part"
[436] Literally 'vierte' means "pour out, spill out, cause to flow out; empty; shoot; tip out"
[437] Literally 'frente a' means "facing, opposite, versus"
[438] Literally 'exprimir' means "squeeze; press; wring; express"
[439] Literally 'arroja' means "throw, hurl, fling; send out, give off, spew out; produce, yield; throw up"

Back in the Temple of Tyre, the Deity, was represented by two columns united in the middle by a scale, both columns equally represented the equinoxes of the Spring and Autumn in Aries and Libra, who's significance also extends to South America although they have their times inverted there.

This is the fluid, the energy, the universal electricity or christic substance in its material expression.

The Great Architect who produced[440] the Temple of our organism, which is based on these two columns.

Aries is willpower, the impulse, the action that excites[441] everything, while Libra is the immutable Law that puts an end to everything.

In arcanum number 8 of the Tarot, we have Justice represented by the Sword and the Scales; and this same number is a [symbolic] compound of two plates that symbolize the infinite [which is contained] in its figure [∞], because it is in Justice where one finds the just impulse of everything, even if it has to be blindfolded.

In the second letter[442] [which was the Lesson for Taurus] we also spoke of the form of the symbol of Venus (that is to say, the Circle above and the Cross below), and in the constellation of Leo we have Regulus[443], the King, which is the Sun that directs[444] it.

Ya en el Templo de Tiro, la Deidad, estaba representada por dos columnas unidas por medio de una balanza, siendo ambas columnas igualmente la representación de los equinoccios de Primavera y Otoño en Aries y Libra, cuyo significado alcanza también a América del Sur aunque tengan allí los tiempos invertidos.

Es el fluido, la energía, la electricidad universal o substancia crística en su expresión material.

El Gran Arquitecto que elabora el Templo de nuestro organismo, que está basado en esas dos columnas.

Aries es la voluntad, el impulso, la acción que agita todo lo existente mientras que Libra es la Ley inmutable que pone punto final a todo.

En el arcano número 8 del Tarot, tenemos la Justicia representada por la Espada y la Balanza; y este mismo número es un compuesto en su figura de dos platillos que simbolizan lo infinito, puesto que en la Justicia es donde se encuentra el impulso de todo lo justo, aunque tenga que ser con los ojos vendados.

En la carta segunda hablamos también de la forma del símbolo de Venus, es decir, el Círculo arriba y la Cruz abajo, y en la constelación de Leo tenemos a Regulus, el Rey, que es el Sol que la dirige.

---

[440] Literally 'elabora' means "elaborate, provide additional details; process; work out, think out; develop"
[441] Literally 'agita' means "wave, flutter; excite, agitate"
[442] Literally 'carta' means "letter; document; charter; epistle; map; card"
[443] Regulus (α Leo, α Leonis, Alpha Leonis) is the brightest star in the constellation Leo and one of the brightest stars in the night sky
[444] Literally 'dirige' means "direct; guide, lead, instruct; manage; command"

Venus offers the same impulse in both[445] Signs, only that the ancients, who gave it the [title] of King, made it into the form of the Emperor's Globe with the Cross[446] that we [can] observe in many alchemical figures representing antimony[447].

When we take a course on Alchemy, we will come back to this symbol.

The fact is that (after passing through the degree of Libra) the Mystic receives this symbol in their hand, and it is explained in the Rose Cross [Fraternity] that the Mystery of the Crown of Thorns is realized in Libra and that of the King or Emperor [is realized] in Taurus.

For this reason the Chief of the Rose Cross Order had to pass through this superior degree of Venus in Taurus so as to receive the title of "Imperator" that, in our times, only the Master Rakoczi[448] holds and not those who have misappropriated [it], like Spencer Lewis[449].

Venus in Libra prepares men for Science, [whereas Venus] in Taurus [prepares us] for Wisdom.

Venus ofrece el mismo impulso en uno y otro Signo, sólo que los antiguos, al dárselo al Rey, lo hacían en forma del Globo del Imperio con la Cruz hacia arriba que observamos en muchas figuras alquimistas representando el antimonio.

Cuando demos un curso sobre Alquimia, volveremos sobre este símbolo.

El hecho es que el Mysto recibía, después de pasar por el grado de Libra, dicho símbolo en su mano, y se explicaba a los Rosa Cruz que en Libra se realizaba el Misterio de la Corona de Espinas y en Tauro el del Rey o Imperator.

Por esta razón el Rosa Cruz Jefe de la Orden, tenía que pasar por ese grado superior de Venus en Tauro a fin de recibir el titulo de Emperador que, en nuestros días, sólo ostenta el Maestro Racokzi y no quienes se lo han apropiado indebidamente, como Spencer Lewis.

Venus en Libra, prepara a los hombres para la Ciencia, en Tauro para la Sabiduría.

---

[445] Literally 'uno y otro' means "one and another"
[446] Editor's note: This seems to be refering to the orb or sphere topped with a cross that was used by the Roman and Christian Empires as a symbol of authority.
[447] Literally 'antimonio' means "antimony (a brittle, lustrous, white metallic element occurring in nature free or combined, used chiefly in alloys and in compounds in medicine)"
[448] Master Rakoczi was also known as "the Count" and the "Hungarian Adept", and it is said that this person was known to history as the Count St. Germain.
[449] Harvey Spencer Lewis, PhD (1883-1939), a pseudo-Rosicrucian author, occultist, and mystic, and the first 'Imperator' of the Ancient Mystical Order Rosae Crucis (AMORC), a group that Dr. Krumm-Heller finds irregular and he wrote warnings about their teachings, as did Samael Aun Weor.

Under the influence of Venus in Libra one can be a good Worker in Painting, [whereas with Venus] in Taurus [one can be] a Great Artist Painter; [with Venus] in Libra one loves prose[450], [whereas Venus] in Taurus [one loves] poetry.

In this [same] way, material Love is refined with Venus in Libra in order to convert itself into Divine Love with Venus in Taurus.

If in Taurus we recommended vocalization exercises, [then] in Libra we have to do gymnastics in order to accommodate the substances in their corresponding filters.

This is why it is possible for us to copy the exercises of Yoga which are the original material.

When one gets up early, one should drink a glass of water which the Disciple has previously blessed seeking[451] not to ingest it until [after] having made a Prayer invoking the Divine Forces[452] so that this water acts as [a] purifier.

Subsequently we enter into the gymnasium which must be done in the following way:

First extend[453] the arms like a scale, to the right and to the left.

Already in this position, the right arm is lowered along the body, at the same time raise the left arm.

Then the same operation is done with the left arm arching the body to that side and raising the right arm.

---

[450] Literally 'prosa' means "prose, sequence; common phrase"
[451] Literally 'procurando' means "see; seek; attempt"
[452] Literally 'fuerza' means "strength, quality of being strong, might; durability; determination, resolve; effectiveness; intensity"
[453] Literally 'extienden' means "extend, stretch; enlarge, lengthen; prolong; outstretch, overextend; open; escalate; issue; renew"

This operation or movement must be repeated seven times, alternately on each side, or fourteen times in total.

In all these practices one has to constantly concentrate[454] (because this is the basis of everything) on the terrestrial current that should be ascending and that [the] impure [energies] should not ascend without being assimilated and accommodated at the waist for your internal goals[455].

---

[454] Literally 'pensar' means "think, deliberate, conceive in the mind; believe; contemplate, consider; ponder, reflect"
[455] Literally 'fines' means "end, completion, termination; finale; aim; goal; corona"

SCORPIO

Dear Disciple:

Married Disciples who have achieved the exercising [of the] sexual functions as a sacred act or [as] a religious operation in their matrimony, have obtained[456] a great advantage, since, both beings, in this way, can mutually help [each other].

In general, each one of our Disciples must have a spouse[457] in order to perform the [duties of] marriage[458], but up [to now] they have done nothing but squander[459] their values, [and even] life itself[460], [when] they could have gained[461] eternal youth.

Let us not forget that the sensation of coitus is much too short, enough[462] to lead the performer to boredom[463], apathy[464], [and] annoyance[465] like a [form of] sickening[466] sadness and [often] we must force ourselves to become magnetically charged in order to feel the romantic[467] attraction [for each other].

---

[456] Literally 'conseguido' means "obtain, acquire, come by; procure, secure; earn, achieve"
[457] Literally 'mujer' means "woman; wife; inamorata"
[458] Literally 'connubio' means "matrimony, marriage, wedding, conjugality"
[459] Literally 'desperdiciar' means "dissipate, scatter; misspend, waste"
[460] Literally 'su vida misma' means "their life itself" or "their very life"
[461] Literally 'conquistado' means "conquer; win over; carry; capture"
[462] Literally 'para' means "so as to, in order to"
[463] Literally 'aburrimiento' means "boredom, weariness, ennui, tedium"
[464] Literally 'desgano' means "lack of appetite; reluctance, disinclination; weakness"
[465] Literally 'fastidio' means "annoyance, nuisance, bother; boredom"
[466] Literally 'asqueante' means "disgusting, sickening, nauseating, loathsome"
[467] Literally 'amorosa' means "loving, affectionate; amorous, passionate; yearning; yielding"

Ovid[468] has already said: "Post coitum omnia animalia tristia".[469]

In sexual function, only two objectives may be taken into account: either the conjunction of two souls in a soft and tender spiritual spasm, or the direct creation of a new being.

Animals only seek[470] this instant (for the final goal [of impregnation]) at the precise time[471] in which the female is in heat[472] and demands[473] to be fertilized[474], but man (the sublime animal, the angelic being) is the only one who repeats this function every day in order to go[475] [about] slowly draining himself [of his values] and [he does so] without consciousness.

Catalysis[476] [is what] we call an accelerating action that exercises certain substances upon other [substances in order to] increase or decrease the speed of their chemical reactions, and if we transfer[477] this idea of catalysis to the field of parapsychism[478], [then] we can already begin to count [on the] verification of the sexual functions as an exchange of their forces.

---

[468] Publius Ovidius Naso (43 BC - AD 18), known as Ovid in the English-speaking world, was a Roman poet who is best known as the author of the three major collections of poetry, the *Heroides, Amores* and *Ars Amatoria.*
[469] Latin meaning: "All animals are sad after intercourse."
[470] Literally 'buscan' means "search for, seek, look for; scout for; forage; call for, ask for"
[471] Literally 'época' means "period, age, era; season; lesson; length of time"
[472] Literally 'brama' means "rut, rutting season, period of sexual excitement (about animals)"
[473] Literally 'pide' means "ask, request, inquire; require, demand; invite; treat"
[474] Literally 'fecundada' means "fecundated, fertilized, impregnated"
[475] Literally 'irse' means "go away, remove oneself, leave, depart; discard, throw away, get rid of; slip; leak; overflow, spill over"
[476] Literally 'Catálisis' means "catalysis, acceleration of a chemical reaction caused by a substance that remains unchanged by the process; changes brought about by an agent that is unaffected by those same changes"
[477] Literally 'trasladamos' means "translate; move; transfer"
[478] Literally 'parapsiquismo' means "para-psychism (Psychism is the doctrine that there is a universally diffused fluid, equally animating all living beings; the difference in their actions is due to the difference of the individual organizations)"

The Pelvis in women, pours feminine currents, while the breasts give masculine [currents].

In [a] man the radical feminine current [is] in the mouth and the masculine [current is] in his virile member.

All these organs, as [a] consequence, must be excited with the purpose of giving and receiving, transmitting and collecting, and then one [should] provoke the currents more and more that [are now] flowing[479], looking for quantity and quality.

Dancing and kissing (which put the couple in intimate contact [with each other]) are none other than an intuitive manifestation in order to achieve this Magnetization between man and woman.

Here in Germany and in many other countries there have [been] societies which cultivated nudity and [even nude] dancing.

This has served many times for immoral excesses and it is good that it has been prohibited.

These things should only be handled by select persons with pure sentiments, and let us not forget that for the pure mind everything is pure and that immorality is not outside of us but within [us], and in the Mysteries of Eleusis (where they practiced these things) nobody was thinking about anything [other] than holy things.

Before, in the Initiations of ancient Mexico, young people of both sexes united for months, completely naked, who were allowed to mutually embrace[480] each other without ever reaching[481] the carnal act [or orgasm].

---

[479] Literally 'van' means "go, proceed, move; travel; walk; suit; lead; drive; ride"
[480] Literally 'acariciarse' means "embrace, cuddle; neck, kiss and caress; spoon, behave in an affectionate or sentimental manner"
[481] Literally 'llegar' means "arrive, come; reach; roll along; land; immigrate; invade; get; travel; vaporize"

La Pelvis, en la mujer, vierte corrientes femeninas, mientras que los pechos las dan masculinas.

En el hombre la corriente femenina radica en la boca y la masculina en su miembro viril.

Todos estos órganos, por consecuencia, deben estar excitados al objeto de dar y recibir, transmitir y recoger, y entonces se provocan corrientes que van en más y en más, buscando cantidad y calidad.

El baile y el beso, donde se pone en tan íntimo contacto la pareja, no es más que una manifestación intuitiva para lograr esa Magnetización entre el hombre y la mujer.

Aquí en Alemania y en muchos otros países había sociedades que cultivaban el desnudo y hacían bailes.

Sirvió esto muchas veces para excesos inmorales y es bueno que se haya prohibido.

Estas cosas sólo deben ser manejadas por personas seleccionadas de sentimientos puros, y no olvidemos que para el puro mentalmente todo es puro y que la inmoralidad no está fuera sino dentro de nosotros, y en los Misterios de Eleusis, donde se practicaban estas cosas, nadie pensaba en porquerías sino en cosas santas.

Ya en las Iniciaciones del antiguo México, se unían jóvenes de ambos sexos durante meses, completamente desnudos, a quienes se les permitía acariciarse mutuamente sin llegar jamás al acto carnal [o el orgasmo].

The awakened passion must be dominated so that once all the glandular juices are in [their] zenith[482], they can be transmuted into spiritual force.

In our work [the] "ROSE CROSS"[483] we said that in this instant, the Semen is cerebrized while the Cerebrum is seminized, [the] key to which lies in what we have already explained.

Our Disciples, [who are in] Rose Cross marriages, should ignore what others do[484] and keep this secret so that we are the privileged, the supermen, those of character.

This seems [to be] a selfish [act], but certain Keys should not be disclosed[485] to people who are going through a purely materialized life and have not done [the] Rose Cross practices.

Instead of coitus[486] which reaches orgasm, one should reflexively[487] lavish [one's partner with] sweet caresses, amorous phrases and delicate touchings, maintaining the mind constantly separated from animal sexuality, sustaining the most pure spirituality, as if the act were a true religious ceremony.

Nevertheless the man can and must introduce the penis and maintain it in the feminine sexual organ, so that for both [of them] a divine sensation, full of joy, ensues (which can last for hours) withdrawing at the moment in which the spasm approaches in order to avoid the ejaculation of the semen.

---

[482] Literally 'auge' means "peak, zenith; meridian; heyday, boom; upgrade; vegetation"
[483] Editor's note: This refers to the *Rose Cross: Novel of Initiatic Occultism*, an initiatic novel by Krumm-Heller first published around 1926.
[484] Literally 'hagan' means "make; manufacture; create; construct, build; fashion, shape; compose; emit; wage, conduct (war, battle); prepare, do; cause; perform; effect; force; render; fabricate; behave, act in a particular manner; live through; be"
[485] Literally 'conocer' means "know, become acquainted, meet; learn; recognize; see; taste"
[486] Literally 'coito' means "intercourse, coitus"
[487] Literally 'reflexivamente' means "reflexively, with a subject and object that have the same referent"

Debían dominar la pasión despertada para que una vez en auge todos los jugos glandulares, pudieran ser transmutados en fuerza espiritual.

En nuestra obra "ROSA CRUZ" decíamos que, en ese instante, el Semen se cerebriza mientras que el Cerebro se seminiza, cuya clave radica en lo que ya hemos explicado.

Los matrimonios Rosa Cruz, nuestros Discípulos, deben hacer caso omiso de lo que otros hagan y guardar este secreto para que seamos los privilegiados, los superhombres, los de carácter.

Esto parecerá un egoísmo, pero es que no deben darse a conocer ciertas Claves a quienes atraviesan una vida puramente materializada y no han hecho prácticas Rosa Cruz.

En vez del coito que llega al orgasmo deben prodigarse reflexivamente dulces caricias, frases amorosas y delicados tacteos, manteniendo constantemente apartada la mente de la sexualidad animal, sosteniendo la más pura espiritualidad, como si el acto fuera una verdadera ceremonia religiosa

Sin embargo puede y debe el hombre y introducir el pene y mantenerlo en el sexo femenino, para que sobrevenga a ambos una sensación divina, llena de gozo, que puede durar horas enteras, retirándolo en el momento en que se aproxima el espasmo, para evitar la eyaculación del semen.

In this way, each time they will have a greater yearning[488] to caress [each other].

This can be repeated as many times as one wants without ever becoming[489] fatigued, because on the contrary, [this] is the Magical Key in order to be rejuvenated daily, to keep the body healthy and to prolong life, since it is a source of health with this constant Magnetization.

We know that with ordinary Magnetism, the Magnetizer communicates[490] [magnetic] currents[491] to the subject and if the first has these [magnetic] forces developed [then] they are able to heal the second.

The transmission of the magnetic current is ordinarily done via the hands or via the eyes, but it is necessary to say that there is no more powerful conductor than the virile member and the vulva, [which are] a thousand times more powerful, a thousand times superior to others as organs of reception.

If many people practice this, [then] they spread strength and success to all [those] who are put into commercial or social contact with them.

But, in the act of sublime [and] Divine Magnetization, to which we are referring; both man and woman magnetize each other reciprocally, being one for the other as a musical instrument which (when being plucked) gives off[492] or starts[493] prodigious[494] sounds of sweet and mystical harmony.

De esta manera tendrán cada vez más ganas de acariciarse.

Esto se puede repetir tantas veces cuantas se quieran sin jamás sobrevenir el cansancio, pues todo lo contrario, es la Clave Mágica para ser diariamente rejuvenecido, manteniendo el cuerpo sano y prolongando la vida, ya que es una fuente de salud con esta constante Magnetización

Sabemos que en el Magnetismo ordinario, el Magnetizador comunica fluidos al sujeto y si el primero tiene esas fuerzas desarrolladas puede sanar al segundo

La transmisión del fluido magnético se hace de ordinario por las manos o por los ojos, pero es necesario decir, que no hay conductor más poderoso, mil veces más poderoso, mil veces superior a los demás, que el miembro viril y la vulva, como órganos de recepción

Si muchas personas practican eso, a su alrededor se esparce fuerza y éxito para con todos los que se pongan en contacto comercial o social con ellos.

Pero en el acto de Magnetización Divina, sublime, a que nos referimos; ambos, hombre y mujer se magnetizan recíprocamente, siendo el uno para el otro como un instrumento de música que, al ser pulsado, lanza o arranca sonidos prodigiosos de misteriosas y dulces armonías.

---

[488] Literally 'ganas' means "desire; wish"
[489] Literally 'sobrevenir' means "intervene; excel; arrive; supervene, ensue"
[490] Literally 'comunica' means "communicate, broadcast, disclose, report, convey, divulge;"
[491] Literally 'fluido' means "fluid, free-flowing; smooth; fluent; current or power"
[492] Literally 'lanza' means "throw, cast, dart, flip, launch, pitch, toss, chuck, fling, heave, hurl, launch forth, give;"
[493] Literally 'arranca' means "start, pull out, take off, pull off, set off, pick off;"
[494] Literally 'prodigiosos' means "prodigious, great, big"

The strings of this instrument are spread over the whole body and their principal buttons[495] are the lips and the fingers, provided that absolute purity presides over the act, [and this] is what makes us Magicians in that supreme instant.

Obtain[496] a good accumulation of forces at [their] boiling point, [and] say: "I AM STRENGTH[497], I AM STRENGTH, I CAN [HAVE] EVERYTHING THAT I WANT", and then direct the Mind towards whatever it is that you want to achieve[498].

Let us repeat, as we did in our [other] Works, we have the right to comfort[499], wealth[500], [and] power[501], provided that it is not to the detriment [of others] and [on the contrary, that it is] to the benefit of others.

The general utility is above the particular.

Keep this secret[502], and work according to [what] your inner being advises[503] you [to do].

We have arrived at the last Glands of the Septenary which we have followed.

We started with the Epiphysis [or Pineal gland and by] recommending the path of LIGHT, LOVE, LIFE, LIBERTY AND TRIUMPH, and if the Disciple has consciously done the practices [then he] has been [able] to find the final door, that of TRIUMPH.

---

[495] Literally 'los principales pulsadores de él' means "the principle buttons of them"
[496] Literally 'Conseguido' means "obtain, acquire, come by; procure, secure; earn, achieve"
[497] Literally 'FUERZA' means "strength, quality of being strong, might; durability; determination, resolve; effectiveness; intensity"
[498] Literally 'conseguir' means "obtain, acquire, come by; procure, secure; earn, achieve"
[499] Literally 'comodidades' means "comfort; convenience; cosiness; accommodation"
[500] Literally 'riqueza' means "richness, wealth; ennoblement; money; love"
[501] Literally 'poderío' means "might, power"
[502] Literally 'Guardad esto en secreto' means "Guard this in secret" or "Keep this in secret"
[503] Literally 'aconseje' means "advise, counsel; suggest; admonish"

Las cuerdas de ese instrumento están esparcidas por todo el cuerpo y son los labios y los dedos los principales pulsadores de él, a condición de que presida ese acto la pureza más absoluta, que es la que nos hace Magos en ese instante supremo.

Conseguido un buen cúmulo de fuerzas en ebullición, se dice: YO SOY FUERZA, YO SOY FUERZA, YO PUEDO TODO CUANTO QUIERO, y entonces se dirige la Mente sobre aquello que se quiere conseguir.

Repetimos, como lo hicimos en nuestras Obras, que tenemos derecho a comodidades, riqueza, poderío, siempre que no sea en perjuicio y sí en provecho de los demás.

La utilidad general está por encima de la particular.

Guardad esto en secreto, y obrad según vuestro ser interno os aconseje.

Llegamos a las Glándulas últimas del Septenario que hemos seguido.

Comenzamos por la Epífisis recomendando el camino de LUZ, AMOR, VIDA, LIBERTAD Y TRIUNFO, y si el Discípulo ha hecho conscientemente las prácticas ha debido encontrar la última puerta, la del TRIUNFO.

We also recommended concentrating oneself upon the Source of Light, upon one's interior source, repeating each time[504] "I AM, I CAN".

This was the Fighter[505] [in] the practice corresponding to Aries dominated by Mars.

Today we reach (from the opposite direction) the dominion of the same [planet] Mars, but in Scorpio, who rules the sexual parts.

In the ancient Initiations, [they] called the Scorpion THE GREAT FECUNDATOR[506].

The terrestrial current comes from the sexual parts, which only has slight opposition in the knees and [in] the joints of the feet, [before] colliding[507] and mixing itself with those [heavenly currents] which have gone through so many screens[508] until [finally reaching] the testicles [and ovaries].

Now [we are] looking after[509] the great laboratory where the fate of everything is determined[510].

All [of] Creation is governed by two forces, that from above (positive) and that from below (receptive).

Based in Love, one repeats the same activity emitting and receiving, the two poles, represented here by the man (positive principle) and the women (receptive principle).

---

[504] Literally 'siempre' means "always, ever, forever; each time"
[505] Literally 'Luchador' means "fighter, combatant; wrestler; contestant; fertilizer"
[506] Literally 'FECUNDADOR' means "fecundator, fertilizer"
[507] Literally 'chocar' means "shock; smash; crash, collide"
[508] Literally 'cedazos' means "sieve, sifter"
[509] Literally 'se trata' means "look after oneself"
[510] Literally 'se fija' means "set; lodge; latch on to; become fixed; take notice"

There is an intimate secret, then, in the mental plane, through our action, the woman converts herself into [the] positive [principle] and the man [converts himself] into [the] receptive [principle], this[511] transformation transcends sex.

That is to say, an androgynous tendency in us where both principles fight [each other], which makes us comprehend the Laws of the Biorhythm[512].

We have already seen that in our Liquid Nervous System we consist of masculine and feminine Glands ([see] our book "Biorhythm") which vibrate in a constant cycle[513] of action and reaction, ascent and descent, augmentation and diminuation, and [that] Mars operates [in] this fight and [that] within us its outpouring[514] [is] in the constellation of Scorpio.

In Astrology, Scorpio is the 8th House.

This is the House of Death, and statistics prove that the majority of beings die when the constellation of Scorpio is acting.

This is because we have lost the Key to managing Scorpio.

Let's remember that in Scorpio is the action and function of the sexual organs, whose passional power can only be compared with a lively[515] steed[516] who pulls the chariot[517] of our life.

Hay en esto un íntimo secreto, pues, en el plano mental, mediante nuestra acción, la mujer se convierte en positiva y el hombre en receptivo, cuya transformación transciende al sexo.

Es decir, una tendencia andrógina en nosotros donde luchan ambos principios, que nos hacen comprender las Leyes del Biorritmo.

Ya hemos visto, que en nuestro Sistema Nervioso Liquido nos componemos de Glándulas masculinas y femeninas (nuestro libro "Biorritmo"), que vibran en un constante camino de acción y reacción, ascenso y descenso, aumento y disminución, y esa lucha la opera Marte y sus efluvios en la constelación de Escorpio dentro de nosotros.

Escorpio corresponde a la 8a. Casa en Astrología.

Esta Casa es la de la Muerte, y la estadística prueba que la mayoría de los seres fallecen cuando actúa la constelación de Escorpio.

Esto es debido a que hemos perdido la Clave de manejar a Escorpio.

Recordemos que en Escorpión está la acción y función de los órganos sexuales, cuyo poder pasional sólo es comparable con un brioso corcel que tirara de nuestro carro de vida.

---

[511] Literally 'cuya' means "whose; which"
[512] Editor's note: " Biorhythm" is the name of another book by Krumm-Heller
[513] Literally 'camino' means "road, avenue; trail, path; lane; journey; distance"
[514] Literally 'efluvios' means "outpour, spill out quickly or freely; cause to flow out quickly or freely"
[515] Literally 'brioso' means "high-spirited, lively, zestful; proud"
[516] Literally 'corcel' means "steed, horse; charger, war-horse; racehorse, horse that is specially bred and trained for racing"
[517] Literally 'carro' means "car; truck; carriage, wagon, cart"

While we have our hands firmly on the reins of this steed, we can dominate it while hopping[518] and jumping[519] and infuriating[520] [the] proud, but the day that these reins are gone[521], the animal runs wild and goes off at [a] full gallop, turning our chariot [around] and dragging us through the rocks and the mud of the road until we are exhausted and dead.	Mientras tengamos en nuestras manos firmes las riendas de este corcel, podemos dominarle aunque salte y brinque y se enfurezca altivo, pero el día que estas riendas se nos van, el animal se desboca y sale a galope tendido, volcando nuestro carro y arrastrándonos por las piedras y el lodo del camino hasta quedar extenuados y muertos.
Behold the cause of many deaths in this Constellation.	He ahí la causa de tantas muertes en esta Constelación.
But Death and Life are intimately linked and depending on [whether] we can overcome[522] the evil effects of Mars in Scorpio, [we can thereby] emerge triumphant in Life, attracting new Life and new vigor[523]. The key is this.	Pero la Muerte y la Vida, están íntimamente ligadas y depende de nosotros podernos burlar de los efectos maléficos de Marte en Escorpión, saliendo triunfantes con la Vida, acaparando nueva Vida y nuevos bríos. La clave es esta.
Throughout our whole body, a portion of Little Glands are distributed [which are] more or less large or small, such as the sweat and sebaceous [glands] that are in the skin by the millions, each one of them [is] of [a] masculine or feminine character.	Por todo nuestro cuerpo, están repartidas una porción de Glandulitas más o menos grandes o pequeñas, como son las sudoríparas y las sebáceas que, por millones, están en la piel, siendo cada una de ellas de carácter masculino o femenino.
These Little Glands (in their intimacy) are individual[524] accumulators of Magnetic Forces with their respective currents, seeking in every instant [for] the masculine collision[525] with the feminine and vice versa, as [if they were] in a constant exchange of positive and negative principles.	Estas Glandulitas, en su intimidad, son aisladamente un acumulador de Fuerzas Magnéticas con sus respectivas corrientes, buscando en todo instante las masculinas chocar con las femeninas y viceversa, como en un constante intercambio de principios positivos y negativos.
This exchange, which is prolonged until a divine, sublime, state [is reached] is nothing other than Love.	Este intercambio, que se prolonga hasta un estado divino, sublime, no es otra cosa que el Amor.

---

[518] Literally 'salte' means "jump, leap; leapfrog; hop; dance; plunge; pounce"
[519] Literally 'brinque' means "bounce, jump; skip; hop; make jump; dance, skip or bounce about in a dance-like manner"
[520] Literally 'enfurezca' means "enrage, madden, infuriate"
[521] Literally 'se nos van' means "go from us"
[522] Literally 'burlar' means "deceive, cheat, mislead; circumvent, outmaneuver"
[523] Literally 'bríos' means "brio, dash, spirit, vigor"
[524] Literally 'aisladamente' means "separately, distinctly; individually"
[525] Literally 'chocar' means "shock; smash; crash, collide"

But these forces are dormant[526], sleeping, and it is our duty to wake them up, and to excite them or provoke them, and unite Man —as [the] positive principle— and Woman —as [the] receptive principle— in a mutual agreement[527] and harmony, [so that] both can realize the Great Operation of Sexual Magic.

We do this for 22 erotic points on our organism.

I observed that many women are copiously[528] excited if one touches the edges[529] of the ears; others are [excited by touching] the nipples, however the excitement is not local but includes[530] the entire body.

It is the same in man, who also has his erotic points.

The latter is excitable [by] touching[531] the chest which is his feminine part, while women have their clitoris as [their] masculine excitable part.

In this letter[532] we have exposed[533] a lot, putting every word clearly and accurately in place so that our Disciples comprehend and take charge of what this practice is and [so that they take care to] do it as best they can.

We only desire that the comprehension [is] correct between everyone and [that you] do things properly to our wishes.

---

[526] Literally 'aletargadas' means "heavy; torpid"
[527] Literally 'acuerdo' means "agreement, pact, accord; resolution, ruling; harmony; memory, recollection; sense, perception"
[528] Literally 'copiosamente' means "richly, copiously, heavily, profusely, abundantly"
[529] Literally 'extremo' means "extreme, radical, excessive; most, greatest; farthest"
[530] Literally 'abarca' means "include, embrace; take in, surround; comprise, contain; span, extend across; take on, deal with; monopolize"
[531] Literally 'rozándole' means "graze; rub, chafe; skim, touch"
[532] Literally 'carta' means "letter; document; charter; epistle; map; card"
[533] Literally 'abierto' means "open, not closed; outspoken, frank; generous, giving; on, turned on; exposed, vulnerable; unrestricted"

Pero esas fuerzas están aletargadas, dormidas, y es nuestro deber despertarlas, ya excitándolas o provocándolas, y unidos el Hombre - como principio positivo - y la Mujer - como principio receptivo - en un mutuo acuerdo y armonía, pueden ambos realizar la Gran Operación de Magia Sexual.

Tenemos para ello 22 puntos eróticos en nuestro organismo.

Observé que muchas mujeres se excitan copiosamente si se les toca el extremo de las orejas; otras son los pezones, pero la excitación no es local sino que abarca todo el cuerpo.

Es igual en el hombre, que tiene también sus puntos eróticos.

Este último es excitable rozándole el pecho que es su parte femenina, mientras que la mujer tiene su clítoris como parte excitable masculina.

En esta carta nos hemos abierto más, poniendo en cada lugar la palabra clara y precisa para que nuestros Discípulos comprendan y se hagan cargo de cuanto es esta práctica y hasta donde alcanza.

Sólo deseamos que la comprensión justa entre en cada uno y hagan las cosas adecuadamente a nuestros deseos.

I insist that this letter should not be desecrated and that nobody should teach it to another.

It is strictly personal[534] and one commits an indiscretion, an evil[535] action, which never goes unpunished karmically [if one were to share it].[536]

In addition it is not complete.

In the course about Magic we will return to this [subject].[537]

---

[534] Literally 'individual' means "individual, personal; single, distinct"

[535] Literally 'mala' means "bad; poor; mischievous, naughty; evil, wicked; disagreeable; sick; disgusting; hard, difficult; inconvenient; troubled"

[536] Editor's note: Sometime between 1906 and 1909, Dr. Krumm Heller published "Do not fornicate" with a simplified presentation of some of the themes of tantric sexual magic. The book was not reissued, it is known only by being referenced in the *Revista Rosacruz* [*Rose Cross Magazine*] of June 1930:

"If the Rose Cross brethren seek gnostic works in libraries, provided that the caretakers of the books have not followed the example of St. Jerome (burning everything that smacks of sexual issues) they will find true wonders, as I have found, because the Gnostics were those who gave me my key of Sexual Magic. Some theosophists have called me [a] black magician because I occupy myself with these studies, but in this [field] all can agree that in terms of sexual magic I am [an] authority, [and] that I have occupied myself [for] many years with that discipline, publishing more than twenty years ago, my first book 'Do not fornicate', which at that time attracted much attention. Today it is only found in libraries."

Then between December 1932 and March 1933, Krumm-Heller published a number of articles in his *Revista Rosacruz* [*Rose Cross Magazine*] discussing some concepts from 'White Sexual Magic' and 'Tantra'. These are included in the Editor's Appendix.

Finally, starting in 1950, more information about the sexual mysteries have been made public by Samael Aun Weor in his book *The Perfect Matrimony* (1950). He also recommends this *Zodical Course* by Krumm-Heller (Huiracocha) saying: "The most profound Initiatic Wisdom of the centuries is enclosed within Huiracocha's 'Zodiacal Course'." in Ch.3 'Gemini' of the *Zodical Course* (1951) by Samael Aun Weor.

[537] Editor's note: It is unclear what this Course was, but it may be referring to *The Magic of Silence*

Yo insisto en que esta carta no debe ser profanada y que nadie debe enseñarla a otro.

Es estrictamente individual y el indiscreto comete una mala acción, que nunca queda sin castigo kármicamente.[538]

Además no está completa.

En el curso sobre Magia volveremos sobre esto.

---

[538] Entre 1906 y 1909, el doctor Krumm Heller publicó "No fornicarás", con la exposición simplificada de algunos de los temas sobre magia tántrica sexual, que había recibido de Papus y de otros maestros en Europa. El libro no fue reeditado; se conoce, sólo por la referencia que el propio Maestro hace en la *Revista Rosa Cruz* de Junio de 1930:

"Si los hermanos Rosa Cruz buscan obras gnósticas en las bibliotecas, siempre que los encargados de cuidar los libros no hayan seguido el ejemplo de San Jerónimo (de quemar todo lo que huela a cuestiones sexuales) encontrarán verdaderas maravillas, como yo las he encontrado, pues los gnósticos fueron los que me dieron a mi la clave de la Magia Sexual. Se que algunos teósofos me han llamado mago negro porque me ocupo de estos estudios, pero en esto sí están todos de acuerdo, que en cuanto a magia sexual soy autoridad, que me he ocupado muchos años de esa disciplina, publicando hace más de veinte años, mi primer libro 'No fornicarás', que en aquel entonces llamó mucho la atención. Hoy sólo se encuentra en las bibliotecas."

Luego, entre diciembre de 1932 y marzo de 1933, Krumm Heller publicó una serie de artículos en su *Revista Rosacruz* discutir algunos conceptos de 'Magia Sexual Blanca' y 'Tantra'. Estos se incluyen en el Apéndice del Editor.

Por último, a partir de 1950, más información acerca de los misterios sexuales se han hecho públicos por Samael Aun Weor en su libro *El Matrimonio Perfecto* (1950). También recomienda este *Curso Zodical* por Krumm-Heller (Huiracocha), diciendo: "La más profunda Sabiduría Iniciática de los siglos está encerrado dentro de 'Curso Zodiacal' de Huiracocha." en Cap. 3 'Gemini' del *Curso Zodical* (1951) por Samael Aun Weor.

SAGITTARIUS

Dear Disciple:

In our Magazine we offer a certain number of details[539] that we consider necessary in order to explain these teachings.

Here we limit ourselves to [just] treat the lines [of the] vital principles.

In this respect, we must of course note that the Planets and Zodiacal Constellations not only act on the exclusively identified parts, but [also] have secondary influences and direct their powerful action[540] onto other parts as well.

For example, Scorpio not only influences the sexual parts (which we have already discussed before), but also reaches the eliminating organs such as the Nose, the Throat and the Colon[541], etc.

Today, we have arrived in Sagittarius, we must point out that its influence is exerted on the Thighs (femurs[542]), but also exerts [its influence] on the Waist, Lungs, and Forearms.

We know, then, that the Planet of the Being is Jupiter, [a] word that comes from the Roman God JANUS, [JANO] or IANO (which leads [us] to the mantram IAO), and which was later transformed into JOVE.

This word gave rise in turn to our day thursday [Spanish: 'jueves'] and to the french 'jeudi'.

---

[539] Literally 'pormenores' means "detail, item; group of soldiers who have been sent on a mission"
[540] Literally 'actuación' means "performance, operation; action; act, deed; act of presenting an artistic work to an audience; show, presentation; execution"
[541] Literally 'Hemorroides' means "hemorrhoid, abnormally enlarged vein in or near the anus"
[542] Literally 'femorales' means "femoral, of or relating to the femur, of or pertaining to the thigh bone"

[Inserted by the editor, not in the original] / [Insertada por el editor, no en el original]

[End of editor's insert] / [Fin de la inserción del editor]

Jupiter, alongside Saturn, is the most powerful Planet and [is] therefore called "GREAT[544] FORTUNE" by astrologers.

Everything that is great and noble falls under the influence of Jupiter whose star offers[545] Magnetism and Heat.

In previous Signs, we have gone through very delicate and important organs and saw that they were acting in inferior Planets, but now we get to the thighs, [and what] is present [is] nothing less than Jupiter in Sagittarius.

This will tell us something and, indeed the femoral part ([the] thighs) have, at this point, a vital sidereal importance that we must not lose sight of.

The thighs are, so to speak, like a shell that envelopes[546] and defends[547] at the [same] time one of the principle arteries, the Femoral [artery], which is truly like an abundant[548] canal of blood, [and] is extremely important for our organism.

We already know (from our studies) that the Personality resides in the Blood, and this Personality is engendered and resides in the Magnetic Power of the same Blood.

Our own Magnetism is nothing other than the result of superior currents from above colliding[549] with those that come from the Earth, and it is precisely in the thighs where they encounter, unite, intermix[550] and embrace each other.

---

[544] Literally 'MAYOR' means "main; bigger; major, great; grown-up, adult; senior, elder; head, chief; biggest, largest; greatest"
[545] Literally 'ofrece' means "offer, suggest; tender, bid, propose a price; present, put forward, submit; express; hire"
[546] Literally 'envuelve' means " wrap, pack; cover; envelop, enfold; encircle, surround; involve, implicate, blanket; cocoon; swaddle"
[547] Literally 'defiende' means "defend; guard; advocate, uphold"
[548] Literally 'caudaloso' means "abundant"
[549] Literally 'chocar' means "shock; smash; crash, collide"
[550] Literally 'entremezclan' means "intermingle, blend; intersperse"

Sagittarius for the Greeks was the Centaur Chiron, [who] is in his turn master of Aesculapius, the God of Medicine.

Chiron, separately, was the son of Cronos, time.

Let us remember, in this respect, that Mythology tells us that when Chiron wanted to free Prometheus, he voluntarily wounded him with an arrow poisoned by Heracles who had taken the venom[551] from the Hydra.

As an astrological symbol for this chart we have an arrow which is that of Scorpio united to an M or to Aquarius.

This symbolism should invite us to think carefully.

From here, then, [we can see] that those who are born under the influence of Sagittarius are usually hurt by their own fault or the fault itself [of being] surrounded by barriers, obstacles and difficulties in life.

Providence[552] wants our lives to be level, easy, [and] on the upright path to triumph and success, but we are who we are[553], [and we are] those who (by our own faults and clumsiness[554]) put obstacles[555] onto our own path.

This tendency emerges[556] and resides[557] in the influences that we project [into] the terrestrial currents situated in the thighs.

---

[551] Literally 'veneno' means "bane, venom"
[552] Literally 'Providencia' means "Providence, divine supervision or protection; God"
[553] Literally 'pero somos nosotros, nosotros mismos' means "but we are ourselves, our own selves"
[554] Literally 'torpezas' means "awkwardness, clumsiness; blundering; inability; obtuseness"
[555] Literally 'cortapisas' means "hindrance, restriction, limitation"
[556] Literally 'brota' means "sprout, burst forth; grow quickly; cause to sprout"
[557] Literally 'radica' means "lies, resides, located"

We know that Jupiter is the representation of the personality, and beings born under these influences are full of wisdom and very adept at Philosophy; they are great soldiers, priests, judges, and finally, men whose personality is always well defined.	Sabemos que Júpiter es la representación de la personalidad, y los seres que nacen bajo estas influencias son llenos de sabiduría y muy adeptos a la Filosofía; son grandes militares, sacerdotes, jueces y en fin, hombres cuya personalidad está siempre bien definida.
Steiner gives man three parts: Mental Part, Rhythmic [Part] and Volitional [Part], [and somewhat] significantly [he] makes the last [one] reside in the extremities.	Steiner concedía al hombre tres partes: Parte Mental, Rítmica y Volitiva, haciendo residir esta última significativamente en las extremidades.
[Which] is to say, the Magnetization of blood concentrated in the femoral [area], going through the thighs, [which] is charged, he says, with the Volitional principle and then, Sagittarius with Jupiter acts again in the lungs, [and thus] this willpower loses the rough, terrestrial, material part in order to convert itself into [the] Divine Will.	Es decir, la Magnetización de la sangre concentrada en la femoral, al pasar por los muslos, se cargaba, según él, del Principio Volitivo y luego, al actuar de nuevo Sagitario con Júpiter en los pulmones, esa voluntad perdía la parte grosera, terrestre, material, para convertirse en Voluntad Divina.
Sagittarius is the ninth House of the Zodiac, where we have[558] travel, education and everything that is related with Religion and Philosophy.	Sagitario es la novena Casa del Zodiaco, donde encajan los viajes, la educación y todo cuanto tenga relación con la Religión y la Filosofía.
The Sagittarian Centaur is painted with wings and a double head, one looking forward and one backward.	Al Centauro Sagitario lo pintaban con alas y una doble cabeza, de las cuales una miraba hacia adelante y la otra hacia atrás.
This means that one who has gone through the Sign of Sagittarius is preparing for the comprehension of religious and philosophical things.	Esto quiere decir que el que ha pasado por el Signo de Sagitario se prepara para la comprensión de las cosas religiosas y filosóficas.
People outside of our studies may laugh upon seeing that we place the Thighs in relation to the Philosophical and Religious sentiments, but [this] is because they are not used to seeing much [other] than things from the material point of view.	Personas ajenas a nuestros estudios podrán reírse al ver que nosotros ponemos en relación los Muslos con los sentimientos Filosóficos y Religiosos, pero es que ellas no están acostumbradas a ver más que las cosas desde el punto de vista material.

---

[558] Literally 'encajan' means "insert; encase; enclose; rabbet; chuck; fit"

That is to say, they do not see [much] more than [just the] Legs, but [what] escapes them and [what] they are not aware [of] is that these Legs are nothing more than the expression (the symbol) of something spiritual, and [they] ignore the Biblical phrase that says: "We are, as [a] body, a Temple of God and the Most High dwells within us" [see 1st Corinthians 3:16].

It is said that when the material body sleeps, leaving the etheric double in space; that just like during the vigil [state], the body needs material nourishment[559], [so] too [does] the spirit during the night (while floating[560] in space) nourish itself with sidereal currents; that just as the material nourishment enters through the mouth [and then goes] into the stomach and colloidal[561] substances [enter] through the skin, there are [also] 42 principal points, and between them, twelve outstanding [points] in relation to the Zodiacal Constellations.

We are, therefore, incarnated Angels, and an Angel (as [a] body) is holy, divine and sacred from head to toe.

The double face of the Centaur tells us that the people who do the exercises of Sagitarius, learn to see in the Astral Records[562] (Akashic Records of Oriental Theosophy) [within] which is the past, and no one can be clairvoyant without having struggled and permitted the Superior Magnetism [from heaven] to harmoniously mix with the inferior [magnetism] or that of the Earth, which indeed happens (as has been said) in the thighs.

Es decir, no ven más que Piernas, pero se les escapa y no advierten que esas Piernas no son más que la expresión, el símbolo de algo espiritual, e ignoran la frase Bíblica que dice: "Somos, como cuerpo, un Templo de Dios y el Altísimo mora en nosotros".

Dicen que cuando el cuerpo material duerme, sale el doble etérico al espacio; que así como durante la vigilia el cuerpo necesita alimentos materiales, así el espíritu durante la noche, mientras vaga por el espacio, se alimenta de corrientes siderales; que así como el alimento material entra por la boca al estómago y por la piel las substancias coloidales, así hay 42 puntos principales y entre éstos, doce sobresalientes en relación con las Constelaciones Zodiacales.

Somos, pues, Ángeles encarnados, y un Ángel, como cuerpo, es santo, divino y sagrado desde los pies a la cabeza.

La cara doble del Centauro nos dice que las personas que hacen ejercicios de Sagitario, aprenderán a ver en los Anales Astrales (Anales Akásicos de la Teosofía Oriental) aquello que es el pasado, y nadie podrá ser clarividente si no ha luchado y permitido que el Magnetismo Superior se mezcle armónicamente con el inferior o déla Tierra, cuyo hecho acontece, como ya se ha dicho, en los muslos.

---

[559] Literally 'alimentos' means "nourishment, food; nutriment"
[560] Literally 'vaga' means "wander, roam; straggle"
[561] Literally 'coloidales' means "Colloidal (pertaining to or of the nature of a colloid: a substance in which particles can remain dispersed indefinitely)"
[562] Literally 'Anales' means "annals (a record of events, especially a yearly record, usually in chronological order; historical records generally)"

In addition, the Rose-cross [disciples] must learn the gift of Prophecy, that is to say, not only [of] seeing the old physiognomy[563] of the Past, but one has to sense and perceive the Future, eventually becoming prophetically intuitive.

Clearly, this is achieved if one has been through all the practices, but always, one of the [most] indispensable is that of Sagittarius-Jupiter in the thighs.

The Order of Martinists[564] follows the path of the SUPERIEUR INCONNU (unknown or Faceless Superior), but this is [actually describing] the Great Initiation or [how] to become an Initiate in the Mysteries of Jupiter-Sagittarius.

In Quirology[565] we have learned that the index finger is the finger of Jupiter and, consequently, that of the Personality, which indicates where it takes its name, [therefore] it is curious that this finger is related with the thighs and the Left Thigh corresponds [to] the index [finger] of the Right Hand and the [index finger] of the Left Hand [corresponds] to the Right Thigh.

By crossing [the] index [fingers], one is mentally calling to the Superior current, that [current] from above, to descend and reunite with the inferior [current] from the Earth.

---

[563] Literally 'fisonomía' means "set of features, physiognomy, facial features; superficial appearance; analysis of personal traits based on one's facial features"
[564] The "Order of Martinists" or Martinism (as it is often called) is an esoteric and mystical form of Christianity first established around 1740 in France by Martinez de Pasqually, and later propagated in different forms by his two students Louis Claude de Saint-Martin and Jean-Baptiste Willermoz.
[565] Editor's note: This refers to the *Treatise of Medical Quirology*, a book by Krumm-Heller first published in 1927 about 'quirology' or chirology, ie chiromancy or palmistry.

The Religions of the East are of [a] Lunar character, and this is why[567] one prays [by] utilizing the horizontal position so as to perceive[568] the lunar forces.

The Peruvian Huacas are in [an] inclined position, squatting one could say, therefore, [since] their solar worship required them to receive the influences of the King Star.

Nonetheless, they also placed themselves with [their] knees raised, so as to blend[569] the lunar currents with those of the Sun.

The Disciple [should] mimic the position of the Peruvian Huacas [while] lifting the index finger of both hands for five, ten or more minutes (according to the time you have) extending [the] pronunciation [of] the vowel "Iiiiiiiiii" whose vocalization should be ended with "Sssssssss", therefore, "IS" is the Mantram that corresponds to this practice, and [we should also] have the Mind absorbed with [the] prominent[570] desire to acquire the Forces of Sagittarius in the Region of the Thighs.

If the Disciple has practiced for a month while [also doing] Sexual Magnetization with their spouse[571], [then they] will now sense a very agreeable current in the legs, these currents are those which are encountered at the threshold[572] of the sexual parts.

---

[567] Literally 'el motivo de que' means "the motive of which"
[568] Literally 'percibir' means "perceive, feel, sense, be aware of; distinguish, discern; see, behold"
[569] Literally 'entremezclar' means "intermingle, blend; intersperse"
[570] Literally 'pendiente' means "pendant, hanging; unsettled; outstanding"
[571] Literally 'mujer' means "woman; wife; inamorata"
[572] Literally 'antesala' means "anteroom, antechamber"

CAPRICORN

Dear Disciple:

The Knee (as [a] joint[573] of the Leg) is a truly complicated mechanism, if we stick to the formation of its bones, ligaments, etc., [which are] arranged in a strange[574] and curious way.

[As] for its structure (which seems straightforward) [it] should be one of the weakest joints, but [it] is enough to observe certain feats[575] performed by athletes in order to figure out the enormous strength and resilience that this part of our organism has.

Ancient and modern drawings, describing the magnetic forces, place rays in front of the knee as strong as those which [are] depicted[576] simulating [the energy which is] briskly leaving the hands and the eyes of Magnetizers, as if to express with such symbolism that the knee is none other than an excellent Magnetic source[577].

[We have] already described (when speaking of Venus) the Liquids in their fluidic and semifluidic states, [now] we must take note [of] that rare substance that is found in our Knees and that, in Natural Science, is given the name of SYNOVIAL[578] [FLUID].

That is to say SYN, [meaning] 'with' and OVIAL [or OVUM], [meaning] 'egg'.

---

[573] Literally 'articulación' means "articulation, enunciation; pronunciation of words; joint"
[574] Literally 'raro' means "rare; infrequent; dignified; extraordinary; odd"
[575] Literally 'proezas' means "feat; prowess"
[576] Literally 'pintan' means "paint; picture; depict, portray; decorate; stain"
[577] Literally 'foco' means "focus; spotlight, floodlight; headquarters; pocket; seedbed"
[578] Editor's note: The word "Synovial" or "Sinovia" was coined by Paracelsus, and seems have been derived from the Greek word "syn" ("with") and the Latin word "ovum" ("egg"). This may be because the synovial fluid in joints is similar to egg white.

Vulgarly we could say that it is A SUBSTANCE WITH EGG.	Pudiéramos decir vulgarmente, que es UNA SUBSTANCIA CON HUEVO.
[The] egg, on the other hand, we know is a generating vehicle for [a given] species.	Huevo, por otra parte, ya sabemos que es un vehículo generador de especies.
This secretion from the wall of the joint capsule, not only has as its objective to make the bone surfaces slippery, but it [also] has the mission of providing some strength to our extremities.	Esta secreción de la pared de la cápsula articular, no sólo tiene por objeto hacer resbalar las superficies óseas, sino que tiene la misión de prestar cierta fuerza física a nuestras extremidades.
Otherwise, if the substance in question only has the mission of making the corresponding bones slide, [then] it would not be possible to tolerate[579] such great ordeals that athletes are subjected to and are constantly exposed to [including] unfortunate incidents, but, on the contrary, [it] is a kind of brake so that the bones do not move[580] more than [they should] in the appropriate direction.	De otro modo, si la substancia en cuestión sólo tuviera la misión de hacer resbalar los huesos correspondientes, no seria posible sufrir esas grandes pruebas a que se someten los atletas y se estaría expuesto constantemente a incidencias lamentables, pero, por el contrario, es una especie de freno para que los huesos no jueguen más que en el sentido adecuado.
The Synovial [membrane] of the Knee has a special composition that Science has not yet discovered, but it is known[581] to those who (like us) are engaged in certain [esoteric] studies.	La Sinovia de la Rodilla es de una composición especial que aún la Ciencia no ha descubierto, pero que no es desconocida para quienes, como nosotros, se dedican a ciertos estudios.
Among[582] the Zodiacal Signs, Capricorn is precisely the one that has its action[583] on the Knees, [and] united with it [in this action is] the Planet Saturn.	De los Signos Zodiacales, es precisamente Capricornio el que tiene su actuación sobre las Rodillas, unido a él el Planeta Saturno.
However, Saturn also corresponds to all the Bones, which is to say [that it corresponds to] the whole Skeleton, the Ear, and secondarily [to] the Stomach and Breasts.	Ahora bien, a Saturno corresponden asimismo todos los Huesos, es decir el Esqueleto entero, el Oído, y secundariamente el Estómago y los Pechos.

---

[579] Literally 'sufrir' means "suffer, feel pain, experience loss or harm, endure misfortune; be punished; tolerate, endure; stand, bear; allow, permit"
[580] Literally 'jueguen' means "play, game, sport; move; gamble; coquet"
[581] Literally 'no es desconocida' means "[it] is not unknown"
[582] Literally 'De' means "of; about; from; by; at; with; out; off"
[583] Literally 'actuación' means "performance, show, presentation; execution; act, deed; act of presenting an artistic work to an audience"

Zodiacal Course by Arnoldo Krumm Heller (Huiracocha)	Curso Zodical por Arnoldo Krumm Heller (Huiracocha)
We have inspected[584] an immense quantity[585] of Ancient Works in order to see if the old masters have always noticed this strange coincidence that Saturn rules [the] Bones, Chest and Stomach, and indeed the observation was made in all its parts.	Hemos registrado una inmensa cantidad de Obras Antiguas para ver si los viejos maestros habían notado siempre esta rara coincidencia de que Saturno rija Huesos, Pecho y Estómago, y en efecto la observación fue hecha en todas sus partes.
Nonetheless, if we consider the presence of Marrow in the Bones and the action of the Stomach as the main factor of Metabolism, [then] it can give us some light in order to comprehend this connection.	Sin embargo, si consideramos la presencia de Médula en los Huesos y la acción del Estómago como principal factor del Metabolismo, ello nos puede dar cierta luz para llegar a comprender esa conexión.
As for trees, Cypresses and Pines correspond to Saturn.	En cuanto a árboles, corresponden a Saturno los Cipreses y los Pinos.
In Germany (and even more [so] in the nordic countries) when the cold of Winter hits, all the leaves fall from the trees and there is [a] peculiar gray tone to the naked woods.	En Alemania y más aún en los países nórdicos, cuando azota el frío del Invierno caen todas las hojas de los árboles y queda ese tono gris peculiar de las arboledas desnudas.
But there are exceptions.	Pero hay excepciones.
Cypresses and Pines are green and full of freshness, even with the most intense cold, and it is Saturn who, like [a] great preserver[586], covers and sustains them in this state.	Los Cipreses y los Pinos quedan verdes y llenos de frescura, aún con los fríos más intensos, y es que Saturno, como gran conservador, los ampara y sostiene en ese estado.
Saturn in Capricorn is the Great Planet of Redemption, and if it is also the Genie of Death, [then] Death is always [the one] who gives life as a mysterious resurrection.	Saturno en Capricornio es el Gran Planeta de la Redención, y si es también el Genio de la Muerte, es siempre la Muerte que da vida como una misteriosa resurrección.
Jupiter is generous with its forces and bestows[587] (one could say) its beneficial[588] influence upon humans.	Júpiter, con sus fuerzas, es dadivoso y obsequia, puede decirse, a los humanos, con su bienhechora influencia.
But its effect is passing.	Pero su efecto es pasajero.

---

[584] Literally 'registrado' means "register, record, enroll; file; schedule; minute, clock; examine, inspect; check in"
[585] Literally 'cantidad' means "quantity, amount; total, sum; measure, degree; large amount"
[586] Literally 'conservador' means "conservative; curator, conservator"
[587] Literally 'obsequia' means "give away, bestow, handsel"
[588] Literally 'bienhechora' means "beneficent (doing good or causing good to be done; conferring benefits; kindly in action or purpose)"

In contrast, all that comes[589] from Saturn is permanent and all that does not come[590] [from Saturn] ends[591], remaining intact in this state of life where death (with its constant unraveling[592]) does not arrive.

So we must pass through these forces of Saturn, since, only he makes it so that the benefits acquired are durable and will never be extinguished.

If our terrestrial currents do not pass through these synovial accumulators, [then] their effects will not last, since Saturn is time (duration) and his wife is Rhea (Cybele), Goddess of the Earth, [the source] from [whom] everything flows.

It is worthwhile to study Greek Mythology in terms of the meaning of Rhea as the mother of Ceres, Juno, Neptune, Pluto and Vesta, and their different denominations[593] like[594] Bona, Dea, Ceres, Dindimena, Ops, Tellus, and especially, as [the] mother of Jupiter and his savior, and as [the] daughter of Uranus.

We must consider here that [the] FORCES of Nature are hidden in all these denominations of [the] greek Deities, [if we] want to give an account of the importance of the Knee with its Synovial [Fluid] that the magnetic currents of the Earth pass through.

These currents then pass through all the bones, that is to say, through the marrow of them all, inundating[595] us with magnetic energy.

---

[589] Literally 'da' means "give; present; deal; produce, yield; cause; perform; say; take; teach; lecture; start, begin; overlook; surrender"
[590] Literally 'toca' means "blow; feel, touch; play; handle; beat, fall upon; press; ground; perform; sound"
[591] Literally 'fenece' means "conclude, finish; deduce"
[592] Literally 'destejer' means "unravel, untwist, unwind; take out stitches; upset, worry"
[593] Literally 'denominaciones' means "designation, appellation; denomination"
[594] Literally 'de' means "of; about; from; by; at; with; out; off"
[595] Literally 'invadiéndonos' means "invade; impinge; encroach; raid"

Zodiacal Course by Arnoldo Krumm Heller (Huiracocha)	Curso Zodical por Arnoldo Krumm Heller (Huiracocha)
If these same forces and currents pass as [though] they are from the Earth (those which are agitated under [the influence of] Neptune and Jupiter), [then] their effects would be very distinct.	Si estas mismas fuerzas o corrientes pasaran tal como vienen de la Tierra, las cuales se agitan bajo Neptuno y Júpiter, sus efectos serian muy distintos.
We need to have previously saturated [ourselves] in the Knee, where the lead or weight of Saturn is received.	Es necesario que se saturen previamente en la Rodilla, donde reciben el plomo o peso de Saturno.
Lead is the metal of Saturn, [it is] very[596] heavy, and its colloidal state does not penetrate into our organism without being under the impulse of Saturn and [without passing] through the Knee exclusively.	El plomo es el metal de Saturno, demasiado pesado, y en su estado coloidal no penetra en nuestro organismo sino es bajo el impulso de Saturno y exclusivamente por la Rodilla.
Just as[597] Cancer operates[598] during the Summer Solstice, now the Sun [which is] in Capricorn [also] has a special magnetic influence.	Igual que en la época que actúa Cáncer en el Solsticio de Verano, tiene ahora el Sol en Capricornio una influencia magnética especial.
The Symbol of this Constellation is a Male Goat, which reminds us of the Male Goat of Mendez, always presented as an emblem of Black Magic, not being more than the same symbol with its same esoteric meaning.	El Símbolo de esta Constelación es un Macho Cabrio, que nos recuerda al Macho Cabrio de Méndez, presentado siempre como emblema de Magia Negra, no siendo más que el mismo símbolo con su mismo significado esotérico.
On the 25th of December the Savior of the World is born in a manger and his ascension to the life [like] a Male Goat in order to also offer a new life to Humanity.	En el 25 de Diciembre nace el Salvador del Mundo en un pesebre y su ascensión a la vida un Macho Cabrio para ofrecer asimismo una nueva vida a la Humanidad.
Jambilicus tried to prove (in his time) that all the Myths of Apollo, Mars, Mercury, Adonis, Attis and Osiris were only solar representations, and Aurelian established the same festival of the 25th of december as the feast of NATALIS INVICTI[599] or of the SOL INVICTI[600], which was later appropriated by the Christians [who] then took that time to celebrate the birth of the Nazarene, at around 354 to 360 years of our Era.	Jámblico trató de probar en su tiempo, que todos los Mitos de Apolo, Marte, Mercurio, Adonis, Attis y Osiris no fueron más que representaciones solares, y Aureliano instituyó la misma fiesta del 25 de diciembre como la fiesta del NATALIS INVICTI o del SOL INVICTI, para que luego los Cristianos se apropiaran esa fecha para celebrar el Nacimiento del Nazareno, hacia los años 354 a 360 de nuestra Era.

---

[596] Literally 'demasiado' means "too much, more than enough, extra, more than adequate"
[597] Literally 'Igual que en la época' means "Just as in the epoch [of]"
[598] Literally 'actúa' means "act, perform; play; appear; operate; proceed; sit"
[599] The Philocalian calendar of AD 354 gives a festival of "Natalis Invicti" on 25 December.
[600] Sol Invictus ("Unconquered Sun") was the official sun god of the later Roman Empire and a patron of soldiers.

All these are, ultimately, the same Myths and every one of them refers itself to the Solar Force that has different modes of expression and [of] action according to which influence and according to [which] constellation the King Star passed through, that (as we have proven throughout this present Course) is related to the different parts and organs of our body.

We are confident that never has any Book made known such explanations so clearly [as has been done in this course], unless our Disciples have read our [other] Works, especially [the] "Gnostic Church", where this INTIMATE SOLAR FORCE is spoken of under the name of CHRISTONIC FORCE, that we are trying to acquire and which has its doors of entry in those 12 Zodiacal points of our material Self.

The exercises of Capricorn are done by moving the knees, especially the right [knee], [while] concentrating the mind on this region.

Those who know Masonry can do the movements made by the master when entering into a 'workshop', thus, this stepping is really Initiatic.

Many times the Master Masons laugh when entering the Temple in their degree, [because] of the stunts that they are forced to do over the head of an imaginary coffin, going to the right and another on the left, bending their knees to step over[601] the obstacle.

However, these movements are nothing more than a reminiscence of the initiatic gymnastics of the Ancient Mysteries into which the Jewish Kabalists introduced [some of] their mistakes[602], [and] Masonry still has not been able to rid [itself of] these [mistakes].

---

[601] Literally 'salvar' means "save, rescue, salvage; circumvent; shoot; jump over; negotiate; overcome; cover"
[602] Literally 'yerros' means "error, mistake, something that is incorrect"

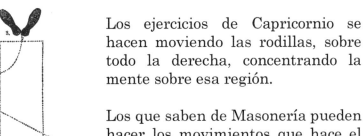

Todos estos son, en el fondo, los mismos Mitos y cada uno de ellos se refiere a la Fuerza Solar que tiene diferentes modos de manifestación y actuación según donde influya y según la constelación porque pasa el Astro Rey, lo cual, como hemos probado durante el presente Curso, tiene relación con las diferentes partes y órganos de nuestro cuerpo.

Tenemos la seguridad de que jamás Libro alguno habrá dado a conocer estas explicaciones tan claramente, a menos que nuestros Discípulos hayan leído nuestras Obras, especialmente "Iglesia Gnóstica", donde se habla de esa FUERZA INTIMA SOLAR bajo el nombre de FUERZA CRISTONICA, que tratamos de adquirir y que tiene en esos 12 puntos Zodiacales de nuestro Mismo material[603] sus puertas de entrada.

Los ejercicios de Capricornio se hacen moviendo las rodillas, sobre todo la derecha, concentrando la mente sobre esa región.

Los que saben de Masonería pueden hacer los movimientos que hace el maestro al entrar a un taller, pues, esa marcha es realmente Iniciática.

Muchas veces se ríen los Maestros Masones, cuando entran al Templo en su grado, de las piruetas que se les obliga a hacer pasando por encima de un ataúd imaginario, dando un paso a la derecha y otro a la izquierda, doblando las rodillas como para salvar el obstáculo.

Sin embargo, estos movimientos no son más que una reminiscencia de la gimnasia iniciática de los Misterios Antiguos en la que los Cabalistas Judíos introdujeron sus yerros, de los que aún la Masonería no se ha podido librar.

---

[603] Originalmente 'nuestro Ego material'

The Rosicrucians, who keep these secrets intact[604], now return to once again give the ancient path, given that the Masonic Master falls under the Constellation of Capricorn, whereas the steps he takes to enter into the Temple are just a means of facilitating the entry of the potentialities of the COSMIC FORCES into his organism.	Los Rosacruces, que guardan incólumes estos secretos, vuelven ahora a dar de nuevo el antiguo camino, puesto que la Maestría Masónica cae bajo la Constelación de Capricornio, mientras que los pasos que da al entrar en el Templo no son más que un medio de facilitar la entrada en su organismo de las potencialidades de las FUERZAS CÓSMICAS.

---

[604] Literally 'incólumes' means "unhurt, not hurt, undamaged, uninjured, unscathed, not scathed"

[Inserted by the Editor, not in the Original][605]

Steps of the Apprentice

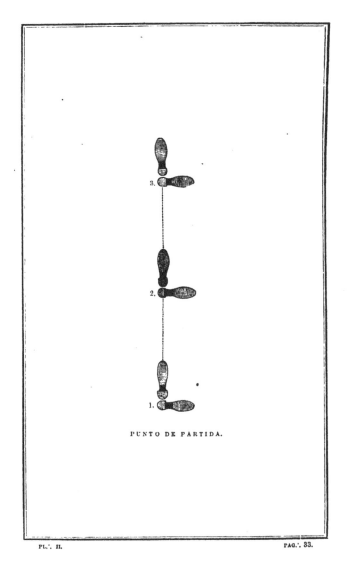

STEPS.

Three steps forward, starting with the left foot, and [put] the feet together at every step.*

* See Pl. 2 [above]

---

[605] This information on "Steps" comes from *Manual de la Masoneria* (1861) by Andres Cassard

[Insertada por el Editor, no en el Original][606]

Marcha del Aprentiz

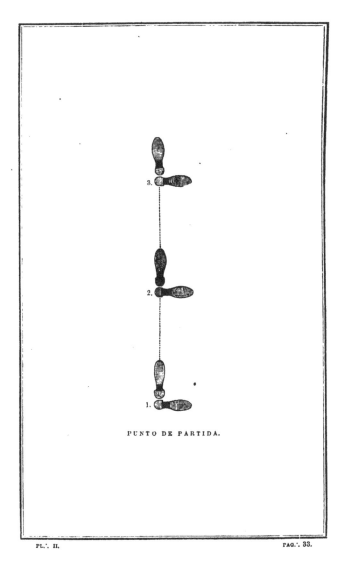

MARCHA.

Tres pasos hacia adelante, partiendo con el pié izquierdo, y juntando los pies á cada paso.*

* Véase la Pl. II [encima]

---

[606] Esta información sobre la "Marcha" viene del *Manual de la Masoneria* (1861) por Andrés Cassard

Steps of the Companion

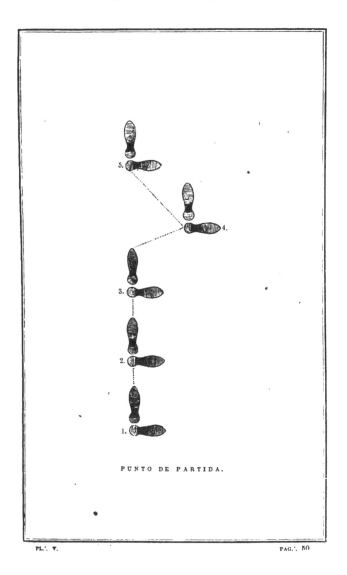

STEPS.

Three steps of [the] apprentice, stomping[607] with the left foot. Then two oblique steps, one to the right, starting with the right foot, and then joining[608] [the right together] with the left, another to the left, starting with the left foot and joining it with the right.* During the reception the recipient makes five journeys.

* See Pl. 5 [above]

---

[607] Literally 'rompiendo' means "break, smash, shatter; interrupt; initiate; leak"
[608] Literally 'juntándolos' means "join, attach, connect; unite, combine; be connected"

Marcha del Compañero

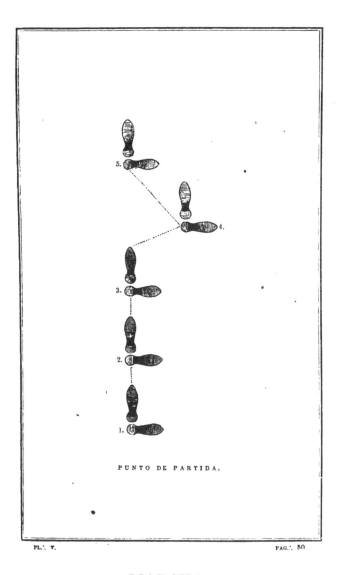

MARCHA.

Tres pasos de aprendiz, rompiendo con el pié izquierdo. Luego dos pasos oblicuos, uno á la derecha, partiendo con el pié derecho, y juntándolos luego con el izquierdo, y otro á la izquierda, partiendo con el pié izquierdo y juntándolo con el derecho.* Durante la recepción el recipiendario hace cinco viajes.

* Véase Pl. V [encima]

Steps of the Master

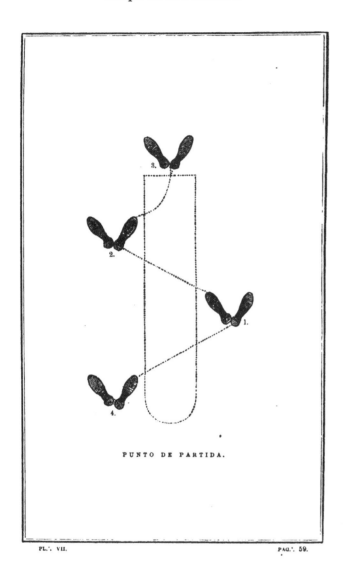

STEPS.

Three high steps, obliquely like as if one is going to pass over some object placed on the floor. The first step to the right, starting with the right foot, the second to the left, starting with the left foot, and the third to the right, starting with the right foot. At the end of each step, feet together.*

* See Pl. 7 [above]

Marcha del Maestro

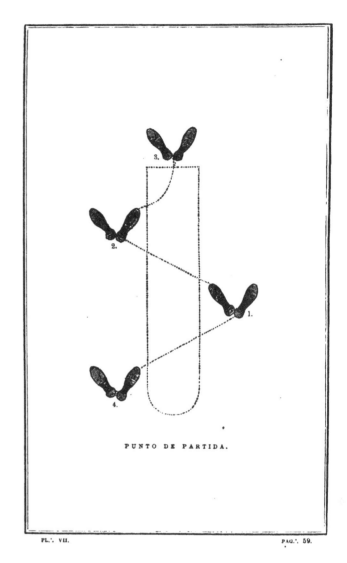

MARCHA.

Tres pasos elevados, oblicuando como si se fuera á pasar por encima de algún objeto puesto en el suelo. El primer paso hacia la derecha, partiendo con el pié derecho; el segundo hacia la izquierda, partiendo con el pié izquierdo, y el tercero á la derecha, partiendo con el pié derecho. Al fin de cada paso se juntan los pies.*

* Véase Pl. VII [encima]

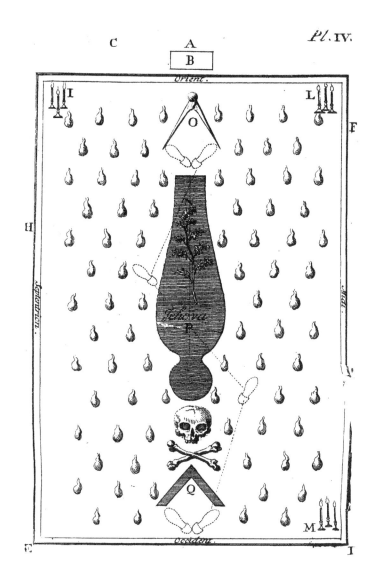

Plate 4 from *L'Ordre des Francs-Maçons trahi, et Le secret des Mopses revelé* (1745) by l'Abbé Larudan

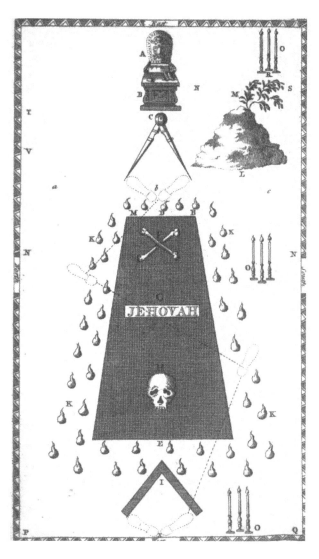

Plato 2 de *Solomon in All His Glory or the Master-mason* (1768) una traducción del libro francés *Le maçon démasqué ou Le vrai secret des francs maçons* (1751)

[End of Editor's Insert]

[Fin del Inserción del Editor]

AQUARIUS

Dear Disciple:

We have arrived at [the constellation of] Aquarius in our [Zodiacal] Course, which has its corporeal[609] point in the Calves.

At this point let us remember Don Abraham Gonzalez (the Minister of the Interior of Mexico during [the] times of Madero[610]) who, in order to determine the cowardice of a political party, said that the back part of [their] knees[611] were trembling.

This phrase, which made us laugh a lot at that time, pushed us to observe some men in a state of nervousness, in order to substantiate[612] the phenomenon.

We also noticed that in some men sentenced to death in court[613], and although we never witnessed the act of execution (since we left just before), after having been greatly[614] consoled[615], we found that both the face and the calves[616] were trembling.

Fluidic emanations [which are] very charged by eroticism meet[617] in this part of the body, and every man knows that there is nothing in the body of a woman which awakens more masculine attention than the calves.

---

[609] Literally 'corporal' means "corporal, bodily"
[610] Francisco Ignacio Madero González (1873-1913) was a Mexican statesman, writer, and revolutionary who served as the 33rd president of Mexico from 1911 until his assassination in 1913.
[611] Literally 'corvas' means "back part of the knee"
[612] Literally 'comprobar' means "check; test; test out; substantiate, prove"
[613] Literally 'campaña' means "countryside; crackdown; campaign; season; cruise"
[614] Literally 'prodigado' means "lavish, give in large amounts, expend in great quantities"
[615] Literally 'consuelo' means "console, comfort, solace"
[616] Literally 'pantorrillas' means "calf, lower back part of the leg"
[617] Literally 'concurren' means "meet, come together; concur; compete"

This produces the form of the leg and its roundness, therefore, a misformed and thin calf defuses[618] the desires of any man, although the face of women may abound in beauty and loveliness.

We call attention to this, from our point of view, in order to show the importance of our practices in these extremities.

It is curious that in Catalonia[619] the Calves are named "Belly of the Bed" and in Portuguese "Belly of the Legs".

It might seem [like] a joke, but [these names] have their origins in the Ancient Mysteries, in which they taught that all the animation of the body resides in the Belly[620], rather like a Cauldron[621] bringing about[622] all necessary Metabolism.

Thus, in the leg is the Belly where all the metabolism of the leg is brought about in a magnetic sense, and as we have seen the importance of the thighs [in the Lesson of Sagittarius], it is easy to comprehend that what is important is to represent the calves in the legs, in general.

Aquarius, in addition to the Calves, exerts its action on the expulsion of carbon dioxide from the organism and therefore upon the Blood and its pathological states.

[It also exerts itself on the] Nervous System (catalepsy[623], neurasthenia[624], hysteria), cardiac diseases and, especially, on diseases of sight.

---

[618] Literally 'apacigua' means "appease, soothe; defuse"
[619] Literally 'Catalán' means "Catalan, of or pertaining to the Catalonian region in northeastern Spain; of or pertaining to the people of Catalonia"
[620] Literally 'Vientre' means "abdomen, stomach, belly, womb"
[621] Literally 'Caldera' means "boiler, copper; cauldron, large pot used for cooking or boiling liquids"
[622] Literally 'efectuaba' means "effect, execute; bring about, effectuate; prosecute"
[623] Literally 'catalepsia' means "catalepsy, muscular rigidity and lack of contact with the environment; trance"
[624] Literally 'neurastenia' means "neurasthenia, weakness or exhaustion of the nervous system; constant mental and physical weariness"

If we first consider the conditions of Aquarius as performing[625] [the function] of [a] belly in the calves and then as [an] operator[626] on the other parts of the body, [then] we will see the great reason [why] the Ancient Initiates had to attribute certain diseases [to this Sign].

For example, deaths due to sudden cardiac accidents always happen when Saturn has a bad aspect with the Heart in the constellation of Aquarius.

Some treatises of Magic say that children born under the influence of Aquarius are difficult to educate and that nothing is ever achieved with harshness and punishment, but [it is rather] with gentleness and pampering, and that instead of us caressing the head [it is] better [for] us caress the calves [of the Aquarian children].

In dealing in the final part of the [Zodiacal] Course with the influence of Pisces upon the feet (which is undoubtedly the Greatest[627] Key) we will see that, just as the eyes are the gateway to Glands such as the Epiphysis [or Pineal gland] and [to the] Hypophysis [or Pituitary gland], the departure of the powerful forces which are in the legs have to be guided through the Calves under the influence of Saturn-Aquarius.

Under the influence of Saturn-Aquarius, great Theosophists, fighters for Religious Principles, Idealists, Revolutionaries and Inventors are born.

Frederick the Great, Bacon, Edison, Swedenborg, Dickenson, Lessing, Haeckel, Darwin, Volta and others, had [their] Sun in Aquarius.

---

[625] Literally 'actuación' means "performance, show, presentation; execution; act, deed; act of presenting an artistic work to an audience"
[626] Literally 'accionando' means "work; operate; activate, actuate; motivate, cause to act; gesticulate, move the hands or other parts of the body in an animated manner (in place of or accompanying speech)"
[627] Literally 'Máxima' means "most, maximum; maximal; top; full"

Occultists have Aquarius in ascent or the Sun in said constellation, therefore, occult intuition is born from it.

Aquarians are necessarily of [an] affectionate[628] character and all these inventors of modern expressions of art [such as] Cubism[629], Ultra-ism[630], Dada-ism[631], which are like a sign[632] of occult intuition in each individual so that (as [a] consequence) the inclination towards ultra-ist theories of Occultism can then flourish in them.

All this has been foreseen[633] Astrologically and it is extremely curious that the same fashion which has hidden the calves of women for centuries and centuries, [has] come now and made them shine[634] as we approach, little by little, the doors of the Sign of Aquarius, whose term[635] begins now.

Likewise the materialists will not accept these explanations about fashion, but those of us who occupy ourselves with occultism and with certain astrological studies, united with the science left in ancient manuscripts by truly wise initiates, we know that nothing is coincidental[636] and that everything firmly has its foundation.

---

[628] Literally 'cariñoso' means "affectionate, loving, fond; kind, affable"
[629] Cubism is an avant-garde art movement which started in the early 20th century and that strongly influenced European painting and sculpture, inspiring related movements in music, literature and architecture. The movement was pioneered by Georges Braque and Pablo Picasso, and then joined by many others.
[630] Ultraism or the Ultraist movement (Spanish: *Ultraísmo*) was a literary movement born in Spain in 1918 with the declared intention of opposing *Modernismo* [Modernism].
[631] Dadaism was a European art movement which began around 1915. It consisted of artists who rejected the logic, reason, and aesthetic of modern capitalist society, instead expressing irrationality and anti-bourgeois protest in their works.
[632] Literally 'presagio' means "prognostication; presage, omen, sign, portent"
[633] Literally 'previsto' means "previse, foresee, forecast; envisage; set down"
[634] Literally 'lucir' means "illuminate, shine; display, flaunt; affect; (Latin America) look"
[635] Literally 'período' means "period, length of time; term; tour; stretch"
[636] Literally 'casual' means "accidental, chance, random"

Zodiacal Course by Arnoldo Krumm Heller (Huiracocha)	Curso Zodical por Arnoldo Krumm Heller (Huiracocha)

Aviation is also under the Astrological influence of Aquarius, and this has already been mentioned accurately[637] [by] the spiritual father of the Aviators, Leonardo da Vinci.

Of course, then, it was just a prediction, without mentioning anything for the age[638] of Aquarius to come.

The eyes of those born in Aquarius are very expressive, when the Karma and the Heritage (which in summary are the same thing) has not extinguished[639] their shiny[640] brightness.

They are something like two ecstatic and radiant bright stars, and it would be sufficient to look upon the face of an Aquarian in order to find the constellation under which they were born.

It is also a fine and delicate hand that invites [us] to caress, and [they] have a special and outstanding instinct for all things, but [there is] also [a] conspicuously labeled selfishness[641] coveting everything for themselves.

They know [how to] perfectly scrutinize the path forward in order to succeed in any enterprise, making of it the most possible, it is not important to them if they harm others in order to achieve their defined purposes.

We have described Saturn as conservative[642].

Now it is in Aquarius where Saturn looks to the Future.

La Aviación se encuentra también bajo la influencia Astrológica de Acuario, y esto ya lo mencionó con acertado tino el padre espiritual de los Aviadores, Leonardo de Vinci.

Claro que entonces era sólo una predicción, sin mencionar para nada la época de Acuario que se avecina.

Muy expresivos son los ojos de los nacidos en Acuario, siempre que el Karma y la Herencia, que en resumen son la misma cosa, no les haya apagado su luciente brillo.

Son algo así como dos luceros extáticos y radiantes, y bastaría mirar a la cara a un Acuariano para saber la constelación bajo la cual nació.

También se destacan por una mano fina y delicada que invita a acariciar, y tienen un instinto especial y sobresaliente por todas las cosas, aunque brillan también por su marcado egoísmo ambicionándolo todo para ellos.

Saben perfectamente escudriñar el camino a seguir a fin de salir airosos de cualquier empresa sacando de ella el mayor provecho posible, no importándoles perjudicar a otros si así ha de ser para conseguir sus definidos propósitos.

Hemos descrito a Saturno como conservador.

Ahora es en Acuario donde Saturno mira al Porvenir.

---

[637] Literally 'acertado' means "correct, right; sensible, wise; sound"
[638] Literally 'época' means "period, age, era; season; lesson; length of time"
[639] Literally 'apagado' means "go out; blow out; burn out; fade away"
[640] Literally 'luciente' means "bright, luminous; shiny; radiant"
[641] Literally 'egoísmo' means "egoism, selfishness, self love"
[642] Literally 'conservador' means "conservative; curator, conservator"

Zodiacal Course by Arnoldo Krumm Heller (Huiracocha)	Curso Zodical por Arnoldo Krumm Heller (Huiracocha)
We come to the Age of Aquarius.	Vamos hacia la Era de Acuario.
It is for this [reason] that we have seen things move so quickly, and the future has to be that of occult ideas, while in the field of parapsychology[643] we observe true marvels.	Es por ello que hemos visto evolucionar las cosas tan rápidamente, y el porvenir ha de ser de las ideas ocultistas, mientras que en el terreno parapsicológico hemos de observar verdaderas maravillas.
[We] are not, of course, far from the day when the separation of the astral body and even other phenomena of major importance will be a fact for Science in general, and what is now only occult knowledge, will be disclosed [to the public].	No está, desde luego, muy lejos el día en que la separación del cuerpo astral y aún otros fenómenos de mayor importancia sean un hecho para la Ciencia en general, y lo que hoy es sólo del conocimiento oculto, tenga una divulgación.
Nonetheless, it will take occult practices such as a necessary and indispensable preparation, so that the physical body gets used to and will permit the indicated phenomenon.	Sin embargo harán falta las prácticas ocultas como una preparación necesaria e indispensable, a fin de que el organismo físico se habitúe y permita los indicados fenómenos.
The practice which is related to the Feet and the Constellation of Pisces, has to be prepared and set up[644] with what we will describe, therefore, the current that comes from the Sanctuary of the Feet starts its trajectory[645] [by passing] through the Calves, and we must mentally prepare [them], but [concentrating] much stronger than before, to open the passageway[646].	La práctica que está relacionada con los Pies y la Constelación de Piscis, tiene que ser preparada y dispuesta con la que vamos a describir, pues, la corriente que parte del Santuario de los Pies comienza su trayectoria por las Pantorrillas, y mentalmente, pero más fuerte que antes, debemos disponernos a abrirle paso.
Nevertheless, it is not, then, [because] of a practice or a complicated exercise [that we will prepare this passageway].	A pesar de ello no se trata, pues, de una práctica o ejercicios complicados.
[It is] enough, in order to achieve this, [that] every night before going to bed [one] rubs the Calves from the bottom up, and while this is being done, think consciously, and with true mental strength, on the following phrases:	Basta para conseguirlo, sobar todas las noches al acostarnos las Pantorrillas de abajo hacia arriba, y al par que esto se hace, pensar conscientemente y con verdadera fuerza mental en las siguientes frases:

---

[643] Literally 'terreno parapsicológico' means "parapsychological field"
[644] Literally 'dispuesta' means "prepared, ready; disposed; arranged, set"
[645] Literally 'trayectoria' means "trajectory, course, path; flight"
[646] Literally 'paso' means "passage, way, route, course; passing, going by; transition, change; migration, seasonal relocation of birds or other animals in groups; passageway, corridor; pass, narrow road between mountains; strait"

"PASSIVE FORCE, PASSIVE FORCE, PENETRATE INTO MY WHOLE ORGANISM.

CURRENT FROM BELOW, ASCEND TO FIND YOUR SISTER, SHE WHO COMES FROM HEAVEN, FROM URANUS.

I, SATURN, AM YOUR RECEIVER[647] IN THE MICROCOSMOS TO REDEEM HUMANITY AND TO REDEEM MYSELF PERSONALLY WHICH TENDS TO ARRIVE[648] [FROM ABOVE, FROM WAY UP], [ALL THE WAY] UP TO GOD, SEEKING FOR MY OWN PERFECTION.

SO BE IT."

You might consider this practice as the least important and [just too] simple[649], but it is only [done in order] to prepare [you for] the next [exercise], which holds the Greatest Key, [and] just doing this well and discovering its Intimate secrets, will open the doors to all Initiations.

"FUERZA PASA, FUERZA PASA, PENETRA EN TODO MI ORGANISMO.

CORRIENTE DE ABAJO, ASCIENDE PARA ENCONTRAR TU HERMANA, LA QUE VIENE DEL CIELO, DE URANO.

YO, SATURNO, SOY TU RECEPTOR EN EL MICROCOSMOS PARA REDIMIR A LA HUMANIDAD Y PARA REDIMIRME A MI PERSONALMENTE QUE TIENDO A LLEGAR, HASTA DIOS, BUSCANDO MI PROPIA PERFECCIÓN.

ASI SEA".

Puede ser que consideremos esta práctica como la menos importante y sencilla, pero es que sólo ella prepara la siguiente, la que encierra la Clave Máxima, que con sólo hacer bien esa y descubrir su Íntimo secreto, se abren las puertas de todas las Iniciaciones.

---

[647] Literally 'RECEPTOR' means "receptor, pickup, receiver"
[648] Literally 'LLEGAR' means "arrive, come; reach; roll along; land; immigrate; invade; get; travel; vaporize"
[649] Literally 'sencilla' means "simple, easy; straightforward; informal; naive; primitive"

PISCES

Dear Disciple:

When speaking of Astrology, we notice that what influences us are not the Planets themselves [meaning not the physical planets], nor[650] [is it] the spiritual forces that irradiate around them, which are (in their turn) the emanation of the Spiritual Entity that presides [over] them.

All the Planets are similar to living beings with Body, Soul and Spirit, and have as [a] consequence their Double or Divine Angel just as we humans have.

The Earth is, therefore, not an exception.

She also has (as [a] living being) her Superior Being or Angel, and the current that emanates [from her] is Magnetism; if we want to obtain results in the Rosicrucian practices [then] we must put ourselves into contact with [some] part of this entity.

We know that in the Hermetic Sciences each Planet has its name, its mantram, its sign, which are those that are recorded upon Amulets.

The mantram, the key to connecting with our Earth, is JEHOVA, who (in the astral) is the soul corresponding to Christ.

JEHOVA represents (in its essence) the five vowels IEOUA and in them reside all the hidden[651] strength[652] which harmonically resonates on Earth and this would also be in our organism if we had preserved ourselves in [the] primitive paradisiacal[653] state.

---

[650] Literally 'si no' means "otherwise, nisi, unless, or else"
[651] Literally 'oculta' means "occult, hidden, covert"
[652] Literally 'fuerza' means "strength, quality of being strong, might; durability; determination, resolve; effectiveness; intensity"
[653] Literally 'paradisíaco' means "paradisiacal, like paradise, like the Garden of Eden, heavenly"

PISCIS

Querido Discípulo:

Al hablar de Astrología, hemos advertido que no son los Planetas mismos los que influyen en nosotros, si no las fuerzas espirituales que irradian alrededor de éstos, que son, a su vez, la emanación de la Entidad Espiritual que les preside.

Todos los Planetas son a semejanza de seres vivos con Cuerpo, Alma y Espíritu, y tienen por consecuencia su Doble o Ángel Divino tal como lo tenemos los humanos.

La Tierra no es, pues, una excepción.

También ella tiene, como ser viviente, su Ser Superior[654] o Ángel, y la corriente que emana es el Magnetismo que parte de esa entidad con la cual hemos de ponernos en conexión si queremos obtener resultados en las prácticas Rosacruces.

Sabemos en las Ciencias Herméticas que cada Planeta tiene su nombre, su mantram, su signo, que son los que se graban en los Amuletos.

El mantram, la clave de conexión de nuestra Tierra, es JEHOVA, que, en lo astral, es el alma correspondiente a Cristo.

JEHOVA representa, en su esencia, las cinco vocales IEOUA y en ellas reside toda la fuerza oculta que está resonando armónicamente en la Tierra y lo estaría también en nuestro organismo si nos hubiéramos conservado en estado primitivo, paradisíaco.

---

[654] Originalmente "Ego Superior"

But just like [how we were] calm in sin and we lost our purity, we have also lost this faculty which must be recovered in order to achieve the power of the primitive Angel-Men, whose Key resides in Pisces.

However, it is rare that Pisces has to do with these things.

As [a] symbol, the Fish was always the Guardian of the Spirit. Let's remember Cipactli, that of the mexicans, the fish of the Incas, etc.

A Fish was also the symbol that was put on the Buddha Statues and on the Effigies of the Nazarene.

The Planet of the Constellation of Pisces is Jupiter, the Personality, the Being.

Thus, the Being Astrologically resides in the Fish, and in the Knees, as we have seen.

Pisces has two Planets, and like the Earth with Jehova and with Christ, [it] also has two representative Angels.

Back in [the times of] Babylonia, God [the] Father had the figure of a Fish, and the Greeks (in their Mysteries) said that the Mantram of the Earth was Oannes, Johannes, Joan, IAO.

The element of the Fish is water, the amniotic[655] liquid where the human fetus swims during nine months, which is the time of Johannes, of that which goes through the desert before the arrival of the Messiah.

In the maternal womb, the being receives its first impressions, and at the moment of birth, all the Planets are engraved upon it and describe its future, which the astrologer then decodes.

---

[655] Literally 'amniótico' means "amniotic, of or pertaining to the membrane surrounding an embryo"

[656] Originalmente "el Ego"
[657] Originalmente "el Ego"

| Zodiacal Course by Arnoldo Krumm Heller (Huiracocha) | Curso Zodical por Arnoldo Krumm Heller (Huiracocha) |

In describing the passage of the cosmic current, both from above and from below, we painted the body as [being] full of screens [or filters] that [these cosmic currents] have to pass [through them] in each region (in one sense or another) until [they] concur[658] in the heart for the first time and with all [the] energy in contact with the Earth.

We are, therefore, upright[659] beings and not quadrupeds like the animals which in their delayed[660] evolution are driven from above [by] the stars and attracted from below by the Earth having to live on four paws[661].

Man is, instead, erect[662] and in this vertical position will also [receive] his current, and his main purpose is to negotiate[663] the steps[664] in order to obtain his own redemption.

The Sign [of Pisces, which is] described[665] as 'the Fishes', are two semicircles united with a tie or dash.

[These] are the Earth and the Cosmos united.

Between the Earth and the Cosmos one finds Arcanum 12 of the Kabalah, or the figure of a man with a halo of gold, suspended by one foot, being disposed [at] the end of [a] tree in such a way that it forms [an] inverted figure.

It is called "Sacrifice" or "The Hanged Man".

Al describir el paso de la corriente cósmica, tanto de arriba como de abajo, hemos pintado al cuerpo como lleno de cedazos por donde tiene que pasar en cada región, tanto en un sentido como en otro, hasta coincidir en el corazón por primera vez y con toda energía en contacto con la Tierra.

Somos, pues, seres erectos y no cuadrúpedos como los animales que en su atraso evolutivo son impulsados por los astros desde arriba y atraídos por la Tierra desde abajo teniendo que vivir en cuatro patas.

El hombre, en cambio, va erguido y en esa posición vertical va también su corriente, siendo su fin principal franquearle el paso para obtener su propia redención.

El Signo descrito de los Peces, son dos semicírculos unidos con un lazo o guión.

Son la Tierra y el Cosmos unidos.

Entre esa Tierra y el Cosmos se encuentra el Arcano 12 de la Cabalah, o sea la figura de un hombre con un halo de oro, suspendido de un pie, estando dispuesto el extremo del árbol de tal modo, que forma la figura invertida.

Se llama "El Sacrificio" o "El Hombre Colgado".

---

[658] Literally 'coincidir' means "coincide, agree, concur"
[659] Literally 'erectos' means "erect, upright, straight up"
[660] Literally 'atraso' means "delay; slowdown; backwardness; leeway"
[661] Literally 'patas' means "leg, paw, foot; tab; duck; hoof, pad; drake"
[662] Literally 'erguido' means "erect, straight; proud"
[663] Literally 'franquearle' means "free, liberate; grant; allow; frank; prepay; meter; negotiate"
[664] Literally 'paso' means "passage, way, route, course; passing, going by; transition, change; migration, seasonal relocation of birds or other animals in groups; passageway, corridor; pass, narrow road between mountains; strait"
[665] Literally 'descrito' means "painted; labeled; described"

[It] represents the Divine Manifestation or the Revealed Law, and according to the Kabalists [it] is the key to all Initiation.

The Letter is Lamed [ל] in the Kabalah, and it corresponds to the sphere of Saturn.

Now let us remember when we said Saturn was the finite, and from Uranus was the infinite, and we will [thereby] explain why the Kabalists connect[666] Saturn, Lamed [ל] and 'the Fishes'.

The Zodiac is round and because of this [the beginning and the end] are united, Pisces and Aries, Winter and Spring, death and birth, the 12th House of Astrology with the first House.

The Logos, the Word (according to Saint John) is the origin of all things, [it] is life itself.

In the beginning was the Verb and only with its use[667] can we obtain[668] Initiation, but the LIVING VERB, the LOGOS within us, which is what unites [us] with the LOGOS, the VERB OF THE EARTH.

When this Mantram was pronounced in the Temple of Jerusalem, they sounded the drums so that no one would hear.

Today the veil has been lifted and we know that [it] is JEHOVA, whose Secret Key is rooted in its Five Vowels.

Representa la Divina Manifestación o la Ley Revelada, y según los Cabalistas es la clave de toda Iniciación.

La Letra es Lamed en la Cábalah, y ella corresponde a la esfera de Saturno.

Recordemos ahora cuanto hemos dicho de Saturno, lo finito, y de Urano, lo infinito, y nos explicaremos el porqué unieron los Cabalistas a Saturno, Lamed y los Peces.

El Zodiaco es redondo y por esta causa, están unidos Piscis y Aries, el Invierno y la Primavera, la muerte y el nacimiento, la Casa 12 de la Astrología con la Casa primera.

El Logos, la Palabra, según San Juan, es el origen de todas las cosas, es la vida misma.

En el principio era el Verbo y sólo con su uso logramos la Iniciación, pero el VERBO VIVO, el LOGOS en nosotros, que tiene que estar unido con el LOGOS, el VERBO DE LA TIERRA.

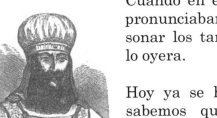

Cuando en el Templo de Jerusalén pronunciaban este Mantram, hacían sonar los tambores para que nadie lo oyera.

Hoy ya se ha levantado el velo y sabemos que es JEHOVA, cuya Clave Secreta radica en sus Cinco Vocales.

---

[666] Literally 'unieron' means "unite, join, link, connect; mate; incorporate; interlock"
[667] Literally 'uso' means "use, utilize, take advantage of; practice; employ; exploit; treat; consume; explode"
[668] Literally 'logramos' means "get, obtain; achieve, attain; reach; win"

The BEING, [the] Cosmic Verb, resides in the Head and is pronounced [by] utilizing the throat[669].

In contrast, the Verb, the Logos of the Earth, resides in the Feet and you have to learn to derive[670] the voice from the Feet in order to sense the vibration in them, that is to say, we must speak with the Feet.

Whosoever does not know our studies will be smiling when they read this [idea] of "speaking with the Feet", but we know that all Initiates do so.

It is not always necessary for the word to [make a] sound[671] [in order for it] to be heard; a gesture [is sometimes] enough.

How many times have we understood with only gestures, movements [of the] arms, face, shoulders, in a continuous gesticulation[672], which is also [a] language.

This indicates to us that speaking is something which is related to the whole body.

The Washing of the Feet was an Initiatic Ceremony, and one never goes to a Mohammedan Mosque without having gone through it.

Jesus washed the Feet of his Apostles, saying to them: "If you wash the Feet you shall be clean and prepared in the whole body and you will be able to communicate with me." [see John 13:1-17]

The Alphabet is made of vowels and consonants, whose signs all have a direct relationship with our organism and for each one [there] is a corresponding Initiatory movement.

---

[669] Literally 'garganta' means "throat, gullet; neck; coomb, ravine; abysm"
[670] Literally 'derivar' means "derive; shunt, divert"
[671] Literally 'suene' means "sound; ring; play; pronounce; mention; seem, appear; resound"
[672] Literally 'gesticulación' means "gesticulation, moving of the hands or other parts of the body in an animated manner"

El SER[673], Verbo Cósmico, reside en la Cabeza y se pronuncia utilizando la garganta.

En cambio, el Verbo, el Logos de la Tierra, reside en los Pies y hay que aprender a derivar la voz hacia los Pies para sentir en ellos la vibración, es decir, hay que hablar con los Pies.

Quien no conozca nuestros estudios habrá de sonreírse al leer esto de hablar con los Pies, pero ya sabemos que todos los Iniciados lo hacen.

No es necesario que la palabra suene siempre, que se escuche; basta un gesto.

Cuántas veces sólo nos hacemos entender con gestos, moviendo brazos, cara, hombros, en una gesticulación continua, que también es lenguaje.

Eso nos indica que el hablar es algo que está relacionado con todo el cuerpo.

El Lavado de los Pies era una Ceremonia Iniciática, y jamás un Mahometano irá a la Mezquita sin antes haber pasado por ello.

Jesús al lavar los Pies a sus Apóstoles, les dice: "Si os lavo los Pies quedaréis limpios y preparados en todo el cuerpo y os podréis comunicar conmigo".

El Abecedario está hecho de vocales y consonantes, cuyos signos tienen todos una relación directa con nuestro organismo y a cada una corresponde un movimiento Iniciático.

---

[673] Originalmente "El YO"

The primitive letters were the Runes, and in Nordic Initiatic Schools [the students] learned those gymnastics or Runic movements that we are going to teach in [the] next Course[674], but the current already has [a way for us] to act upon ourselves through the movement in which one has accessed[675] while passing through that screen[676] which astrally resides in the Feet.

We know that we are composed of Cells; that they in their turn are composed of molecules, these [are composed] of atoms, and these atoms are a conjunction of Matter, Energy and Consciousness.

[The] result, therefore, [is] that these three conditions are [in] a constant struggle[677], thus, Matter wants to be Energy and Energy would like to become Consciousness.

The objective of our life is to make all Matter Conscious and the Mystery of Redemption consists [entirely] of this [objective].

But the atoms that are active in the Heart with its constant rhythmic movement are more energetically conscious than the others, and the atoms that make up our Brain [are even] more conscious, and in this [there] exists a disharmony.

We are an organic whole[678] from the Feet to the Head, and it is necessary to carry the conscious impulse to the extremities, to the feet, so that their atoms have[679] the necessary consciousness, and then we will be Gods like in primeval times.

---

[674] Editor's note: In 1931, once the 12 lessons of the Zodiacal Course were completed, Krumm-Heller immediately began distributing the lessons of the "Course of Runic Magic".
[675] Literally 'entrado' means "enter, go in; approach, come near to; access, gain entrance to; introduce; tackle; attack; rise; input"
[676] Literally 'cedazos' means "sieve, sifter"
[677] Literally 'lucha' means "fight, battle; combat; wrestle; agonize"
[678] Literally 'conjunto' means "whole; conjunction; ensemble; chorus; union; set"
[679] Literally 'tomen' means "take, seize; accept; have; drink, eat; impound; touch; understand; draw; reduce; live on"

Las letras primitivas eran las Runas, y en las Escuelas Iniciáticas Nórdicas aprendían esa gimnasia o movimientos Rúnicos que vamos a enseñar en un próximo Curso[680], pero la corriente ya puede actuar en nosotros desde el momento en que haya entrado bien atravesando ese cedazo que reside astralmente en los Pies.

Sabemos que somos un compuesto de Celdillas; que éstas a su vez se componen de moléculas, éstas de átomos, y que esos átomos son un conjunto de Materia, Energía y Consciencia.

Resulta, pues, que entre estas tres condiciones hay una lucha constante, pues, la Materia quiere hacerse Energía y la Energía quiere convertirse en Consciencia.

El objeto de nuestra vida es hacer Consciente toda la Materia y en eso consiste el Misterio de la Redención.

Pero más conscientes energéticamente que los demás, son los átomos que actúan en el Corazón en su constante movimiento rítmico, y más conscientes los átomos que forman nuestro Cerebro, y en esto existe una desarmonía.

Somos un conjunto orgánico desde los Pies hasta la Cabeza, y es necesario llevar el impulso consciente hasta las extremidades, hasta los pies, para que sus átomos tomen la consciencia necesaria, y entonces volveremos a ser Dioses como en tiempos primitivos.

---

[680] Nota del editor: En 1931, cuando fueron completadas las 12 lecciones del Curso Zodiacal, Krumm-Heller inició de inmediato la distribución de las lecciones del "Curso de Magia Rúnica".

In this resides the whole secret, by acting on the atoms in order to awaken the Body-Temple where God resides.

The *modus operandi* is as follows: The Disciple will sit comfortably, and after making a mental Prayer, one should lead[681] the Vowels to the Feet, [that] is to say, think and pronounce the vowel "Iiiiiiiii" extending[682], vibrating, [and] seeking[683] to mentally lead its pronunciation downwards, through the knees to the feet, and continue slowly with the other vowels just like that[684].

The effect, more or less immediate, according to the temperament [of the Disciple], is positive and sanctifies[685] us.

Every time you do [this, you do] not have to do [it out loud], whether you are walking or you are seated, [simply] do this exercise mentally and you will do yourself an immense favor[686].

With an hour [of] vocalization, as we call it, one achieves more [spiritual development] than assimilating 20 Theosophical Works, since, (in the end) these bring other's ideas, and [instead] with this practice [of vocalization] one achieves [the] filling of oneself with the divine forces that [one] would not otherwise get.

With this practice, dear Disciple, [we] finish[687] the first Initiatic Course.

If you have only read and not practiced, [then] you have lost time.

---

[681] Literally 'llevar' means "carry, transport; take; convey; wear; win; lead; bear; spend; hunch, hump; heave; carry off; deliver; live through; encroach on"
[682] Literally 'largamente' means "long; largely"
[683] Literally 'procurando' means "see; seek; attempt"
[684] Literally 'así' means "so; thus; just like that; thereby"
[685] Literally 'santificamos' means "bless, hallow, sanctify"
[686] Literally 'bien' means "good, benefit; welfare; sake; right"
[687] Literally 'acaba' means "finish, terminate, end; be terminated; conclude, bring to an end; destroy; defeat; complete, perfect; add the finishing touches"

En esto radica todo el secreto, en actuar sobre los átomos para despertar el Templo-Cuerpo donde Dios reside.

El *modus operandi*, es el siguiente: Se sienta el Discípulo cómodamente, y después de hacer una Oración mental, tiene que llevar las Vocales a los Pies, es decir, piensa y pronuncia largamente, vibrándola, la vocal Iiiiiiiii, procurando llevar mentalmente su pronunciación hacia abajo, por las rodillas hasta los pies, y así se continúa despacio con las demás vocales.

El efecto, más o menos inmediato, según los temperamentos, es positivo y nos santificamos.

Cada vez que no tengáis que hacer, que vayáis andando o estéis sentados, haced mentalmente este ejercicio y os hará un inmenso bien.

Con una hora vocalizando, como le llamamos nosotros, se consigue más que asimilándose 20 Obras Teosóficas, pues, estas traen, a última hora, ideas ajenas, y con esta práctica se consigue llenarse uno mismo de fuerzas divinas que no de otro modo se consiguen.

Con esta práctica, querido Discípulo, acaba el primer Curso Iniciático.

Si lo has leído solamente y no llevado a la práctica, has perdido el tiempo.

Although it was very cheap[688], [and] at first glance does not [appear to be] worth anything, but if you meditate well, extracting[689] everything that is in it, [then] you have paid next to nothing for it[690]. [Yet] it is of immense value.

[It] encloses the secret of secrets and you need to go back and repeat it, studying each practice again, since, [in] the end, that which we owe to Jacob Boehme and that which has opened the gates of Heaven is[691] alive, [and] is masterfully divine, but you will only receive[692] results if you have done well and consistently [done] the preceding [practices].

Not only is it necessary to have practiced, but also to have comprehended and thoroughly assimilated [the material in] its broadest sense.

That is why I say: "Do this..." So[693] do not ask me [for] more.

Herein lies the Secret of Secrets and with it [one] walks the true path, the most straight and sure [way] to arrive [at the objective], that which all Initiates have traveled, and without such practice Initiation is not possible.

These things are sacred.

What has been divulged[694] without [the] permission of the Temple, carries a terrible karma and [whosoever does so] will never advance any further.

---

[688] Literally 'barato' means "cheap, inexpensive; dirt cheap, extremely inexpensive"
[689] Literally 'sacando' means "take out, remove; bring out; draw out, extract; get; take; bring up; let; produce; educe, deduce; protract"
[690] Literally 'no hay dinero con qué pagarlo' means "there is no money with which to pay [for] it"
[691] Literally 'estando' means "be; stay, remain; hold; be found; be present"
[692] Literally 'dará' means "give; present; deal; produce, yield; cause; perform; say; take; teach; lecture; start, begin; overlook; surrender"
[693] Literally 'Pero' means "only, but"
[694] Literally 'divulga' means "divulge, reveal, tell, disclose"

It is now necessary to continue with the Runes and their Magic, therefore, with the present course we have only set in motion the divine currents; now let us apply it in the practice of Magic.

No one can give the Keys of Runic Magic who has not followed the present [course] which was compulsory for preparation.[695]

We recommend for the bretheren to get our personal Incense and perfumes which help in the different exercises.

END

Es necesario seguir ahora con las Runas y la Magia de ellas, pues, con el curso presente sólo hemos puesto en movimiento las corrientes divinas; ahora vamos a aplicarlas en la práctica de la Magia.

A nadie se puede dar las Claves de la Magia Rúnica que no haya seguido el presente que fue de preparación forzosa.[696]

Recomendamos a los hermanos de conseguir nuestros Inciensos y perfumes personales que ayudan en los distintos ejercicios.

FIN

---

[695] Editor's note: In 1931, when the 12 lessons of the Zodiacal Course were completed, Krumm-Heller began distributing the lessons of the "Course of Rune Magic".

[696] En 1931, cuando fueron completadas las 12 lecciones del Curso Zodiacal, Krumm-Heller inició la distribución de las lecciones del "Curso de Magia Rúnica".

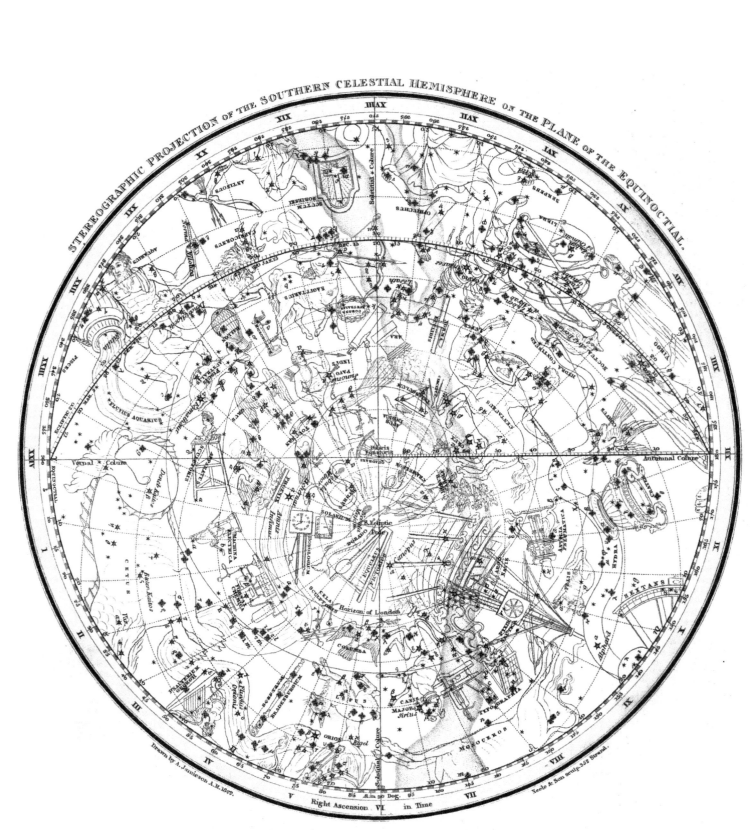

Editor's Appendix

Apéndice del Editor

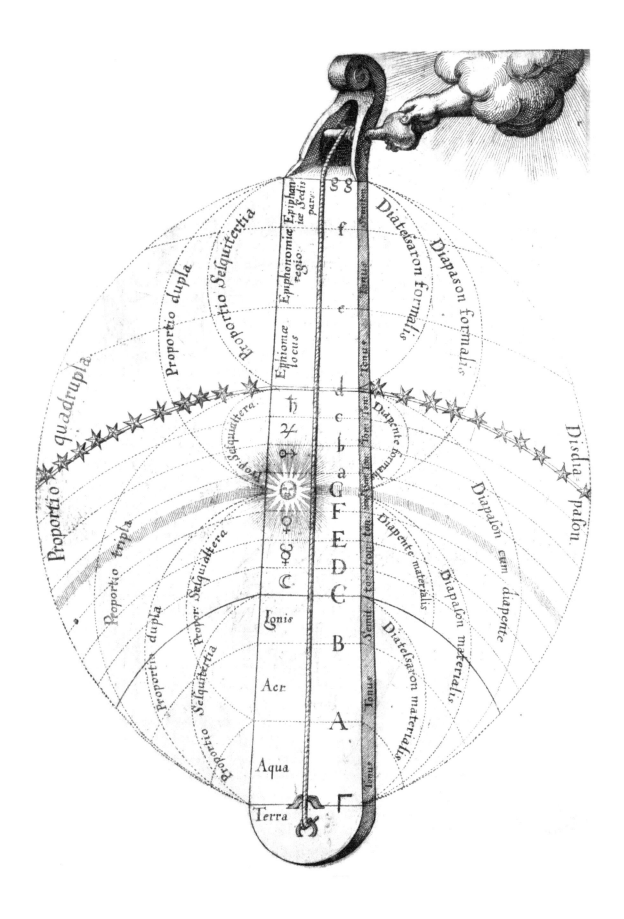

Extract from Lecture #194,
from pages 1983-1984 of
El Quinto Evangelio (2000)
by Samael Aun Weor

"IN THE BEGINNING WAS THE VERB"

...Do your practice with intensity, do not tire[1]!

The important thing is to not get tired, my dear brethren; consistency[2], [and] tenacity[3] are necessary.

There are many brethren who start doing these practices and then get tired[4].

If you truly want to develop your Powers, do not get tired.

You have to be tough[5], very tough.

Without tenacity, my dear brethren, it is completely impossible to awaken the Superior Faculties of the Soul.

We are giving [you] the mantrams necessary in order to awaken the Powers; but if you are not tenacious[6], then you are really wasting [your] time.

What is required is that you are tenacious, understand?

...

Dr. Krumm Heller advised his disciples [to do] one hour of vocalization daily.

Dr. Krumm Heller said that one should vocalize in the following order: I-E-O-U-A.

---
[1] Literally 'canséis' means "tire out, exhaust, weary, make tired or fatigued"
[2] Literally 'constancia' means "constancy; certainty; (Latin America) proof, evidence"
[3] Literally 'tenacidad' means "tenacity, obstinacy, stubbornness, willfulness, unwavering determination"
[4] Literally 'cansan' means "tire out, exhaust, weary, make tired or fatigued"
[5] Literally 'tenaz' means "tenacious, not easily loosened; stubborn, obstinate"
[6] Literally 'tenaces' means "tenacious, not easily loosened; stubborn, obstinate"

Extracto de la Conferencia #194,
de páginas 1983-1984 de
El Quinto Evangelio (2000)
por Samael Aun Weor

"EN EL PRINCIPIO ERA EL VERBO"

...¡Haced vuestras practicas con intensidad, no os canséis!

Lo importante es que no os canséis, mis caros hermanos; es necesaria la constancia, la tenacidad.

Son muchos los hermanos que comienzan a hacer estas practicas y luego se cansan.

Si tú verdaderamente quieres desarrollar tus Poderes, no te cansen.

Hay que ser tenaz, muy tenaz.

Sin tenacidad, mis caros hermanos, es completamente imposible despertar las Facultades Superiores del Alma.

Les estamos dando los mantrams que se necesitan para el despertar de los Poderes; pero si vosotros no sois tenaces, pues, realmente estáis perdiendo el tiempo.

Lo que se requiere es que vosotros seáis tenaces, ¿entendido?

...

El Dr. Krumm Heller, aconsejaba a sus discípulos una hora diaria de vocalización.

Decía el Dr. Krumm Heller que se debería vocalizar en el siguiente orden: I-E-O-U-A.

Dr. Krumm Heller advised bring the sound of each vowel from the head to the feet.

Dr. Krumm Heller would [also] say that we [should] identify ourselves with the sound, carrying it (with the imagination[7]) from the head to the feet, as well as awakening all the Powers of man.

The method of Dr. Krumm Heller is as follows, let us begin:

IIIIIIIIIIIIIIIIIIIII
EEEEEEEEEEEEE
OOOOOOOOOOO
UUUUUUUUUU
AAAAAAAAAAA

Dr. Krumm Heller said that the Disciple should vocalize one hour a day; and this is the system that the Great Master HUIRACOCHA (Krumm Heller) taught.

We, with the brethren of the Sierra Nevada de Santa Marta, there in our Summum Supremum Sanctuarium Gnosticum, we vocalize [while] doing "Chains", or we vocalize individually, everyone.

We utilized many mantrams, and each vocalization of I-E-O-U-A, we combined [them] with (for example) the "CH" and the result was always wonderful: The brethren of the Summum Supremum Sanctuarium developed their Occult Powers.

These brethren are very advanced: They have Clairvoyance, they have Clairaudience, they have developed Telepathy, they are intuitive, they remember their[8] past existences, they know [how to get] in and out of the physical body at will (that is to say, they know [how] to "unfold" [or] "get out in Astral"). Do you understand, brethren?

---

[7] Literally 'imaginativamente' means "imaginatively"
[8] Literally 'las' means "them, those people (3rd person); the; him; it"

Well, let's move on... With the mantrams: CHIS, CHES, CHOS, CHUS, CHAS, wonderful results are always obtained, in this matter of the awakening of Powers.

These mantras are vocalized like this:

CHIIIIIIIIIIIIIIIIIISSSSSSS
CHEEEEEEEEEEESSSSSSS
CHOOOOOOOOOSSSSSSS
CHUUUUUUUUSSSSSSS
CHAAAAAAAAASSSSSSS

The combination of the "CH" with the vowel, and putting the letter "S" at the end of the mantram, is something extraordinary, something wonderful: Potently rotating[9] the chakras, awakening the Internal Senses of man.

But I repeat, brethren: Without tiring; do not get tired.

These are exercises that one should practice throughout[10] one's whole life, one must accustom oneself to these exercises, just like[11] with breakfast.

If in life one picks up[12] many vices, if in life many are given to picking up the vice of liquor, the vice of smoking, etc., then [what is] better than those vices is the practice of mantrams; they are much better than being in bars, [or] taverns.

One will come to love the mantrams so much, that one does not feel well [on] the day that one has not practiced one's exercises.

Be tenacious, beloved brethren, tenaciously thirsty!

That is the advice I give to you...

---

[9] Literally 'Giran' means "gyrate, rotate; move in spiral motion, twist, whirl; derange; revolve, turn"
[10] Literally 'durante' means "during, pending"
[11] Literally 'lo mismo' means "the same"
[12] Literally 'coge' means "grasp; seize; catch; take, pinch; pick, pluck; arrest; toss; gore; impale; accept; get, understand; take on; hold"

Bien, sigamos adelante... Con los mantrams: CHIS, CHES, CHOS, CHUS, CHAS, se obtienen siempre maravillosos resultados, en esta cuestión del despertar de Poderes.

Estos mantrams se vocalizan así:

CHIIIIIIIIIIIIIIIIIISSSSSSS
CHEEEEEEEEEEESSSSSSS
CHOOOOOOOOOSSSSSSS
CHUUUUUUUUSSSSSSS
CHAAAAAAAAASSSSSSS

La combinación de la "CH" con la vocal, y poniendo la letra "S" al final del mantram, es algo extraordinario, algo maravilloso: Giran los chakras potentemente, se despiertan los Sentidos Internos del hombre.

Empero vuelvo a repetir, hermanos: Sin cansarse; no se cansen.

Éstos son ejercicios que los debe uno practicar durante toda su vida; uno debe acostumbrarse a estos ejercicios, lo mismo que al desayuno.

Si en la vida coge uno tantos vicios, si en la vida (a muchos) les da por coger el vicio del licor, el vicio del cigarrillo, etc., pues, mejor que esos vicios es la práctica de los mantrams; son mucho mejor que estar en cantinas, en tabernas.

Uno llega a querer tanto a los mantrams, que al fin no se siente uno bien el día que no ha practicado sus ejercicios.

¡Sed tenaces, queridos hermanos, sed tenaces!

Ése es el consejo que yo os doy a vosotros...

Extracts from
The Magic of Silence (undated)
by Arnoldo Krumm-Heller

PERSONAL CONSECRATION

Supreme Power, Cosmic Seity, You who are all Substance, all Energy and all Spirit.

I, [who am a] part of that Substance, [a] part of that Energy, [a] part of that Spirit, consecrate[13] myself [to You], because I wish [to] integrate with You.

Unify me with You, [so that I may] be eternally in You...

I surrender[14] my destiny, my actions, my present and [my] future life to your infinite and perpetual action, so that my realizations are always your realizations.

So Be It.

CONSECRATION TO THE MASTER

Exalted Master, venerable guide and instructor of mine, infuse[15] me with your protective emanations[16] and receive, in this Act of Consecration, all my intense longing to be your sincere disciple.

Instruct me, forgive my faults and ensure that all my actions always conform to your sacred instructions and [that] I can merit[17] your blessing and your love.

So Be It.

---

[13] Literally 'consagro' means "consecrate, sanctify; dedicate, devote"
[14] Literally 'entrego' means "deliver, convey; give over; consign; submit; surrender; address; serve"
[15] Literally 'infunde' means "inject; infuse; ingrain"
[16] Literally 'efluvios' means "effluents; outpouring; vapor, scent;"
[17] Literally 'merecer' means "deserve, merit; earn, gain; bear"

Extractos de
Magia del Silencio (sin fecha)
por Arnoldo Krumm-Heller

CONSAGRACIÓN PERSONAL[18]

Poder Supremo, Seidad Cosmica, a Ti que eres toda Substancia, toda Energia y todo Espiritu.

Yo, parte de esa Substancia, parte de esa Energia, parte de ese Espiritu, me consagro, pues deseo integrarme en Ti.

Unificarme contigo, ser eternamente en Ti...

A tu infinita y perpetua accion entrego mi destino, mis actos, mi vida presente y futura, de modo que mis realizaciones sean siempre realizaciones tuyas.

Asi Sea.

CONSAGRACIÓN AL MAESTRO

Maestro excelso, venerable guia e instructor mio, infunde en mi tus efluvios protectores y recibe en este Acto de Consagracion, todo mi deseo intenso de ser tu discipulo sincero.

Instruyeme, perdona mis faltas y vela para que todos mis actos se conformen siempre a tus instrucciones sagradas y pueda yo merecer tu bendicion y tu amor.

Asi Sea.

---

[18] Originalmente "CONSAGRACIÓN AL EGO"

UNIVERSAL AND COSMIC FORCE[19]

Universal and Cosmic Force, mysterious energy, fertile[20] womb[21] from which everything is born, You Solar Logos, Igneous Emanation, Christ in Substance and in Consciousness, Potent Life whereby everything advances, come unto me and permeate[22] me, illuminate me, bath me, pierce[23] me and awaken within **MY BEING** [of] all those[24] ineffable substances which are as much [a] part of you as [they are a part] of myself.

Universal and Cosmic Force, mysterious energy, I conjure you, come unto me, remedy my affliction, cure me [of] this evil[25] and remove[26] [from] me this suffering so that I may have harmony, peace, and health.

I ask you in your Sacred Name, that the Mysteries and the Gnostic Church have taught me, so that you can make all of the mysteries of this plane and [the] superior planes vibrate with me, and that [all of] those forces unite[27] to achieve the miracle of my healing.

So Be It.

FUERZA UNIVERSAL Y CÓSMICA

Fuerza Universal y Cósmica, energia misteriosa, seno fecundo de donde todo nace, Tu Logos Solar, Emanacion Ignea, Cristo en Substancia y en Conciencia, Vida Potente por la que todo avanza, ven hacia mi y penetrame, alumbrame, baname, traspasame y despierta en **MI SER**[28] todas esas substancias inefables que tanto son parte de ti como de mi mismo.

Fuerza Universal y Cosmica, energia misteriosa, yo te conjuro, ven hacia mi, remedia mi afliccion, curame este mal y apartame este sufrimiento para que yo tenga armonia, paz y salud.

Te lo pido en tu Sagrado Nombre, que los Misterios y la Iglesia Gnostica me han ensenado, para que hagas vibrar conmigo todos los misterios de este plano y planos superiores y que esas fuerzas reunidas logren el milagro de mi curacion.

Asi Sea.

---

[19] Editor's note: Compare the "Gnostic Prayer for Healing" from *Occult Medicine and Practical Magic* by Samael Aun Weor
[20] Literally 'fecundo' means "fertile, fecund, prolific, bountiful"
[21] Literally 'seno' means "breast, bosom; womb; heart; bay, gulf"
[22] Literally 'penétrame' means "penetrate, permeate; perforate; emerge; infiltrate; lodge; fathom"
[23] Literally 'traspásame' means "overstep; transfer; transfix; transgress; give up"
[24] Literally 'esas' means "those, these, such"
[25] Literally 'mal' means "evil; illness, disease, ill, sickness, malady, mal, malum; wrong; bad"
[26] Literally 'apártame' means "separate, divide; alienate; distract; avert, turn away; lure away, allure"
[27] Literally 'reunidas' means "joined; gathered; reunite"

[28] Originamente "mi YO"

INVOCATION TO THE LIGHT

From the point of Light, in the Mind of God, may [the] Light stream[29] forth into the Minds of Men. May the Light descend to the Earth.

From the point of Love, in the Heart of God, may [the] Love stream forth into the Hearts of Men. May the Christ return to the Earth.

From the center, where the Will of God is known, may the [divine] purpose guide the little wills of men. [Thereby manifesting] the purpose that the Master knows and serves.

Through the center which we call [the] human race, may the plan of Love and Light be fulfilled[30] and seal the door where evil dwells.

MAY THE LIGHT, THE LOVE AND THE POWER, REESTABLISH[31] THE [DIVINE] PLAN ON EARTH. (3 times).

INVOCACIÓN A LA LUZ

Desde el punto de Luz, en la Mente de Dios, que afluya Luz a la Mente de los Hombres. Que la Luz descienda a la Tierra.

Desde el punto de Amor, en el Corazon de Dios, que afluya Amor a los Corazones de los Hombres. Que Cristo retorne a la Tierra.

Desde el centro donde la Voluntad de Dios es conocida que el proposito [divino] guie las pequenas voluntades de los hombres. El proposito que el Maestro conoce y sirve.

Mediante el centro que llamamos raza de los hombres, que se cumpla el plan de Amor y de Luz y selle la puerta donde mora el mal.

QUE LA LUZ, EL AMOR Y EL PODER, RESTABLEZCAN EL PLAN [DIVINO] SOBRE LA TIERRA. (3 veces).

---

[29] Literally 'afluya' means "flow; flock; embody"
[30] Literally 'cumpla' means "carry out, keep (a promise), observe (a law), fulfill; reach; serve; do, do one's duty"
[31] Literally 'Restablezcan' means "reestablish, restore; recover, revive; resettle; recruit;"

Editor's Appendix	Apéndice del Editor
# PRACTICE OF THE LIGHT	# PRACTICA DE LA LUZ
## DOMINION OF THOUGHTS AND FEELINGS	## DOMINIO DE PENSAMIENTOS Y SENTIMIENTOS
The First Step for self-dominion is the cessation of **ALL EXTERIOR ACTIVITY**, both for the mind as well as the body.	El Primer Paso para el auto dominio es el cese de **TODA ACTIVIDAD EXTERIOR**, tanto de la mente cuanto del cuerpo.
At night, fifteen to thirty minutes before sleep, and in [the] morning before our daily obligations, practicing the following exercise will provide wonderful results to whosoever makes the necessary effort.	Quince a treinta minutos por la noche antes de dormirse y de manana antes de iniciar nuestras obligaciones diarias, de la practica del ejercicio siguiente, daran resultados maravillosos a quienquiera que realice el esfuerzo necesario.
The Second Step: Take care not to be disturbed.	El Segundo Paso: Tomad cuidado de no ser perturbado.
Then establish harmony and tranquility [within yourself].	Despues estableced armonia y tranquilidad.
Next imagine and feel that the body is enveloped in a dazzling **WHITE LIGHT**.	Enseguida imaginad y sentid que el cuerpo esta envuelto en una deslumbrante **LUZ BLANCA**.
In the first five minutes during which this picture[32] should be maintained in the imagination, **RECOGNIZE** and **FEEL INTENSELY** that your **EXTERIOR BEING**, has been linked to your powerful **INTERIOR GOD**; then focus the attention on the center of the Heart, visualizing it as a **SUN OF GOLD**.	Durante los primeros cinco minutos en que ese cuadro se mantenga en la imaginacion, **RECONOCE** y **SIENTE INTENSAMENTE** que tu **SER**[34] **EXTERIOR**, se ha ligado a vuestro poderoso **DIOS INTERIOR**; entonces focaliza la atencion en el centro del Corazon, visualizandolo como un **SOL DE ORO**.
The NEXT STEP IS RECOGNITION.	El **PASO SIGUIENTE ES EL RECONOCIMIENTO.**
I, NOW, HAPPILY ACCEPT THE FULLNESS OF THE POWERFUL PRESENCE OF GOD, THE PURE CHRIST.	**YO, AHORA, ACEPTO ALEGREMENTE LA PLENITUD DE LA PODEROSA PRESENCIA DE DIOS, EL CRISTO PURO.**
Perceive the **GREAT BRILLIANCE**[33] **OF THE LIGHT** and intensify it in every cell of your body for ten minutes or more.	Percibe el **GRAN BRILLO DE LA LUZ** e intensificala en cada celula de vuestro cuerpo durante diez minutos o mas.

---

[32] Literally 'cuadro' means "square; stable, structure in which horses and other animals are housed; picture; painting; plot; table; chart"

[33] Literally 'Brillo' means "brilliance, brightness, shininess; glitter, splendor; sheen, luster, shine; eclat, big success, triumph"

[34] Originamente "YO"

Then enter into meditation with the [following] commandment or mandate:

I AM A CHILD[35] OF THE LIGHT.

I LOVE THE LIGHT.

I LIVE IN THE LIGHT.

I AM PROTECTED, ILLUMINATED, FILLED, [AND] SUSTAINED BY THE LIGHT AND I BLESS THE LIGHT...

Don't forget and always meditate: We turn into **THAT** upon which we meditate and afterwards the things [we meditated upon] sprout from the **LIGHT**, the **LIGHT** is Supreme Perfection and dominion over all things.

CONTEMPLATE and **ADORE THE LIGHT**, make **ILLUMINATION** arise[36] in the mind, [make] health, strength, [and] discipline [arise] in the body, [and] bring harmony and prosperity into [the] affairs of every individual who **REALLY** practices and seeks to live them.

In all ages, at all times[37], in any condition, they tell us [that for] all those who realize great events[38] in Life, that the **LIGHT** is supreme, [that] the **LIGHT** is Omnipresent and [that] all things exist in the **LIGHT**.

This truth is as true today as it was millions of years ago [in the] past.

Entra entonces a la meditacion con el mandamiento o mandato:

YO SOY UN HIJO DE LA LUZ.

YO AMO LA LUZ.

YO VIVO EN LA LUZ.

YO SOY PROTEGIDO, ILUMINADO, PLENO, SUSTENTADO POR LA LUZ Y YO BENDIGO LA LUZ...

No olvides y medita siempre: Nos tornamos en **AQUELLO** en que meditamos y una vez que las cosas brotan de la **LUZ**, la **LUZ** es la Suprema Perfeccion y el dominio sobre todas las cosas.

CONTEMPLACION y **ADORACION A LA LUZ**, hacen surgir la **ILUMINACION** en la mente, la salud, la fuerza, la disciplina en el cuerpo, trayendo armonia y prosperidad en los negocios de todo individuo que practica **REALMENTE** y procura vivirlas.

En todos los siglos, en todas las epocas, en cualquier condicion, dicennos todos aquellos que realizaron los mayores sucesos en la Vida, que la **LUZ** es suprema, la **LUZ** es Omnipresente y en la **LUZ** existen todas las cosas.

Esta verdad es tan verdad hoy como lo era hace millones de anos pasados.

---

[35] Literally 'Hijo' means "son, male child, male offspring; child; boy"
[36] Literally 'surgir' means "appear, arise, emerge; intervene; crop up"
[37] Literally 'epocas' means "period, age, era; season; lesson; length of time"
[38] Literally 'sucesos' means "incident, event, happening; doings"

Since ancient times[39], since [the time] when humanity had news, the sages and the great men of all ages are represented with a halo of **LIGHT** which emanates from their head and body.

And the **LIGHT** is **REAL**, as **REAL** as the electric Light that illuminates your home.

The day is not far off in which [an] apparatus[40] will be built to reveal the **LIGHT** that emanates from every individual for [the] physical view of whosoever wishes to see it.

Such apparatuses will also show the contamination or discoloration which occurs in the form of a cloud around the LIGHT OF GOD, generated by the personal "I" and by virtue of disharmonious[41] thoughts and feelings.

This and only this is the means through which **the great energy, the current[42] of Life** [or Cosmic Current][43] is poorly used and wrongly impregnated within us.

If the recommended exercise is practiced faithfully, feeling it in each atom of the mind and the body, with profoundity, with **PROFOUND INTENSITY**, you will receive abundant evidence of the Tremendous Activity, of the Power and of the Strength which resides and is permanently active in the **LIGHT**.

---

[39] Literally 'tiempos mas remotos' means "very remote times"
[40] Literally 'aparatos' means "apparatus, device; system; machine; gear; receiver; appliance; gadget; show, display; symptom, indication (Medicine); syndrome;"
[41] Literally 'discordantes' means "inconsonant; discordant, disharmonious"
[42] Literally 'corriente' means "current, flow (of water, electricity, etc.); tendency, drift; tide; swim; rain"
[43] Editor's note: In Lesson 3 of his *Runic Course*, Huiracocha says "In our Zodiacal Course, we have tried to make known and explain the Cosmic Current that flows both from the height as well as from the earth itself in order to converge in us assimilating in our Glands or Magnetic Centers so as to finally realize in us the miracle of converting us into Gods again. Because we are Gods... [only] now we are enclosed in the prison of our physical envelope, as Plato said, where one can not simply and spontaneously, [nor] without any preparation, actualize the Sacred Fire that encourages us."

When you have experienced this, even when it is little thing, the privilege of a new experience will come to you. Giving[45] you, therefore, your own experience.

The **LIGHT** is the Kingdom, penetrate into it and be at Peace.

After the first ten days of practicing this exercise, it would be convenient to do it three times per day –if possible–, morning, noon and night.

We often hear the complaint: "Oh, I do not have much time...".

To anyone who wants to think this way I would simply say this:

> THE TIME THAT THE COMMON INDIVIDUAL DEDICATES TO CRITISIZING, BLAMING AND CONDEMNING PEOPLE, CONDITIONS AND THINGS, NOT WANTING TO BE DIFFERENT FROM WHAT THEY ARE, IF [THAT SAME TIME] IS USED IN THE RECOGNITION AND USE OF LIGHT, IT WILL BRING HEAVEN TO EARTH FOR WHOSOEVER DARES[46] TO EXPERIMENT [WITH IT] AND HAS THE STRENGTH ENOUGH TO PERSEVERE.
>
> NOTHING IS IMPOSSIBLE.
>
> THE LIGHT NEVER FAILS.

---

[45] Literally 'Tornaos' means "turn down; dial; transform; make, turn, return"
[46] Literally 'Ose' means "venture, dare"

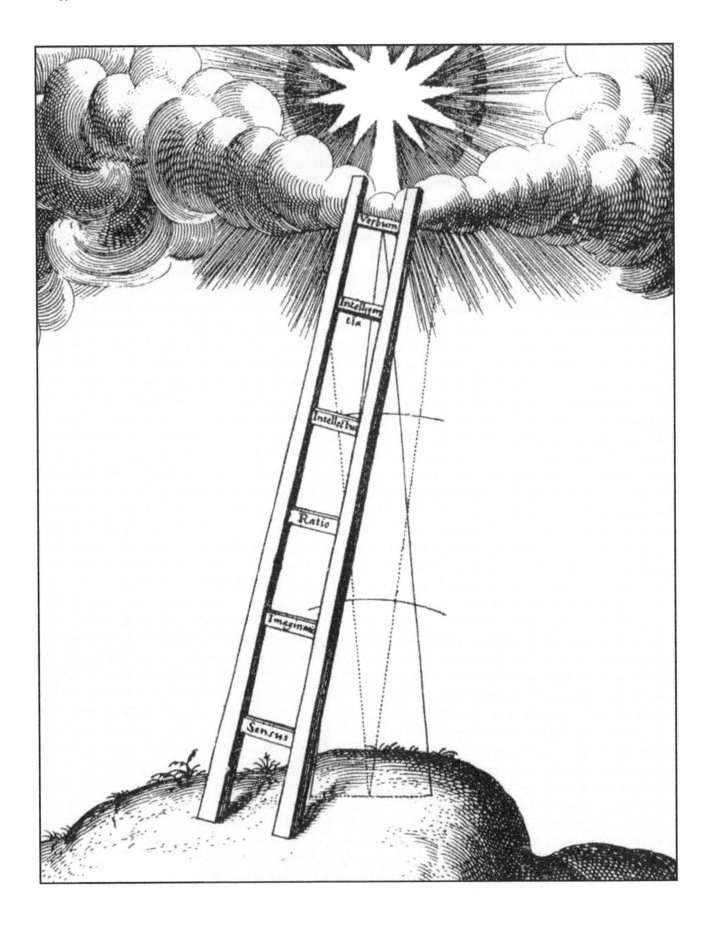

Editor's Appendix

Extract from
The Rosecross Magazine
Berlin, January 1933

Apéndice del Editor

Extracto del
Revista Rosacruz
Berlín, Enero de 1.933

LIGHT

It was in the vehemence[47] of [our] youth, when we were rebelling against the teachings of the Bible.

Those Chapters of Genesis, moved us to indignation, thinking that an almighty God first made Light and then the Sun when this was unscientific.

Even the youngest pupils of Elementary School knew that all Light comes from the Sun, and that the first could not exist without the presence of the second.

So we attributed[48] ignorance to the same God of Genesis, and in [another] case [we attribute] great benevolence[49], we accepted this whole legend as a translation error.

But then, we also saw that, in the stories of other Religions, the same [thing] was mentioned[50], as if all Religions had agreed on this point in order to sustain such a tremendous absurdity[51], and our protest reached[52] its limit[53] because [we] did not want to dwell[54] among the ignorant sheep.

---

[47] Literally 'vehemencia' means "vehemence, passion, fervor, force"
[48] Literally 'poníamos' means "put, place; lay; insert; impose; mark; adjust; send; contribute; subscribe; perform; translate"
[49] Literally 'benévolo' means "benevolent, kind, gentle"
[50] Literally 'se hacía la misma mención' means "the same mention was made"
[51] Literally 'disparate' means "folly, absurdity, piffle, nonsense"
[52] Literally 'salía' means "exit, leave, go out; appear, come into view; escape; enter; hatch, emerge from an egg; defray, pay, cover the expenses of; project; quit; lead; win"
[53] Literally 'límite' means " limit, point at which something ends; boundary, borderline; extreme, pronounced or excessive degree; maximum"
[54] Literally 'pasar' means "hand over, transfer, deliver; move from one place to another, relocate; conduct; pass; traverse, cross; give, bestow; send, dispatch; insert, put in; slip by; strain, filter through a sieve; swallow; overlook, ignore"

LUZ

Era en la vehemencia de la juventud, cuando nos rebelábamos contra las enseñanzas de la Biblia.

Aquellos Capítulos del Génesis, nos movían a indignación, pensando que un Dios todopoderoso hiciera primero la Luz y luego el Sol cuando esto era anticientífico.

Hasta los alumnos más pequeños de la Escuela Primaria, sabían que toda Luz proviene del Sol, y que no podía existir la primera sin la presencia del segundo.

Entonces poníamos de ignorante al mismo Dios del Génesis, y en el caso más benévolo, aceptábamos toda esta leyenda como un error de traducción.

Pero luego, veríamos también, que en los relatos de otras Religiones se hacía la misma mención, como si todas las Religiones se hubiesen puesto de acuerdo en este punto para sostener tan tremendo disparate, y nuestra protesta salía de límite porque no queríamos pasar entre el rebaño de ignorantes.

However, over the course of the years, we were able to read the most beautiful tradition which has been written about the Creation of the World. It is that of the Aztecs.

For them, there existed [a] Fire, but a very weak and tenuous[55] Fire, almost without [any] action.

Then Tezcatlipoca took pity[56] on the humans and took possession of that Fire making it react and converted it into [the] Sun.

From [what] we have observed, according to the Mexicans, there was also firstly Light or Fire and when the Sun is created, it is only [then that] a God, or the Gods, took possession of it.

The Fire!, but what was the Fire for the first men, when they saw it burning in the shadows of the night?

A compound of Light, and of Smoke, because that is just what is seen when we look at the phenomenon of Fire.

Then, if we get closer[57], we feel heat.

In this way we can affirm that there is a trio of LIGHT, HEAT AND SMOKE.

This Smoke is the material part. The Heat has [the] character[58] of Soul or mediating energy, and the Light is the spiritual part, that is to say, Fire, calm, phosphoric, but which illuminates and shines and is silent in all that is...

Sin embargo, con el transcurso de los años, pudimos leer la tradición mas hermosa que se ha escrito acerca de la Creación del Mundo. Es la de los Aztecas.

Para ellos, existía el Fuego, pero un Fuego muy débil y tenue, casi sin acción.

Entonces Tezcalipoca se compadece de los humanos y toma posesión de ese Fuego haciéndolo reaccionar y convirtiéndolo en Sol.

Según observamos, para los Mexicanos, también existió primeramente la Luz o Fuego y sólo al posesionarse de ella un Dios, o los Dioses, es cuando el Sol es creado.

¡El Fuego!; pero ¿qué era el Fuego para los primeros hombres cuando lo veían arder en las sombras de la noche?

Un compuesto de Luz, y de Humo, porque es esto tan sólo lo que se advierte cuando nos fijamos en ese fenómeno del Fuego.

Luego, si nos acercamos, se siente calor.

De esto modo podemos afirmar que existe un trío de LUZ, CALOR Y HUMO.

Este Humo es parte material. El Calor, tiene condición de Alma o mediadora energía, y la Luz, es la parte espiritual, es decir, Fuego, frío, fosfórico, pero que alumbra y resplandece y está silente en todo cuanto es...

---

[55] Literally 'tenue' means "tenuous, thin; weak, faint; remote"
[56] Literally 'compadece' means "commiserate, sympathize; comply"
[57] Literally 'acercamos' means "draw near, come close; bring near; verge"
[58] Literally 'condición' means "condition, state; character; rank; factor; term; requirement, stipulation; embargo"

Editor's Appendix	Apéndice del Editor
Fire has always [been] a kind of link or bridge between the material world and the spiritual [world].	El Fuego, era siempre una especie de nexo o de puente entre el mundo material y el espiritual.
It is the finger pointing up signaling creation, to take [something up] from the material world like [a] fertile[59] sprout[60] of Smoke and Light.	Él es el que levanta el dedo señalando la creación, al salir de él el mundo material como brote fecundo del Humo y la Luz.
Now [this] seems to us [to be a] glimpse of the secret enclosed within the INRI of the Rose Cross.	Ahora parecíamos entrever algo del secreto encerrado en el INRI de los Rosa Cruz.
INRI: the fire renews all, or, we could say, light (the constant) creates.	INRI: el fuego todo renueva, o luz, la constante, crea, podríamos decir.
If someone asks: "Do you see the Light?"	Si preguntamos a alguien: ¿Veis la Luz?
We then respond in [an] affirmative tone, but it is certain, most certain, THAT [WE] DO NOT SEE THE LIGHT.	Nos responderían seguidamente en tono afirmativo, pero es cierto, ciertísimo, QUE NO VEN LA LUZ.
No one has seen the Light, except the Initiates, and for this reason seeing the Light plays an important role within Masonry.	La Luz nadie la ha visto, excepto los Iniciados, y por eso este hecho de ver la Luz, juega un papel tan importante dentro de la Masonería.
What the whole world sees, is not the Light, it is the fire that produces it.	Lo que todo el mundo ve, no es la Luz, es el fuego que la produce.
It happens, however, that we see objects in the physical world through the Light, but the Light itself, in itself, no one sees.	Sucede, sin embargo, que vemos los objetos del mundo físico, mediante la Luz, ahora que, la Luz misma, en sí, nadie la ve.
If we look at [a] vaccum, [a] vaccum would be space that covers our eyes and no one could distinguish anything if some object was not interposed[61] upon it.	Si miramos al vacío, vacío estaría el espacio que abarcara nuestra mirada y nada podríamos distinguir él si no interponerse algún objeto.
The light lets us see solid, liquid and gaseous things; but the Light itself is physically[62] invisible.	La luz nos hace ver las cosas sólidas, líquidas y gaseosas; pero la Luz misma es materialmente invisible.

---

[59] Literally 'fecundo' means "fertile, fecund, prolific, bountiful"
[60] Literally 'brote' means "outbreak; bud, sprout, shoot; upsurge; burgeon"
[61] Literally 'interponerse' means "interpose, interject; intervene"
[62] Literally 'materialmente' means "materially, in a material or physical way; substantially, considerably"

Editor's Appendix	Apéndice del Editor
That which belongs to[63] the superphysical world is what leads[64] us to Initiation.	Pertenece al mundo superfísico que es al que nos llevan en la Iniciación.
But if we look at the Sun and we persist[65] in saying that we are seeing the Light, [what] we are saying [is] wrong.	Pero si mirarnos al Sol y nos obstinamos en decir que estamos viendo la Luz, decimos mal.
What we see is a **flaming** body, a burning[66] and luminous substance from which Light is exiting.	Lo que vemos, es un cuerpo en **flama**, una substancia ardiente y luminosa de la que sale la Luz.
And [so] the question remains: "What is the Light? Where did it come from?"	Y queda pendiente la pregunta: ¿Qué es la Luz? ¿De donde proviene?
The first idea would be to assume that a Central Sun is charging[67] towards us, [charging] towards our system, with that Living Fire which is peculiar to it, and if this were sustained[68] [then there] would be many adepts through this theory, since it is very rational and soundly logical and has so often been sustained by Theosophists. But... it is an error, a complete error.	La primera idea, seria suponer que un Sol Central es el que carga al nuestro, al de nuestro sistema, de ese Fuego Vivo que le es peculiar, y si así se sostuviera serían muchos los adeptos para esta teoría, ya que es bien racional y bien lógica y tantas veces ha -sido sostenida hasta por los mismos Teósofos. Pero... es un error, un completo error.
The Light does not come from any Sun... just as our thoughts do not come from the material brain.	La Luz no proviene de ningún Sol... como nuestros pensamientos no provienen del cerebro material.
The brain is an instrument of the mind, just as the Sun is an instrument of the Light.	Es el cerebro un instrumento de la mente, como el Sol es un instrumento de la Luz.
We repeat: The Light does not come from any Sun.	Repetimos: La Luz no proviene de ningún Sol.

---

[63] Literally 'Pertenece' means "appertain, belong to; connected to"
[64] Literally 'llevan ' means "carry, transport; take; convey; wear; win; lead; bear; spend; hunch, hump; heave; carry off; deliver; live through; encroach on"
[65] Literally 'obstinamos' means "be obstinate (firmly or stubbornly adhering to one's purpose, opinion, etc)"
[66] Literally 'ardiente' means "burning, glowing; fervent, ardent; hot, fervid"
[67] Literally 'carga' means "load; burden; encumber; charge; stoke; oppress; carry; plow; attack, assault; lean, incline; pester, annoy; veer, change direction; crowd together"
[68] Literally 'sostuviera' means "sustain, uphold, support; maintain; bear; live"

| Editor's Appendix | Apéndice del Editor |

The truth is quite different, and it is far from any hypothesis or theory and enclosed within it is one of the Great Initiatic Secrets, rarely published, because it is very difficult to comprehend and accept, if it is not for someone who has received true Initiation.

Initiation consists[69] precisely of[70] this [secret], in receiving the Light, and only upon receiving it, is[71] it comprehended.

The Light, therefore, does not come from any Planet, nor [does it] spring from any celestial body.

It is, simply[72], the emanation of the zodiacal signs, but let's take care [to understand], I am not saying [that it is the light] of the constellations (which is not the same [thing], even if it is related), [instead] it is the environment where certain [specific] and determined BEINGS live.

These Beings are called ELEMENTARIES, [and] they populate the whole [of] space.

They are the Superior Angels, luminous and resplendent, [they are] vehicles, and [they] are the ones that must be communicated with and [the ones that] communicate with us, in order to verify [our] Initiation.

We know perfectly [well], that this theory is one of the biggest obstacles that [we] present [in] our teachings, since we can not provide scientifically clear evidence of our assertion, [nor] offer material experiments, since[73] the Light is not material.

These Beings, to which we refer ourselves, populate the vast interplanetary space and the Light flows[74] from them, of which humans only see their effects.

La verdad es muy otra, y está muy distante de cualquier hipótesis o teoría y en ella se encierra uno de los Grandes Secretos Iniciáticos, rara vez publicado, porque es muy difícil de comprender y aceptar si no es por aquél que haya recibido la verdadera Iniciación.

En esto consiste precisamente la Iniciación, en recibir la Luz, y tan sólo al recibirla, es cuando se le comprende.

La Luz, pues, no sale de ningún Planeta, ni brota de ningún cuerpo celeste.

Ella es, tan sólo, la emanación de los signos zodiacales, pero pongamos cuidado, no digo, de las constelaciones, que no es lo mismo, aunque haya relación, es algo del ambiente de ellos donde viven ciertos y determinados SERES.

Estos Seres, son llamados ELEMENTARIOS, los cuales pueblan todo el espacio.

Son los Ángeles Superiores, luminosos y resplandecientes, los vehículos, y son con los que se debe comunicar y nos comunicamos, al verificarse la Iniciación.

Sabemos perfectamente, que esta teoría es uno de los más grandes escollos que presentan nuestras enseñanzas, pues no podemos ofrecer científicamente una prueba clara de nuestro aserto, ofreciendo experimentos materiales, ya que la Luz no es material.

Esos Seres, a que nos referimos, pueblan el inmenso espacio interplanetario y de ellos mana la Luz, de la que sólo los humanos vemos sus efectos.

---

[69] Literally 'consiste' means "consist"
[70] Literally 'En' means "in, into; for, to; on, at; by; about"
[71] Literally 'es cuando' means "is when"
[72] Literally 'tan sólo' means "just, only, merely"
[73] Literally 'ya' means "already, by now; before, beforehand"
[74] Literally 'mana' means "run, flow, stream"

Given these assumptions, we could also say that the earth is not the earth, because it would be the effect of the Gnomes, or that the water is not water, because it would be the result of the water spirits [or Undines].

But it is not thus, these [Elemental spirits] are inferior beings who dwell in these [inferior] forms of matter, while the Angels and Archangels are already Superior Entities that have become the elements themselves.

They ARE the elements [themselves], since what [is] already in their BEING is REALITY...

If we enter a room in the dark[75], where the light only penetrates through a slit, [then] we see this light and millions of dust particles dancing in it.

But if the room encountered is completely clean, that is to say, free of [any of] that tiny dust, then we would not see the Light, because it is (in the material sense) invisible.

Nonetheless, we see the Light in its effects within Nature, and this is because [Nature] is also found [to be] saturated with dust.

The higher the point is that we examine in the air, [the] less dust we will find.

In the City, for example, there is [a] 1/4 of a million [particles] per cubic centimeter squared. At the Eiffel Tower, only 150,000, and in Riga, only a little more than 200 particles [per cubic centimeter squared].

Going much higher, one encounters greater quantities [of these particles], since it is dust that comes from other celestial bodies.

The tail of the comet is nothing other than burning dust.

The same [is true of] rain and granite, we have them in our earth, thanks to dust.

---

[75] Literally 'oscuridad' means "obscurity, that which is obscure; anonymity; unclearness; dimness, darkness"

Dadas estas afirmaciones, pudiéramos decir también que la tierra no es la tierra, porque ella sería el efecto de los Gnomos, o que el agua no es el agua, porque ella sería la consecuencia de los espíritus del agua.

Pero no es así, estos son seres inferiores que moran en esas formas de materia, mientras que los Ángeles o Arcángeles son ya Entidades Superiores que se han convertido en los elementos mismos.

Ellos SON los elementos, puesto que ya el SER[76] de ellos, es REALIDAD...

Si entramos en una habitación en plena oscuridad, donde la luz penetre tan sólo por una rendija, vemos esta luz y danzando en ella, millones de partículas de polvo.

Pero si la habitación se encuentra totalmente limpia, es decir, exenta de esa polvoreda minúscula, entonces no veríamos la Luz, ya que ella, en el sentido material, es invisible.

Sin embargo, vemos la Luz en sus efectos dentro de la Naturaleza, y es porque ésta también se encuentra saturada de polvo.

Mientras mas alto es el punto que examinamos en el aire, menos polvo hallamos.

En la Ciudad, por ejemplo, hay 1/4 de millón por centímetro cúbico cuadrado. En la Torre Eiffel, sólo 150.000, y en Riga, sólo algo mas de 200 partículas.

Subiendo algo más, ya se encuentran en mayores cantidades, pues es polvo que viene de otros cuerpos celestes.

La cola de los cometas, no es mas que polvo ardiente.

La misma lluvia y el granito, los tenemos en nuestra tierra, gracias al polvo.

---

[76] Originalmente "el YO"

Editor's Appendix	Apéndice del Editor
Assuming that the air is completely pure, without [any] dust particles, where [would] water coagulate[77]?, we would have the Atmosphere full of humidity and this would force us to cover ourselves with rubber suits.	Suponiendo que el aire es completamente puro, sin partículas de polvo, donde haya podido posarse agua, tendríamos a la Atmósfera llena de humedad y esto nos obligaría a cubrirnos con trajes de goma.
The blue color of the sky is also [blue] because of the Light reflected in the water particles attached to the floating dust.	El color azul del cielo, os también debido a la Luz que se refleja en las partículas de agua adheridas al polvo flotante.
[The] same dust formed by [the] combustion of matter due to its weathering[78], gives birth[79] (in [the] same way) to the other Planets and even [to] the Sun.	Mismo el polvo que se forma por combustión de la materia debido a su desgaste, sale de igual manera de los demás Planetas y hasta el Sol.
One could say that these Planets attract these particles of dust, as does the Sun, through the force of its Light.	Se podría decir que esos Planetas atrajeran esas partículas de polvo, como sucede con el Sol, por la fuerza de su Luz.
This is, then, the material Light but the spiritual [Light] is quite different.	Esta es, pues, la Luz material ya que la espiritual es bien distinta.
We have lifted the corner of the veil of a Great Initiatic Secret, but we do not put it [out] for discussion.	Hemos levantado la punta del velo de un Gran Secreto Iniciático, pero no lo ponemos a discusión.
There are indisputable[80] things of which the mind can not form an accurate judgment about their existence.	Hay cosas indiscutibles mientras la mente no pueda formar un juicio exacto sobre su existencia.
We are only sketching[81], so that our readers, [can] meditate upon it and then can go closer to the GREAT LIGHT...	Sólo lo esbozamos, para que nuestros lectores, mediten sobre ello y así podrán irse acercando a la GRAN LUZ...
Also the problem of the superior invisible [worlds] lies in the Key of Astrology, and [it is] for this fact [that] the Astrologer must be a true Initiate, so that one knows what the zodiacal signs are, in themselves, since, while working with them, many pseudo-astrologers, do not know what they are.	También el problema de los invisibles superiores, reside en la Clave de la Astrología, y por este hecho el Astrólogo ha de ser un verdadero Iniciado, para que sepa lo que son, en sí, los signos zodiacales, pues, aunque trabajan con ellos, muchos pseudo-astrólogos, no saben lo que son.

---

[77] Literally 'posarse' means "settle; sit; land; perch, alight"
[78] Literally 'desgaste' means "wear; waste; leak; attrition; wastage"
[79] Literally 'sale' means "exit, leave, go out; appear, come into view; escape; enter; hatch, emerge from an egg; defray, pay, cover the expenses of; project; quit; lead; win"
[80] Literally 'indiscutibles' means "indisputable, undisputed, unquestioned"
[81] Literally 'esbozamos' means "rough out, outline, sketch"

Initiated astrologers are few.

The others, who only dedicate themselves to Horoscopy in a cold and material manner, are no more than mere imitations[82] of what can be so great, so real, so holy and superior among humans.

The true astrologer must know through experience, what the Astral Light is, which we direct[83] in our operations of Magic, and not just talk about these things through having read them.

And why should Man aspire to see the Light?, because Man is an Angel, because Man, despite having [a] temporarily carnal[84] cover[85], is the beginning[86] [of] the Hierarchy of Angels.

Below him are the Elementals, that is to say, the Gnomes of the Earth element, the Sylphs of the air, the Ondines of the water, and the Salamanders of Fire, but, here are these four spiritual legions —while being lower than Man, for which reason the Rose Cross dominates them— [that] have their corresponding doubles or legions in the superior planes, among the Angelic Hierarchies, just as the Salamanders, which act in the fire, have their correspondences in the Angels of the Light, who are the LIGHT ITSELF.

In Chapter 11 [of the Gospel of] Saint Luke, especially in Verse 36[87], those resplendent bodies and the light that dwells within us, are spoken of.

---

[82] Literally 'remedos' means "mimicry, imitation"
[83] Literally 'manejamos' means "handle, manage; run, operate, work; use; tend; drive; steer"
[84] Literally 'carnal' means "carnal, fleshly"
[85] Literally 'envoltura' means "cover, wrapper; case, sheath; membrane"
[86] Literally 'con el Hombre principia' means "with Man begins"
[87] This verse is: "If thy whole body therefore be full of light, having no part dark, the whole shall be full of light, as when the bright shining of a candle doth give thee light."

Jesus says: "I AM THE LIGHT OF THE WORLD" [see John 8:12, 9:5], because he also belonged to those Luminous Entities who do not incarnate, although, as an exception, he did [incarnate] in order to save Humanity. Modern Science, through its investigations, has already proven that matter itself is nothing but light waves[88] and heralds[89] the day in which the Rose Cross Philosophy (which holds that everything is Light) will overcome that poor Buddhist and Theosophical definition that everything is Maya or Illusion. Hence the Buddhist idea is pessimistic, while the Christian idea is frankly optimistic. R^+	Jesús dice: YO SOY LA LUZ DEL MUNDO, porque él también pertenecía a esas Entidades Luminosas que no encarnan ya, aunque él lo hiciera para salvar a la Humanidad, por una excepción. La Ciencia moderna, mediante sus investigaciones, ha probado ya que la materia en sí, no es más que ondulaciones de luz y llegará el día en que la Filosofía Rosa Cruz, que sostiene que todo es Luz, venza a aquella mala definición Budista y teosófica de que todo sea Maya o Ilusión. Por eso la idea Budista es de pesimismo, mientras que la idea cristiana es francamente optimista. R^+

---

[88] Literally 'ondulaciones' means "undulation, waving motion; wave"

[89] Literally 'llegará' means "arrive, come; reach; roll along; land; immigrate; invade; get; travel; vaporize"

Extract from
The Rosecross Magazine
Berlin, March 1933

MORE LIGHT

We have received a Great number of letters which refer themselves to our Article "Light", [and so] we are obligated to enter into some new explanations [in regards to this subject].

Let's talk first about the Material Light, since (in our previous Article) we were referring mainly to the Spiritual Light which is the Origin of the first and genesis-cause of all that exists...

The first man of science in our era occupied himself with the Light, it was Huygens[90] and who then discovered his 'wave Light theory' which, much later, was denied and undone by Newton[91] to also let us know his other 'theory of emission' which sustained that the Light is nothing but small particles rotating[92] in space.

In his turn, Maxwell[93], sought to dismiss the theory of Newton [so as] to present his electromagnetic [theory] which, at one point, was a rehabilitation sustained by men of Science until about twenty years ago, they wanted to resurrect the theory of Newton once again.

---

[90] Christiaan Huygens, FRS (1629-1695) was a prominent Dutch mathematician and a leading scientist of his time. He is known particularly as an astronomer, physicist, probabilist and horologist. Huygens is remembered especially for his wave theory of light, which he first communicated in 1678 to the Paris *Académie des sciences*.
[91] Sir Isaac Newton PRS MP (1642-1727) was an English physicist and mathematician who is widely regarded as one of the most influential scientists of all time and as a key figure in the scientific revolution.
[92] Literally 'giratorias' means "revolving, rotating, turning, spinning"
[93] James Clerk Maxwell FRS FRSE (1831-1879) was a Scottish mathematical physicist. He formulated a set of equations that describe electricity, magnetism, and optics as manifestations of the same phenomenon (the electromagnetic field).

Extracto del
Revista Rosacruz
Berlín, Marzo de 1.933

MAS LUZ

Una Gran cantidad de cartas que hemos recibido y que se refieren a nuestro Artíclo Luz, nos obligan a entrar en algunas nuevas explicaciones.

Hablemos primero, de la Luz Material, ya que en nuestro Artículo anterior, nos referíamos principalmente a la Luz Espiritual que es el Origen de la primera y causa-génesis de todo lo existente...

El primer hombre de ciencia que en nuestra era se ocupó de la Luz, fue Huggens y descubrió entonces su teoría ondulatoria de la Luz que, más tarde, fue negada y deshecha por Newton al darnos a conocer también su otra teoría de la emisión en la cual venía a sostener que la Luz no era otra cosa que pequeñas partículas giratorias en el espacio.

A su vez, Maxwell, pretendió desechar la teoría de Newton al presentar la suya electromagnética que, en cierto punto, fue una rehabilitación de la sostenida por los hombres de Ciencia hasta hace unos veinte años, en que han querido resucitar otra vez la teoría de Newton.

Then, finally, Einstein[94] has come [along] stating that there were so many extreme contraditions in different theories about the light, which he declared incompetent so [he] decided [to either find] which one of them was the most correct or to create a new one that was even closer[95] to the truth.

This gave rise, in the last Congress of Physics, to the Scientists having reached [an] agreement in that "so far it is unknown what Light is. Its effects are known, but the Light itself offers many enigmas that force[96] everyone to concede[97] and to give in to their [own] ignorance..."

Our readers [should] remember that joke from a man who was required[98] to give a definite[99] answer on some topic when he said: "it might be yes, it might be no, but what is most likely is that Nobody Knows!"

So we hope[100] that the science [of the] future[101] will learn, [along] with the Rose Cross, what the Light is.

It can not be measured nor weighed, but it is lived in the interior of one's Divine Being.

Luego, finalmente, ha llegado Einstein declarando que existían tantos extremos contradictorios en las distintas teorías sobre la luz, que el se declaraba incompetente para decidir cual de ellas era la más acertada o para crear una nueva que aun se aproximara mas y mas a la verdad.

Esto dio motivo que, en los últimos Congresos de Física, se hayan puesto de acuerdo los Científicos en que "hasta ahora no se sabe lo que es la Luz. Que se conocen sus efectos, pero que la Luz en si ofrece tantos enigmas que obliga a todos a ceder y a darse por vencidos ante su ignorancia"...

Recuerden nuestros lectores aquel chiste de un hombre a quien se le exigió que diera una respuesta categórica sobre cierto asunto cuando dijo: puede ser que si y puede ser que no, pero lo mas probable es ¡Quien sabe!.

Así que esperamos a que la ciencia venga a aprender con los Rosa Cruz lo que es la Luz.

Sin medirla ni pesarla, pero viviéndola en el interior de su Ser Divino[102].

---

[94] Albert Einstein (1879-1955) was a German-born theoretical physicist. He developed the general theory of relativity, one of the two pillars of modern physics (alongside quantum mechanics). While best known for his mass–energy equivalence formula $E = mc^2$, he received the 1921 Nobel Prize in Physics "for his services to theoretical physics, and especially for his discovery of the law of the photoelectric effect" which was pivotal in establishing quantum theory and the field we now call Quantum Physics.
[95] Literally 'mas y mas' means "more and more"
[96] Literally 'obliga' means "oblige, compel; coerce, compel to do something; push; bind; draft; trust"
[97] Literally 'ceder' means "concede, admit; yield, give up; cede, assign, grant"
[98] Literally 'exigió' means "exact, demand, require; levy; need, necessitate; beg"
[99] Literally 'categórica' means "categorical, definite; flat, point blank; emphatic"
[100] Literally 'esperamos' means "hope, expect; wait, tarry; stay; watch; anticipate; trust"
[101] Literally 'venga' means "come; reach; arrive; result from; happen, occur; infiltrate; settle; land"

[102] Originalmente: "su Yo Divino"

The Prophets, kabalists, Mystics, Sleepwalkers, [and] Seers from all time, have referred to this Magical Light and affirmed that it is something inexplicable through human language, but what they also say [is that] what they are dealing with[103] is a sublime thing that penetrates their whole Being...

This Light radiates its powerful[104] phosphorescence[105] and this is the reason why we see some Initiate Saints and Fathers possessed and surrounded by a magnificent aura[106] of white, powerful and divine Light.

It was said in ancient [times], long before the beginning of the modern churches, that Moses, Socrates, Zoroaster, Pythagoras, etc., Imagined...

[There was] a German Saint, [according to] the story of the church, who extended his luminous aura, and the nuns of his convent were frightened when he came out of his room[107].

Although [this] is something material, we also have to remember a manifestation which we know as the Odic Rays or luminous emanations that the Physicist Baron Reichenback[108] refers[109] [to] as OD rays and much later, at [the University of] Nancy, [were referred to] as N rays studied today [by] the Spiritists and which are [nothing] more than manifestations of this Divine Light.

---

[103] Literally 'trata' means "treat, behave towards; attend; process; like; carry; doctor"
[104] Literally 'potentes' means "liable; potent, powerful"
[105] Literally 'fosforescencias' means "phosphorescence, luminosity, quality of producing light after exposure to radiation"
[106] Literally 'aureola' means "halo, aureole, aura"
[107] Literally 'celda' means "cell"
[108] Baron Dr. Karl Ludwig Freiherr von Reichenbach (1788-1869) was a notable chemist, geologist, metallurgist, naturalist, industrialist and philosopher. Towards the end of his life, he dedicated himself to researching an unproved field of energy combining electricity, magnetism and heat, emanating from all living things, which he called the Odic force. This Odic force (also called Od, Odyle, Önd, Odes, Odylic, Odyllic, or Odems) refers to vital energy or life force and comes from the Norse god Odin.
[109] Literally 'señalado' means "signalize, make prominent; mark, indicate, signal; particularize, specify"

Los Profetas, cabalistas, Místicos, Sonámbulos, Videntes en suma de todos los tiempos, han hecho referencia a esa Luz Mágica y afirman que es algo inexplicable por medio del lenguaje humano, pero si dicen también que se trata de una cosa sublime que les penetra por todo el Ser...

Esta Luz, irradia sus potentes fosforescencias y esta es la causa de que veamos a algunos Santos y Padres Iniciados provistos y rodeados de una aureola magnífica de Luz blanca, poderosa y divina.

Ya se decía de antiguo y mucho antes del comienzo de las iglesias modernas, que Moisés, Sócrates, Zoroastro, Pitágoras, etc. Imaginaban...

De una Santa Alemana, cuenta la historia de la iglesia, que tanto extendía su luminosa aura, que las monjas de su convento se asustaban cuando ella salía de su celda.

Aunque es algo material, hemos de recordar también una manifestación que conocemos con el nombre de Rayos Odicos o emanaciones luminosas que ha señalado el Físico, Barón de Reichenback, como rayos OD y más tarde, en Nancy, como rayos N hoy estudian los Espiritas y que son mas que manifestaciones de esa Divina Luz.

It has been [a] long time [that] I have had experiences with moving motors [powered by] direct solar rays and with having superb result.

Now we could say, as it is [said by] the German physicist Legar[110], that the other stars are all suns and [that they are] seeking to discover a device with which one can perfectly measure the moving force of the stars.

This is not measured with the galvanometer[111], which is old, but with a special device and it was seen among others that Jupiter gave [off] 30 millampares and the secondary stars [gave off] 10 millampares.

I did more, transforming the already demonstrated[112] electrical waves, into sound and so on, and those that visit a German observatory can hear the star Light.

With this Astrology has had her proof[113] through the exact sciences and has glimpsed the Astral Light.

The fact is, that there exists the Astral Light of the Magi[114].

Now [the fact is] that this Light becomes Heat and is therefore in close[115] and constant relation to the heat of our body.

Our organic heat is equal throughout the body, so if the Medic places the Thermometer in the mouth or the anus of the patient, we observe that the temperature is the same.

---

[110] The Editors have not been able to find this person.
[111] Literally 'galvanómetro' means "galvanometer, instrument that measures electric currents"
[112] Literally 'demostradas' means "displayed; indicated; designed"
[113] Literally 'comprobación' means "checkup; testing; ascertainment, substantiation, proving"
[114] Literally 'Magos' means "magician, wizard; Magus, one of the Magi, one of the wise men who came from the East to worship the baby Jesus"
[115] Literally 'íntima' means "intimate, close, familiar; personal, private; warm, friendly"

Desde hace mucho tiempo se han hecho experiencias moviendo motores con rayos solares directos y con saberlo soberbio resultado.

Ahora podríamos decir y así se dijo el físico Alemán Legar, que las demás estrellas son otros tantos soles y buscando descubrirlo un aparato con que se puede medir perfectamente la fuerza motriz de las estrellas.

No se trata de medir con el galvanómetro, ese es viejo, sino con un aparato especial y se vio entre otros que Júpiter dio 30 millampares y las estrellas de segunda 10 millampare.

Hizo más, transformó las ondas eléctricas así demostradas, en sonido y así ya los que visitan un observatorio Alemán pueden oir la Luz estelar.

Con esto la Astrología ha tenido su comprobación por las ciencias exactas y se entreve la Luz Astral.

El hecho es, que existe la Luz Astral de los Magos.

Ahora que esta Luz se convierte en Calor y por eso está en relación íntima y constante con el calor de nuestro cuerpo.

Nuestro calor orgánico, es igual en todo el cuerpo, por esto si el Médico coloca el Termómetro en la boca o el ano del enfermo, observamos que la temperatura es la misma.

When [someone] has a Blood transfusion, the heat is also equal and whosoever receives the Blood of another observes no alteration of heat.

There is only one difference in us, the semen which, even if [there is] no increase in temperature when it is perceived externally, whereas women in return feel its heat.

In the carnal act, [something] like Fire escapes[116] from Man and it is the Semen which is made from that Mysterious Light.

Now [know] that the evil[117] mind makes [it so] that this light can not manifest itself in all its power, for this [manifestation a] man who wants to operate in the Astral Light has to be Excited and Pure as Wagner has said in his [opera] Parsifal.

We must avail ourselves of the means at our disposal in order to study and manage the Light and for this [study] there has been and will always be sexual Magic with profound meditative prayer, [with] the mind pure and [with an] elevated and holy disposition[118], mentally directing the currents of the Heart to the Semen and then [this] will give off interior Light[119].

But [for] those who are not capable of this purity and holiness required, it is better not to venture [any] further[120] nor achieve [any] greater development.

At this point our Readers may appreciate[121] our recent[122] articles upon Tantra and Light and to meditate...

---

[116] Literally 'sale' means "exit, leave, go out; appear, come into view; escape; enter; hatch, emerge from an egg; defray, pay, cover the expenses of; project; quit; lead; win"
[117] Literally 'malévola' means "malevolent, malicious, wishing evil or harm to another, spiteful"
[118] Literally 'orientación' means "orientation; training; trim"
[119] Literally 'desprenderá interiormente la Luz' means "interiorly give off Light"
[120] Literally 'hasta' means "even; through; up"
[121] Literally 'unir' means "unite, join, link, connect; mate; incorporate; interlock"
[122] Literally 'últimos' means "last, final, ultimate; latter; top; bottommost"

Cuando se hace una transfusión de Sangre, también el calor es igual y quien recibe la Sangre de otro no observa ninguna alteración de calor.

Solo hay una diferencia dentro de nosotros, el semen que, si bien no tiene aumento de temperatura cuando se percibe exteriormente, las mujeres en cambio sienten su calor.

En el acto carnal, sale como Fuego del Hombre y es que el Semen está hecho de esa Luz Misteriosa.

Ahora que la mente malévola, hace que esa luz no pueda manifestarse en todo su poder, por eso el hombre que quiere operar en la Luz Astral, tiene que ser Excitado y Puro como dijo Wagner en su Parsifal.

Nosotros, debemos de valernos de los medios a nuestro alcance para estudiar y manejar esa Luz y por eso ha existido y existirá siempre la Magia sexual con la oración profundamente meditada, la mente pura y la orientación elevada y santa, se dirigen mentalmente las corrientes del Corazón al Semen y entonces se desprenderá interiormente la Luz.

Pero los que no sean capaces de esa pureza y santidad exigida, es mejor que no se aventuren hasta no lograr un mayor desarrollo.

En este punto podrán nuestros Lectores unir nuestros últimos artículos sobre Tantra y Luz y meditar...

Editor's Appendix	Apéndice del Editor
There is a Path in order to learn the secrets of the light and that path is known and lived [in] the rituals of occult masonry, from the Rite of Memphis[123], which [contains] in itself[124] every excursion[125] around that sublime mystery of the Light. [R⁺]	Hay un Camino para conocer los secretos de la luz y ese camino es conocer y vivir los rituales de la masonería oculta, del Rito de Menphis, que en él todo jira alrededor de ese sublime misterio de la Luz. [R⁺]

---

[123] Editor's note: Krumm-Heller was a member of the Masonic Rite of Memphis-Misraim, which was a combination of two so-called 'Egyptian' Rites: the Rite of Memphis and the Rite of Misraïm. For more information on the subject of Occult Masonry, see *The Gnostic and Esoteric Mysteries of Freemasonry, Lucifer and the Great Work* (2012) and *Esoteric Studies in Masonry Volume 1*, as well as the writings of John Yarker. For specific details of the Memphis Rite, see *Le Sanctuaire de Memphis ou Hermès: Développements complets des Mystères Maçonniques* (1849) by Jacques-Étienne Marconis de Nègre, which has been translated into English as *The Sanctuary of Memphis, Or, Hermes: The Development of Masonic Mysteries* (1933) as well as the other writings of Marconis de Nègre.

[124] Literally 'él' means "he; it; one"

[125] Literally 'jira' means "unket, excursion; tour; picnic; strip"

Extract from
The Rosecross Magazine
Berlin, December 1932

TANTRA

In the Yoga system, so popular[126] in Spain as in America and yet [very] little understood, we have as [a] coronation, as [a] result, as [its] ultimate goal, TANTRA a word which is translated by Mrs. Besant [as] a kind of RULE OR RITUAL and indicates something that is exclusive to the powers [of] Sexual Magic, adding that in the Books of TANTRA the whole Occult Science is found and that they are very beneficial[127] and instructive.

Yet readers can read, concerning this word, in the Theosophical Glossary[128] translated [into Spanish] by Roviralta Borrel or in our Magazine for the month of May 1930 whose article ended saying "TO BE CONTINUED..."

---

[126] Literally 'manoseado' means " hackneyed (overdone, overused), trite"
[127] Literally 'provechosos' means "rewarding, satisfying, worthwhile, profitable; serving as a reward"
[128] Some entries from the *Theosophical Glossary* (1892):
  Tantra *(Sk.)*. *Lit.*, "rule or ritual". Certain mystical and magical works, whose chief peculiarity is the worship of the *female* power, personified in Sakti. Devi or Durga (Kali, Siva's wife) is the special energy connected with sexual rites and magical powers—*the worst form of black magic or sorcery.*
  Tantrika *(Sk.)*. Ceremonies connected with the above worship. Sakti having a two-fold nature, white and black, good and bad, the Saktas are divided into two classes, the Dakshinacharis and Vamacharis, or the right-hand and the left-hand Saktas, *i.e.,* "white" and "black" magicians. The worship of the latter is most licentious and immoral.
  Sakti *(Sk.)*. The active female energy of the gods; in popular Hinduism, their wives and goddesses; in Occultism, the crown of the astral light. Force and the six forces of nature synthesized. Universal Energy.
  Sakti-Dhara *(Sk.). Lit.,* the "Spear-holder", a title given to Kartikeya for killing Taraka, a Daitya or giant-demon. The latter, demon though he was, seems to have been such a great Yogin, owing to his religious austerities and holiness, that he made all the gods tremble before him. This makes of Kartikeya, the war god, a kind of St. Michael."
[Editor's note: For the last entry cited (Satki-Dhara), consider that Daitya may be the Hindu Lucifer].

| Editor's Appendix | Apéndice del Editor |

However, we have been forced[130] to wait two years in order to continue these works.

At that time, we had received various letters from Theosophists who, according to them, had addressed[131] this matter, ensuring[132] us that [they] intended[133] to write about some interesting topic.

We had hoped to read what [they] wrote, but [things] never happen[134] as we supposed and now is when we [are going to] make a new attempt[135] for the sake of our disciples and Readers.

Of course, let's not waste time with too many explanations. We need to touch[136] [on] something practical and occult, from the many rules that we give [you] every day from the Tantrists, but not with[137] a blind routine[138], as Westerners, we are not able to carry out many [of the] things that are unique to the Hindus.

Let's see an example: Patanjali says... "the width of two fingers below the anus and two fingers below the Penis, one finds [the] Adhara Lotus or the Mula-Adhara, that is to say, the square Lotus because of its leaves and the Yoni radiates from there, [which] constitutes the ultimate Power of Tantra, where Kundalini, the Supreme deity, remains[139] [asleep] in its[140] [own] dream."

Sin embargo, nos hemos visto obligados a esperar dos años para poder continuar aquellos trabajos.

Por aquel entonces, hubimos de recibir varias cartas de Teósofos que, según ellos, habíanse ocupado de esta materia, asegurándonos algunos que pretendía escribir sobre tema tan interesante.

Esperamos a leer lo escrito, pero nunca llegó como habíamos supuesto y es ahora cuando hacemos un nuevo intento en obsequio a nuestros discípulos y Lectores.

Desde luego, no vamos a perder el tiempo con demasiadas explicaciones. Hemos de rozar algo practico y oculto, de las muchas normas que damos todos los días a los Tantritas, pero no dentro de una rutina ciega ya que a los Occidentales no nos es posible llevar a cabo muchas cosas que son exclusivas de los Hindúes.

Vamos a un ejemplo: Dice el Pantajalí... del ancho de dos dedos mas abajo del ano y de dos dedos por debajo del Pene, se encuentra Adhara Loto o el Mula-Adhara, es decir, el Loto cuadrado por sus hojas y desde allí irradia el Yoni, el que constituye el Poder último del Tantra, donde en su sueño permanece Kundalini, la deidad Suprema.

---

[130] Literally 'obligados' means "obliged, committed; bound; drafted"
[131] Literally 'ocupado' means "go about, undertake, set about"
[132] Literally 'asegurándonos' means "secure, ensure; guarantee, warrant; assert; adjust; underwrite; fasten"
[133] Literally 'pretendía' means "purport, pretend; profess, allege, claim"
[134] Literally 'llegó' means "arrive, come; reach; roll along; land; immigrate; invade; get; travel; vaporize"
[135] Literally 'intento' means "intent, intention; try, attempt; shy; bid; thing, object"
[136] Literally 'rozar' means "graze; rub, chafe; skim, touch"
[137] Literally 'dentro' means "via; within, inside, in; indoors"
[138] Literally 'rutina' means "routine, rut, habitual procedure or course of action; round; rote"
[139] Literally 'permanece' means "remain, stay, abide"
[140] Literally 'en su' means "in his/her/its"

Editor's Appendix

And [he] goes on to say... "Kundalini[141], seems like a climbing[142] Plant and at the same time [like a] ray[143] [or thunderbolt], with three and [a] half curves[144], sleeping upon the path of Sushumna[145].

Its form is Creative Power in a living world (jagat sata-rupa[146])."

The Power is for those who pronounce the Mantrams.

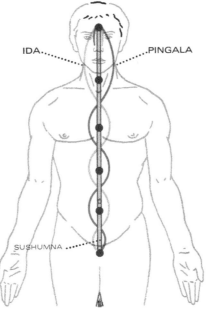

Apéndice del Editor

Y sigue diciendo... Kundalini[147], se parece a una Planta enredadera y al mismo tiempo al rayo, con tres y media curvación, duerme sobre el sendero de Suchumna[148].

Su forma, es Poder Creador en un mundo viviente (jagat zata-rupa[149]).

El Poder es para los que pronuncian los Mantrans.

---

[141] Entry from the *Theosophical Glossary* (1892):
"**Kundalini Sakti** *(Sk.)*. The power of life; one of the Forces of Nature; that power that generates a certain light in those who sit for spiritual and clairvoyant development. It is a power known only to those who practise concentration and Yoga."
[142] Literally 'enredadera' means "climbing plant, creeper; convolvulus, variety of climbing flowering vine"
[143] Literally 'rayo' means "ray, gleam; shaft, beam; thunderbolt"
[144] Literally 'curvación' means "bowing, curving"
[145] Some more entries from the *Theosophical Glossary* (1892):
"**Sushumna** *(Sk.)*. The solar ray—the first of the seven rays. Also the name of a spinal nerve which connects the heart with the Brahmarandra, and plays a most important part in Yoga practices.
Brahmarandhra *(Sk.)*. A spot on the crown of the head connected by *Sushumna,* a cord in the spinal column, with the heart. A mystic term having its significance only in mysticism.
Yoga *(Sk.)*. (1) One of the six Darshanas or schools of India; a school of philosophy founded by Patanjali, though the real Yoga doctrine, the one that is said to have helped to prepare the world for the preaching of Buddha, is attributed with good reasons to the more ancient sage Yajnawalkya, the writer of the *Shatapatha Rrahmana,* of *Yajur Veda,* the *Brihad Aranyaha,* and other famous works. (2) The practice of meditation as a means of leading to spiritual liberation. Psychospiritual powers are obtained thereby, and induced ecstatic states lead to the clear and correct perception of the eternal truths, in both the visible and invisible universe."
[146] Some entries from the *Theosophical Glossary* (1892):
"**Jagat** *(Sk.)*. The Universe.
Sata rupa *(Sk.)*. The "hundred-formed one"; applied to each, who to be the female Brahma assumes a hundred forms, *i.e.,* Nature."

[147] Originalmente "Kundarlini". La entrada del *Glosario Teosófico*:
"**Kundalinî zakti** (–sakti o –shakti) *(Sánsc.)* – El poder de vida; una de las Fuerzas de la Naturaleza; el poder que engendra cierta luz en aquellos que se disponen para el desarrollo espiritual y clarividente. Es un poder que sólo conocen aquellos que practican la concentración y el Yoga."
[148] Algunos más entradas desde el *Glosario Teosófico*:
"**Suchumnâ** (Sushumnâ) *(Sánsc.)* – El rayo solar: el primero de los siete rayos [místicos]. Es también el nombre de un nervio espinal que relaciona el corazón con el Brahmarandhra y desempeña un importantísimo papel en la práctica del Yoga.
Brahmarandhra *(Sánsc.)* – Un punto de la coronilla, o vértice de la cabeza, relacionado por medio del *Suchumna* (un cordón de la columna espinal) con el corazón. Brahmarandhra es un término místico, que sólo tiene significación en el misticismo.
Yoga *(Sánsc.)* – 1°. Uno de los seis Darzanas o escuelas filosóficas de la India; una escuela fundada por Patañjali, aunque la verdadera doctrina Yoga, la única de la cual se dice que ayudó a preparar al mundo para la predicación de Buddha, es atribuida con buenas razones a un sabio más antiguo, Yâjñawalkya, autor del *Zatapatha Brâhmana,* del *Yajur Veda,* del *Brihad Âranyaka* y otras obras famosas. 2°. La práctica de la meditación como medio conducente a la liberación espiritual. Por este medio se obtienen poderes psicoespirituales, y los estados de éxtasis provocados conducen a la clara y correcta percepción de las verdades eternas, tanto del universo visible como del invisible."
[149] Originalmente "jagatsrst-rupa". Algunos más entradas desde el *Glosario Teosófico*:
"**Jagat** *(Sánsc.)* – El Universo.
Zata–rûpa (Sata rûpa) *(Sánsc.)* - La «de cien formas»; título aplicado a Vâch, que por ser el Brahmâ femenino asume cien formas, *esto es*: la Naturaleza."

The Goddess of language (vagdevi[150]) [is] then Word and Form (naman-rupa[151]), [which] are the two columns of this great Power.

One channel, however, we call IDA, makes its way from the left [side of the body] and reaches the right nostril, after having passed through the center [channel] of Sushumna.

The other channel, called PINGALA, goes[152] from the right and up to the left nostril, also after having crossed the center Sushumna.

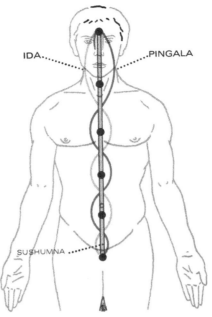

La Diosa del lenguaje (vagdevi[153]) pues Palabra y Forma (naman-rupa), son las dos columnas de este gran Poder.

Cada canal, empero, que llamamos IDA, toma su camino por la izquierda y llegar a la fosa nasal derecha, después de haber pasado por el centro de Suchuma.

El otro canal, llamado PINGALA, se desliza por la derecha y arriba a la fosa nasal izquierda, después de haber atravesado también el centro de Suchuma.

---

[150] Vagdevi or Vachdevi is one of the names of Saraswati. Some entries from the *Theosophical Glossary* (1892):

"**Sarasvati** *(Sk.)*. The same as Vach, wife and daughter of Brahma, produced from one of the two halves of his body. She is the goddess of speech and of sacred or esoteric knowledge and wisdom. Also called *Sri*.

Vach *(Sk.)*. To call Vach "speech" simply, is deficient in clearness. Vach is the mystic personification of speech, and the female *Logos,* being one with Brahma, who created her out of one-half of his body, which he divided into two portions; she is also one with Viraj (called the "female" Viraj) who was created in her by Brahma. In one sense Vach is "speech" by which knowledge was taught to man; in another she is the "mystic, secret speech" which descends upon and enters into the primeval Rishis, as the "tongues of fire" are said to have "sat upon" the apostles. For, she is called "the female creator", the "mother of the *Vedas*", etc., etc. Esoterically, she is the subjective Creative Force which, emanating from the Creative Deity (the subjective Universe, its "privation", or *ideation*) becomes the manifested "world of *speech*", *i.e.,* the *concrete expression of ideation,* hence the "Word" or Logos. Vach is "the male and female" Adam of the first chapter of *Genesis,* and thus called "Vach-Viraj" by the sages. (See *Atharva Veda.*) She is also "the celestial Saraswati produced from the heavens", a "voice derived from *speechless* Brahma" *(Mahabhmata);* the goddess of wisdom and eloquence. She is called *Sata-rupa,* the goddess of *a hundred forms.*

Atharva Veda *(Sk.)*. The fourth Veda; *lit.,* magic incantation containing aphorisms, incantations and magic formulae. One of the most ancient and revered Books of the Brahmans."

[151] This compound term "naman-rupa" means something like "name-form"

[152] Literally 'desliza' means "slide, slip; coast; work in; creep"

[153] Vagdevi es uno de los nombres de Saraswati. Algunas entradas del *Glosario Teosófico*:

"**Sarasvatî** *(Sánsc.)* – Lo mismo que Vâch, esposa e hija de Brahmâ, producida de una de las dos mitades de su cuerpo. Es la diosa del lenguaje, así como de la Sabiduría y del Conocimiento sagrado o esotérico. También se la designa con el nombre de *Zrî*.

Vâch *(Sánsc.)* – El llamar Vâch "lenguaje" sencillamente, es deficiente en claridad. Vâch es la personificación mística del lenguaje, y el *Logos* femenino, siendo uno con Brahmâ, quien la creó de una mitad de su cuerpo, que él dividió en dos partes; ella es también uno con Virâj (llamada la "Virâj femenina"), que fue creada en ella por Brahmâ. En un sentido Vâch es "lenguaje", mediante el cual el conocimiento fué enseñado al hombre; en otro sentido es el "lenguaje místico secreto" que desciende sobre los Richis primitivos y entra en ellos, como las lenguas de fuego que, según se dice, "se posaron sobre» los apóstoles. Porque ella es llamada "el creador femenino" la "madre de los *Vedas*", etc., etc. Esotéricamente, es la subjetiva Fuerza creadora que, emanando de la Deidad creadora (el Universo objetivo, su "privación" o *ideación*) pasa a ser el manifestado "mundo del *lenguaje*", *esto es*, la *expresión concreta de la ideación*, y por consiguiente, la "Palabra" o Logos. Vâch es el Adán "varón y hembra" del primer capítulo del *Génesis*, y así es denominado "Vâch-Virâj" por los sabios. (Véase: *Atharva-Veda*). Ella es asimismo la celestial Sarasvati producida de los cielos", "una voz derivada del Brahmâ *sin habla*". (*Mahâbhârata*); la diosa de la sabiduría y elocuencia. Por último, es llamada *Sata-rûpa*, la diosa de *cien formas.*

Atharva Veda *(Sánsc.)* – El cuarto Veda. *Literalmente*, encantación mágica, que contiene aforismos, encantos y fórmulas mágicas. Uno de los cuatro más antiguos y venerados libros de los brahmanes."

But at the very center of the two, that is to say, between Ida and Pingala, there are six points or stations where six different powers are located for the actor.

There are five points which are above the Mula-adhara, many that will [be] addressed[154] in relation to the use of Tantra...

We are confident[155] that for all those who have not dealt with these esoteric subjects, these relationships say nothing of Patanjali.

What everyone knows or what they believe they know is that Kundalini, the beautiful sleeping Princess from the story, is the essence of the Semen which, animated[156] by the brain centers, will start [rising] from the conjunction of the Sexual Organs until reaching the highest point of the brain, awakening on its way the seven centers or Nadis (See "Esoteric Rose" [by Krumm-Heller]).

Well then, in order to be able[157] to awaken these centers, it is absolutely necessary to prepare the instrument or physical body properly[158] and for this there exist rigorous and special practices...

We know hundreds of these practices, through our study of White Sexual Magic, but we will cite only one of those which Patanjali says is indispensable and that without which [it] would be impossible[159] to achieve some practical result.

Pero en el centro mismo de los dos caminos, es decir, entre la Ida y Pingala, hay seis puntos o estaciones donde radican seis poderes diferentes para el actor.

Los cinco puntos que están sobre el Mula-adhara, hay muchos que los pondrán en relación con el uso del Tantra[160]...

Seguros estamos, que a todos aquellos que no se hayan ocupado de estos temas esotéricos, no dicen nada estas relaciones del Patanjalí.

Lo que todos saben o lo que creen saber, es que Kundalini, la bella Princesa dormida del cuento, es la esencia del Semen que, animado por los centros cerebrales, va partiendo desde el Sexo en conjunto hasta alcanzar lo más alto del cerebro, despertando en su camino los siete[161] centros o Nadis (Véase Rosa Esotérica).

Pues bien, para poder llegar a despertar esos Centros, es absolutamente preciso preparar el instrumento o cuerpo físico adecuadamente y es para esto para lo que se dan prácticas rigurosas y especiales...

Nosotros conocemos centenares de estas practicas, por nuestro estudio de Magia Sexual Blanca, pero vamos a citar tan solo una de las que dice el Patanjalí ser indispensable y que sin ella no sería posible lograr resultado practico alguno.

---

[154] Literally 'pondrán' means "put, place; lay; insert; impose; mark; adjust; send; contribute; subscribe; perform; translate"
[155] Literally 'Seguros' means "confident, sure, certain; secure, safe; reliable, dependable"
[156] Literally 'animado' means "animate, make alive; arouse; inspire; excite; liven, make lively; snap out of it"
[157] Literally 'llegar' means "arrive, come; reach; roll along; land; immigrate; invade; get; travel; vaporize"
[158] Literally 'adecuadamente' means "appropriately, properly, in a fitting manner; suitably"
[159] Literally 'no sería posible' means "would not be possible"

[160] Originalmente "Santra"
[161] Originalmente "siente"

Nonetheless, the reader will notice that this is outside[162] of those [practices] used in [the] West, as we have said before, and that our physiological conditions do not lend[163] themselves to it.

It is, then, to clean the Stomach...

Who has not had occasion to witness[164] when a Doctor introduces [a] probe into a patient in order to extract the gastric juices?

[Who] does not realize how brutal that operation is?

Well, it's nothing compared to what is required for the student of TANTRA [who is] asked to Clean their stomach...

To do this, there must be a strip[165] of Linen four fingers wide and fifteen yards long (vastra) which must be soaked and entirely swallowed little by little, in order to then similarly extract [the gastric juices] since it grabs[166] all the impurities[167] from the stomach.

Failure to do this practice, says Patanjali, you can never awaken Kundalini, whereas doing [something] else and not this, will cause more harm than good.

We now ask: who among us in the West could swallow fifteen yards of Linen, retain [for] a moment in the stomach and then repeat this removing [it for] forty consecutive days without interruption, without getting sick or destroying the throat?

Sin embargo, observará el lector que está fuera de los usos de Occidente, como hemos dicho antes, y que nuestras condiciones fisiológicas no se prestan a ello.

Se trata, pues, de limpiar el Estómago...

Quien no ha tenido ocasión de presenciar cuando un Médico introduce la sonda a un enfermo para extraer los jugos gástricos?

No se han dado cuenta de lo brutal de esa operación?

Pues no es nada en comparación con lo que se exige al estudiante de TANTRA al pedirle que Limpie su estómago...

Para ello, ha de tomarse una tira de Lino de cuatro dedos de ancho y de quince varas de largo (vastra) la cual ha de ser remojada y tragada por entero poco a poco, para irla extrayendo después de igual manera pues ella arrancará todas las suciedades del estómago.

De no hacer esta práctica, dice en Patanjalí[168], nunca podrás despertar a Kundalini, mientras que haciendo otras y no esta, le causarán mas daño que provecho.

Preguntamos ahora. Quien de nosotros en el Occidente podría tragar quince varas de Lino, retenerlas un momento en el estomago e irlas sacando después hasta repetir esto cuarenta días consecutivos sin interrupción, sin conseguir enfermarse o destruir la garganta.

---

[162] Literally 'fuera' means "abroad, outside; without; away; out"
[163] Literally 'prestan' means "lend, loan; provide; swear; give, render; advance"
[164] Literally 'presenciar' means "assist; witness"
[165] Literally 'tira' means "strip, band; shred"
[166] Literally 'arrancará' means "root up, pull up; extract, draw out; blow away; speed up; tear off"
[167] Literally 'suciedades' means "dirt, grubbiness, uncleanliness; guiltiness, sordidness"

[168] Originalmente "Patangalí"

Already in our time of study, we saw a Yogi doing this operation, but then, we wanted to repeat it, we [found it] was entirely impossible.

We had swallowed two strips[169] of Linen, [and] we became[170] very sick and then the Yogi told us: "Note that in the West [people] are disposed to other means that are as effective as ours..."

And then he spoke in favor of certain alchemical preparations which destroy everything harmful in the stomach.

Nonetheless, the latter, is ignored [by] the Easterners and is further evidence that we should not blindly follow the Yoga system.

We must, however, listen to our Gurus and prepare ourselves with less brutal means than those that should be exclusively for the Fakirs.

But [this] is another indispensable practice which consists of the use of certain short enemas[171] in order to clean places near to the Mula-Adhara and [it] is also necessary [for this] to have preceded other [practices] so that no other acute pain occurrs in the Prostate as we experience when practicing this exercise without [a] Master.

Today we comprehend how many things are done improperly and the extent to which a good Master is indispensable[172] who can advise [us] without fear of causing damage to the Neophyte.

---

[169] Literally 'varas' means "rod, switch, cane"
[170] Literally 'estuvimos' means "be; stay, remain; hold; be found; be present"
[171] Literally 'lavativas' means "enema, fluid injected into the rectum; boor, rude person, uncultured person; bother, effort; nuisance"
[172] Literally 'imprescindible' means "indispensable, requisite, essential, vital"

Nonetheless, the student should not desire this advice[173] from the same Patanjali: "Only you will have to do the practices that are given by your Master which you will never change nor substitute, once you have begun with them, since the one who changes from one Master to another, never reachs the goal."

The master should be your Father, Mother, your Confessor and your God at the same time and all your speech[174], your thought and action, should never be mixed[175] with the one who guides you.

Be ye, therefore, respectful with him because without this requirement you will note reach Initiation.

Can a second Master have confidence in the disciple who abandoned the first one?

Be ye consistent[176].

Observe that as slow[177] as the first one is, he will always take you to the goal with his Sacred practices even better[178] than the second one, however good and wise he may be.

"If ever the inner voice urged[179] you to direct yourself to a Master, then you are connected with him for all [of] eternity, as you already were in other lives."

To be continued...

[R+]

---

[173] Literally 'consejo' means "advice, counsel; hint, tip; admonition; council, committee"
[174] Literally 'verbo' means "word; verb, part of speech used to express action or state of being"
[175] Literally 'dispar' means "disparate, uneven, mixed, unequal"
[176] Literally 'consecuentes' means "consequential; consistent; sequential"
[177] Literally 'atrasado' means "slow; belated; backward; overdue"
[178] Literally 'acierto' means "success; right guess; bull's eye, direct hit; smart move, right decision; aptness, ability; appropriateness; discretion"
[179] Literally 'impulsó' means "impulse, urge; pulse; impetus; drive"

Extract from
The Rosecross Magazine
Berlin, January 1933

TANTRA [Part 2]

Continuation...

Ignatius of Loyola, the Founder of the 'Company of Jesus' [or Jesuits], without [a] doubt received Tantric teachings.

Otherwise, I would not have copied his SPIRITUAL EXERCISES[180] verbatim.

In Rome, regarding this[181], a Statue was unveiled to us, [it was] of Crestos or Harpocrates synthesized as a Rooster[182] whose beak[183] is converted into a Phallus or Virile member.

At the foot of the Statue, there is a sign in Greek that says: "THIS IS THE SAVIOR OF THE WORLD..."[184]

All this is, for the initiates, something like a vulgarity[185] because it will never be very proper[186] to exhibit a carved sexual organ and even less [so] with the described sign.

---

[180] This refers to the book *The Spiritual Exercises of Saint by Ignatius of Loyola* which was composed betweev 1522-1524. It contains a set of Christian meditations, prayers and mental exercises, divided into four 'weeks' of variable length, designed to be carried out over a period of 28 to 30 days.
[181] Literally 'Cuando se sabe' means "when [it/this] is known"
[182] Literally 'Gallo' means "cock, rooster; cork; off-key (Music); expert; bantamweight, lightweight boxer"
[183] Literally 'pico' means "pick, pickax; spout; beak; extremity; peak, pinnacle; lip; capstan"
[184] Editor's note: What the statue literally says is ΣΩTHP ΚΟΣΜΟΥ, ie SOTER KOSMOU, meaning "Savior [of the] World".
[185] Literally 'groseria' means "rudeness, coarseness, scurrility, vulgarity"
[186] Literally 'correcto' means "correct, accurate; proper; just; right, seemly"

What is even more surprising, [regarding] this subject, [is that] such a symbol appears in plain [view] of the public [at the] Vatican, but when we receive[187] initiation, then we realize the importance of this symbol and that THE TRUTH *par excellence* is enclosed in it...

The path of the Initiate has three steps[188], namely: IMAGINATION, INSPIRATION AND INTUITION.

The first step that one should take is to ensure[189] that the Mind is trained[190] to imagine something specific, for example, a geometric figure.

[One] must try to see this figure and to objectify it as little as possible[191] and [then] at bedtime bring it [back up] in the brain in the same particular[192] way.

This is very difficult, if you have not done preliminary exercises, such as those offered in our esoteric course, because they are absolutely necessary for the imagination to be properly trained and [to be] able to form an image.

Subsequently, this image is directed[193] to the brain and there it is retained until it is really expressively[194] sensed...

Todavía es más de extrañar este asunto, en dicho símbolo aparece al público en pleno Vaticano, pero luego que llegamos a la iniciación, es cuando nos damos cuenta de la importancia que tiene dicho símbolo y de que en él se encierra LA VERDAD por excelencia...

El camino del Iniciado tiene tres senderos, a saber: IMAGINACIÓN, INSPIRACIÓN E INTUICIÓN.

El primer paso que debe darse es procurar que la Mente se adiestre en imaginarse algo concretamente, por ejemplo, una figura geométrica.

Esta figura hay que tratar de verla y no objetivarla lo mas posible y en el momento de acostarse para luego traerla al cerebro del mismo modo concreto.

Es esto muy difícil, si no se han efectuado ejercicios preliminares, tal como los ofrecemos en nuestro curso esotérico, pues ellos son absolutamente precisos para que la imaginación se adiestre adecuadamente y pueda formar una imagen.

Posteriormente, se lleva esta imagen al cerebro y se retiene allí hasta sentirla plásticamente, realmente...

---

[187] Literally 'llegamos' means "arrive, come; reach; roll along; land; immigrate; invade; get; travel; vaporize"
[188] Literally 'senderos' means "footpath, path, trail"
[189] Literally 'procurar' means "see; seek; attempt"
[190] Literally 'adiestre' means "train (an animal); instruct, coach"
[191] Literally 'no objetivarla lo mas posible' means "not objectify it as much as possible"
[192] Literally 'concreto' means "concrete, tangible, actual; particular"
[193] Literally 'lleva' means "carry, transport; take; convey; wear; win; lead; bear; spend; hunch, hump; heave; carry off; deliver; live through; encroach on"
[194] Literally 'plásticamente' means "plastically, artistically, expressively (full of expression; meaningful: an expressive shrug; serving to express; indicative of power to express;)"

Once [something] is fixed in the brain, it is [then] voluntarily translated[195] to the neck and so on, it successively passes through all the Brains.

If [this training] is attained[196] then [the image] stops in every suitable place, acting intrinsically in a formidable way and will imperceptibly awaken all our internal forces.

The Jesuits, who have their degrees [like the Masons] and receive some exercises directly from the general of the order, do not make use of geometrical figures, but [instead use] the Image of the Virgin Mary and when they arrive at the Sexual Organs (at the Glands of reproduction), [then] they offer a state of ecstasy that should not occur for them in [the] Vigil [state], which is why they always hide behind the dream…

A Jesuit [is] observed by someone else[197] and when he sees in his physionomy that the moment of exhaltation is approaching, [he] awakens the brother and thus makes him dispel[198] the illusion.

Ignatius of Loyola knew much[199] more about the Tantras, but there is enough proof [in] what we have just explained…

The disciple of Yoga should practice these exercises, as we have said, with geometric figures and even better with the star of five points[200].

Una vez fijada en el cerebro, se traslada voluntariamente al cuello y así, sucesivamente, se le hace pasar por todos los Cerebros.

Si se logra irla deteniendo en cada lugar adecuado, actúa intrínsicamente de un modo formidable y va despertando insensiblemente todas nuestras fuerzas internas.

Los Jesuitas, que tienen también sus grados y que reciben algunos ejercicios directamente del general de la orden, no se valen de figuras geométricas, sino de la Imagen de la Virgen María y cuando arriban al Sexo, a las Glándulas de la reproducción, les ofrece un estado de éxtasis que no debe ocurrirles en Vigilia, razón por la cual se escudan siempre en el sueño…

Un Jesuita observa al otro y cuando ve en su fisonomía que el momento de la exaltación se acerca, despierta al hermano y así le hace desvanecer la ilusión.

Ignacio de Loyola, sabía bastante mas acerca de los Tantras, pero ya es bastante la prueba que acabamos de exponer…

El discípulo del Yoga, debe practicar esos ejercicios, como ya hemos dicho, con figuras geométricas y aún mejor con estrellas de cinco puntas.

---

[195] Literally 'traslada' means "translate; move; transfer; get"
[196] Literally 'logra' means "get, obtain; achieve, attain; reach; win"
[197] Literally 'otro' means "another, other"
[198] Literally 'desvanecer' means "dispel, dissipate"
[199] Literally 'bastante' means "enough, quite, sufficiently, fairly; a good few, a good bit"
[200] Literally 'con estrellas de cinco puntas' means "with stars with five points"

When you have done this exercise long enough[201], you can change the objects [you are imagining] and if you have attained powers in this sense, [then] you can use material desires and success in business [as your visualization][202], but you must not, for example, if they are not perfectly lawful[203].

The result is certain[204], but it is also certain for those who are responsible for acting in an abominable[205] way.

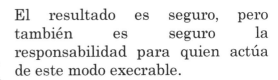

The Rose cross does these exercises only[206] in order to awaken one's DIVINE BEING.

When this figure reaches the heart, one should strongly concentrate on the "I AM".

This is the "Ehye Asher Ehye" ("I am that which is"[207]) of the ancient Mysteries and [it is] repeated in Genesis by the Biblical Author.

Herein lies the difference between the Rose Cross and the Jesuits.

These latter do not awaken their DIVINE BEING but have to focus on the power of the Community.

Buddhist Theosophy [is] the same, [one] must fight one's DIVINE BEING in order to make it impersonal.

Both procedures are Black Magic and are energetically rejected by White Tantrism.

Cuando se ha hecho este ejercicio bastante tiempo, se puede cambiar de objetos y si logramos poderes en este sentido, se puede, pero no se deben, utilizar deseos materiales como éxito en los negocios[208], por ejemplo, si ellos no son perfectamente lícitos.

El resultado es seguro, pero también es seguro la responsabilidad para quien actúa de este modo execrable.

El Rosa cruz, hace esos ejercicios, para despertar su SER DIVINO[209] exclusivamente.

Cuando esa figura llega al corazón, debe concentrarse fuertemente sobre el YO SOY.

Es el Ejhe Asher Ejhe (Yo soy quien soy) de los antiguos Misterios y repetido en el Génesis por el Autor Bíblico.

En esto estriba la diferencia de los Rosa Cruz con los Jesuitas.

Estos últimos no deben despertar su SER DIVINO[210] sino que han de concentrarse sobre el poder de la Comunidad.

Mismo el Teósofo Budista, debe combatir su SER DIVINO[211] para hacerlo impersonal.

Ambos procedimientos son Magia Negra y están rechazados enérgicamente por el Tantrista Blanco.

---

[201] Literally 'bastante tiempo' means "enough time"
[202] Editor's note: Compare the exercise given in 'Lesson Two' of *Introduction to Gnosis* (1961) by Samael Aun Weor
[203] Literally 'lícitos' means "lawful, legal, licit"
[204] Literally 'seguro' means "confident, sure, certain; secure, safe; reliable, dependable"
[205] Literally 'execrable' means "execrable, despicable, abominable"
[206] Literally 'exclusivamente' means "exclusively, in an exclusive manner, in a manner which shuts out all others; solely, in a limited manner"
[207] Literally 'Yo soy quien soy' means "I am who I am"

---

[208] Comparar la ejercicio dado en 'Lección Dos' de *Introducción a la Gnosis* (1961) por Samael Aun Weor
[209] Originalmente: "su YO"
[210] Originalmente: "su YO"
[211] Originalmente: "su YO"

The Divine BEING merged[212] with the Cosmos is our goal, our objective, the ultimate end that we Rose cross [adepts] pursue and once awakened to the degree of Masters, then, this union gives [us] strength[213], [and] we become part of the White Lodge...

But that DIVINE BEING is in the Logos.

Here's why the Tantrist must learn to Vocalize and unite, in this way, TONE and ACTION.

We have a [friend who is a] Film star named Asta Pilsen.

This artist poured REAL TEARS into her works and cries rivers[214] whenever she is asked to do so.

When asked on one occasion how she had accomplished this, she answered simply, that every night before bed, she imagined that she could cry whenever she wanted to and little by little she was [able] to achieve this, to make it a real occurrence[215] subject[216] to her will and command[217].

We were struck by this case and then we remembered the performance of Fakirs who can, at will, act upon[218] the heart and make it go into systole and diastole with greater or lesser speed or acceleration.

El SER Divino[219] confundido con el Cosmos, es nuestra meta, nuestro objetivo, el fin último que perseguimos los Rosa cruz y una vez despertados al grado de Maestros, entonces, como la unión hace la fuerza, entramos a formar parte de la Logia Blanca...

Pero ese SER DIVINO[220] está en el Logos.

He aquí por qué, el Tantrista, debe aprender a Vocalizar y a unir de este modo TONO y ACCIÓN.

Tenemos una estrella del Cine, llamada Asta Pilsen.

Esta artista, vierte en sus obras LÁGRIMAS REALES y llora a torrentes cada vez que se lo piden.

Al preguntársele en una ocasión como había conseguido esto, respondió sencillamente, que todas las noches antes de acostarse, se imaginó que podía llorar cuando quisiera y poco a poco hubo de conseguirlo esto, hasta hacerlo un hecho real sujeto a su voluntad y dominio.

Nos llamó la atención este caso y recordamos entonces la actuación de los Fakires que pueden, a voluntad, mover el corazón y hacerlo marchar en su sístole y diástole con mas o menos lentitud o aceleramiento.

---

[212] Literally 'confundido' means "confound, confuse, bewilder; mix up; merge, to lose oneself in"
[213] Literally 'fuerza' means "strength, quality of being strong, might; durability; determination, resolve; power (of electricity, etc.); effectiveness; intensity; compulsion, coercion, use of force; violence, rough unwarranted force"
[214] Literally 'torrentes' means "torrent, flood, stream; volley; spate"
[215] Literally 'hecho' means "deed; fact, thing; done; factor; event, occurrence"
[216] Literally 'sujeto' means "secure, fasten; hold down, keep down; clip; anchor"
[217] Literally 'dominio' means "dominion, rule; command, mastery; control, authority"
[218] Literally 'mover' means "move, be in motion; put in motion; act on, take action; transfer from one place to another; change residence; excite, cause emotion; motivate, spur to action; suggest, propose"

[219] Originalmente: "YO Divino"
[220] Originalmente: "ese YO"

We talked to the artist to which we refer, and after much questioning, she confessed that she had done the same exercises, but that in those days she had suffered a tremendous[221] heartbreak and that on multiple occasions she cried[222] true tears[223].

We discovered that she was directing her desire, her expressive thought, to the sexual parts and unconsciously turned herself [into a] Tantrist.

A word to the wise is sufficient with little reason.

The Creative part within us is in the sexual organs, in the testicles [and ovaries], and this is where you have to give creative form to the desires...

Reader: We are delivering[224] you a Tantric secret of inconceivable importance and from the letters[225] that we will send[226] you by correspondence, we will see if it is possible to continue this series or if we [need] to return [to this subject again in order] to give[227] help[228].

TO BE CONTINUED... but not 'to be continued' for too long.

[R+]

Llegamos a hablar con la artista a que nos referimos y, después de mucho interrogarla, nos confesó que había hecho los mismos ejercicios, pero que tenía en aquel entonces que sufrir una gran decepción amorosa y que en multitud de ocasiones llegó a llorar de veras.

Nosotros descubrimos, que ella llevaba su deseo, su pensamiento plástico, a las partes sexuales e inconscientemente se volvió Tantrista.

Al buen entendedor con pocas razones le basta.

La parte Creadora en nosotros, está en el sexo, en los testículos, y es allí donde hay que dar forma de creación a los deseos...

Lector: estamos llevándole a un secreto Tántrico de inconcebible importancia y de la impresión que vayamos obteniendo por correspondencia, veremos si[229] es posible continuar con esta serie de artículos o si hemos de tornar a poner el socorrido.

CONTINUARA... para no continuar en mucho tiempo.

[R+]

---

[221] Literally 'gran' means "great; big, large"
[222] Literally 'llegó' means "arrive, come; reach; roll along; land; immigrate; invade; get; travel; vaporize"
[223] Literally 'llorar' means "cry, weep; lament, mourn; bemoan, bewail"
[224] Literally 'llevándole' means "carry, transport; take; convey; wear; win; lead; bear; spend; hunch, hump; heave; carry off; deliver; live through; encroach on"
[225] Literally 'impresión' means "impression, strong feeling or idea left by an experience; effect; vague memory; stamp, imprint; stamping, impressing"
[226] Literally 'vayamos' means "go, proceed, move; travel; walk; suit; lead; drive; ride"
[227] Literally 'poner' means "put, place; lay; insert; impose; mark; adjust; send; contribute; subscribe; perform; translate"
[228] Literally 'socorrido' means "relieve, succor, help"

[229] Originalmente: "sui"

Extract from Lecture #138,
pages 1396-1397 of
El Quinto Evangelio (2000)
by Samael Aun Weor

"[THE] POTENTIALITIES OF THE CREATIVE ENERGY"

...Because sex is one hundred percent sacred, because without the Sexual Force there would be no creature on the face of the Earth.

Sex is not something merely physiological as many illustrious ignoramuses suppose, no!

It is a Cosmic Energy which is boiling[230] and throbbing[231] in all that is, in all that has been, [and] in all that will be...

Through this powerful Energy, which in final synthesis becomes the Sun, we can radically transform ourselves...

When a couple is in Chemical or Metaphysical Copulation, they can take perfect advantage of this extraordinary Power in order to convert themselves into something different.

This is possible if we learn to love sex; this is possible if we study the Sexual Power.

Certainly, and in the name of truth, let us say: That we can trap[232] that wonderful Energy which surrounds us during Chemical Copulation, in order to make something different within ourselves.

In the name of truth, we will emphasize [this] in order to say that: It is possible to trap this Energy...!

---

[230] Literally 'bulle' means "move; boil, seethe"
[231] Literally 'palpita' means "palpitate, beat, pound (about the heart)"
[232] Literally 'aprisionar' means "incarcerate, imprison; bind, tie"

Extracto de la Conferencia #138,
de páginas 1396-1397 de
El Quinto Evangelio (2000)
por Samael Aun Weor

"POTENCIALIDADES DE LA ENERGÍA CREADORA"

...El sexo pues, es sagrado en un ciento por ciento, pues sin la Fuerza Sexual no existiría ninguna criatura sobre la faz de la Tierra.

No es el sexo algo meramente fisiológico como suponen muchos ignorantes ilustrados, ¡no!

Es una Energía Cósmica que bulle y que palpita en todo es, en todo lo que ha sido, en todo lo que será...

Mediante esa Energía poderosa, que en última síntesis deviene del Sol, podemos transformarnos radicalmente...

Cuando una pareja se halla en la Cópula Química o Metafísica, puede perfectamente aprovechar ese Poder extraordinario para convertirse en algo distinto.

Eso es posible si aprendemos a amar el sexo; eso es posible, si nosotros estudiamos el Poder Sexual.

Ciertamente, y en nombre de la verdad diremos: Que podríamos aprisionar esa Energía maravillosa que nos rodea durante la Cópula Química, para hacer de dentro de nosotros algo distinto.

En nombre de la verdad, pondremos énfasis para decir que: ¡Es posible aprisionar esta Energía!...

English	Español
At this time, BROWN-SEQUARD[233] comes to mind. This man did wonderful experiments with sex.	En estos instantes nos viene a la mente BROWN-SEQUARD. Este hombre hizo experimentos maravillosos con el sexo.
He discovered, for example, that exciting the sexual apparatus and NOT SPILLING THE ENS-SEMINIS (that is to say, the 'Entity of the Semen') could revitalize the organism.	Descubrió, por ejemplo, que excitando el aparato sexual y NO DERRAMANDO EL ENS-SEMINIS, es decir, la Entidad del Semen, podría revitalizarse el organismo.
Furthermore, he found that we can totally rejuvenate [ourselves].	Aún más, descubrió que podríamos rejuvenecernos totalmente.
Brown-Sequard was famous in the field of endocrinology.	Brown-Sequard fue famoso en el terreno de la endocrinología.
There also existed the ONEIDA SOCIETY[234], in the United States.	Existe también en los Estados Unidos, la SOCIEDAD ONEIDA.
This society has done extraordinary experiments. 25 families were submitted to a magnificent discipline.	Esta sociedad ha hecho experimentos extraordinarios. 25 familias se sometieron a una disciplina magnífica.
They were forbidden [from] the ejaculation of the Ens Seminis; they were allowed the connection of the Lingam-Yoni, but without ever spilling the Glass[235] of Hermes.	Se les prohibió la eyaculación del Ens-Seminis; se les permitió la conexión del Lingam-Yoni, pero sin derramar jamás el Vaso de Hermes.
The result was tremendous: Their partners were transformed magnificently; sick men were healed, rejuvenated, [and] filled with life.	El resultado fue formidable: Sus parejas se transformaron magníficamente; hombres enfermos, sanaron, se rejuvenecieron, se llenaron de vida.
It is clear that by not ejaculating the Ens Seminis, by not ejaculating the Sacred Sperm, wonderful transformations occur: The sperm is transformed into Energy, and the Energy rises through the nervous system to the brain, radically invigorating it.	Es claro que al no eyacular el Ens-Seminis, al no eyacular el Esperma Sagrado, se producen transformaciones maravillosas: El esperma se transforma en Energía, y la Energía subiendo por el sistema nervioso hasta el cerebro, lo dinamiza radicalmente.

---

[233] Charles-Édouard Brown-Séquard FRS (1817-1894), also known as Charles Edward, was a Mauritian physiologist and neurologist. He was one of the first to postulate the existence of substances, now known as hormones, secreted into the bloodstream to affect other organs.

[234] The Oneida Community was a religious commune founded by John Humphrey Noyes in 1848 in Oneida, New York. The practiced Communalism (in the sense of communal property and possessions), Complex Marriage, Male Continence, Mutual Criticism and Ascending Fellowship.

[235] Literally 'Vaso' means "noggin, small drink of liquor; glass; tumbler; vessel"

Doctor KRUMM HELLER said that "one has to seminize the brain and cerebrize the semen..." This is quite important.

When one transmutes the Sacred Sperm, in this way, one obtains[236] [the] entry of the sex hormones into the blood vessels[237]; then they stimulate the sexual endocrine glands to produce [a] greater quantity of hormones and the whole organism is extrordinarily rejuvenated.

The Hindustanis speak to us of the "KUNDALINI". [This is a] strange word for us Westerners, but [it describes something] wonderful in depth.

Blavatsky said that "[Kundalini] is the transcendent FOHAT, contained in all organic and inorganic matter."

That Fohat is the Power of Kundalini Shakti.

That SACRED FIRE awakens through the transmutation of the Sexual Energy.

When the Kundalini Solar Fire ascends through the medullary[238] spinal canal, it produces transcendental and transcendent psychological changes in the human being.

The Hindustanis, the Brahmins, the students of the Vedas, the Tibetans, etc., say, emphatically, that the spine has SEVEN MAGIC CENTERS, [that are] magnificent [and with] which we can transform and convert [ourselves] into Supermen.

Theosophists give these Seven Centers sanskrit names.

---

[236] Literally 'consigue' means "obtain, acquire, come by; procure, secure; earn, achieve"
[237] Literally 'canales' means "canal, sluice; duct, conduit; track, channel; gutter; groove, furrow; ravine; cleavage; station"
[238] Literally 'medular' means "medullary, of the marrow, containing or resembling marrow"

| Editor's Appendix | Apéndice del Editor |

The Magnetic Center of the Coccyx to is named "Muladhara"; the Magnetic Center of the Prostate [or Uterus] is called "Svadhishthana"; the Magic Center of the Solar Plexus, situated at the height of the navel, he is called "Manipura"; the Center of the Heart is called the "Anahata"; that of the Creative Larynx is called "Vishuddha"; "Ajna" is that of the brow, and "Sahasrara" is that of the Pineal [gland].

In Esoteric Christianity the SEVEN CHURCHES of the Revelation of Saint John are spoken of.

The Magnetic Center of the Coccyx is called the "Church of Ephesus", and it is said that the Sacred Fire has the power to awaken it and when it is awakened, it gives us Power over the Element EARTH.

We are assured that the "Church of Smyrna or Prostatic Church" contains extraordinary Powers, and that, when awakened, gives us Power over the WATERS. That is the Church of Smyrna.

Concerning the "Church of Pergamos" located in the Umbilical Center, a little above the navel, [this is what] the Christian Esotericists and students of Revelation say, which gives us Powers over the Universal FIRE of Life when we awaken [it].

The students of the Esoteric Revelation continue affirming, that the heart is the "Church of Thyatira", and that when we awaken [it], it gives us Powers over the Element AIR.

Continuing with these studies, we know [very] well that in the Creative Larynx one finds the "apocalyptic Church of Sardis".

Al Centro Magnético del Coxis, lo denominan "Muladhara"; al Centro Magnético de la Próstata le dicen "Svadhishthana"; el Centro Mágico del Plexo Solar, situado a la altura del ombligo, le llaman "Manipura"; al Centro del Cardias le llaman "Anahata"; al de la Laringe Creadora le llaman "Vishuddha"; "Ajna" el del entrecejo, y "Sahasrara" al de la Pineal.

En el Cristianismo Esotérico se habla de las SIETE IGLESIAS del Apocalipsis de San Juan.

Al Centro Magnético del Coxis se le llama la "Iglesia de Éfeso", y se dice que el Fuego Sagrado tiene poder para despertarlo y cuando despierta nos confiere Poder sobre el Elemento TIERRA.

Se nos asegura que la "Iglesia de Esmirna o Iglesia Prostática", contiene extraordinarios Poderes y que cuando despierta, nos trae el Poder sobre las AGUAS. Ésa es la Iglesia de Esmirna

En cuanto a la "Iglesia de Pérgamo" situada en el Centro Umbilical, un poco arriba del ombligo, dicen los Esoteristas Cristianos y estudiantes del Apocalipsis, que cuando despierta nos confiere Poderes sobre el FUEGO Universal de Vida.

Continua los estudiantes del Apocalipsis Esotérico afirmando, que en el corazón está la "Iglesia de Tiatira", y que cuando despierta nos da Poderes sobre el Elemento AIRE.

Continuando con estos estudios, bien sabemos que en la Laringe Creadora se encuentra la "Iglesia apocalíptica de Sardis".

Awakening this Center gives us the OCCULT EAR, that is to say, conceptual synthesis, great achievements, refined aspiration, etc., etc., etc.

Between[239] the eyebrows is the "Church of Philadelphia".

Whosoever gets to awaken it will acquire[240] CLAIRVOYANCE, [and] can see, in truth, the Mysteries of Life and Death, [they] may perceive the "Ultra[241]" of all things; [and] will no longer be a slave to the fascinations of the Three-dimensional World of Euclid; [they] can perceive what the physical eyes can not perceive.

The skeptics, the disbelievers[242], those who believe this issue [is] impossible, [should] take the time to develop the Church of Philadelphia and corroborate this reality for themselves.

It is possible to see, yes, far beyond the microscope and beyond the telescope.

Clairvoyance gives us this tremendous Power...

Finally, if we open the "Church of Laodicea", located on the superior part of the brain in Pineal gland, we receive POLYVISION.

Then we can see all the Dimensions of Nature and the Cosmos.

Thus, the marvelous Sexual Force, can radically transform us and make us true Supermen, in the fullest sense of the word...

Despertar ese Centro nos da el OÍDO OCULTO, es decir, el sintetismo conceptual, máximos logros, aspiración refinada, etc., etc., etc.

En el entrecejo está la "Iglesia de Filadelfia".

Quien llegue a despertarla, se hará CLARIVIDENTE, podrá ver, en verdad, los Misterios de la Vida y de la Muerte, podrá percibir el Ultra de todas las cosas; ya no será esclavo de las fascinaciones del Mundo Tridimensional de Euclides; podrá percibir eso que los ojos físicos no pueden percibir.

Los escépticos, los incrédulos, los que creen imposible esta cuestión, que se tomen la molestia de desarrollar la Iglesia de Filadelfia y corroborarán, por sí mismos, esta realidad.

Es posible ver, sí, más allá del microscopio y más allá del telescopio.

La Clarividencia nos confiere tan tremendo Poder...

Por último, si abrimos la "Iglesia de Laodicea", situada en la parte superior del cerebro en la glándula Pinealis, recibimos la POLIVIDENCIA.

Entonces podremos ver todas las Dimensiones de la Naturaleza y del Cosmos.

Así pues, la Fuerza Sexual maravillosa, puede trasformarnos radicalmente y hacer de nosotros verdaderos Superhombres, en el sentido más completo de la palabra...

---

[239] Literally 'En' means "in, into; for, to; on, at; by; about"
[240] Literally 'hará' means "make; manufacture; create; construct, build; fashion, shape; compose; emit; wage, conduct (war, battle); prepare, do; cause; perform; effect; force; render; fabricate; behave, act in a particular manner; live through; be"
[241] Literally 'Ultra' means "ultra, extreme, excessive; most"
[242] Literally 'incrédulos' means "disbeliever, non-believer, one who does not believe (especially pertaining to religion)"

Extract from
The Rosecross Magazine
Berlin, January 1933

MAILBOX[243]

A question[244] asked by many: Our Gnostic mindset [with] respect to the Virgin.

Here is what I know and [what I] can say.

In order for the Logos to incarnate [in the human form, it] has to know[245] a vehicle, a special body, [and] for this Mary stands out[246] from the other women.

She was influenced by the True Virgin, THE VIRGIN OF THE LIGHT an Angelic entity who has her attributes in the invisible Plane.

It is a very deep mystery and we will treat it this year, when we will talk about the Angels, Archangels, Cherubim.

What Theosophy has brought [to the West] regarding this [subject] is very elementary and, in part, wrong.

We have no need to use words like devas, since Angels are the same [thing] and there are many categories from the guardian[247] Angel, who accompanies us, to the rulers of Planetary systems.

The Magician and the Astrologer must know these [different categories of Angels] and have the keys in order to call them.

---

[243] Literally 'BUZÓN' means "mailbox; postbox"
[244] Literally 'asunto' means "subject, topic; issue; thing; affair; case; concern; gimmick"
[245] Literally 'saber' means "know; realize; can; learn; hear; savor"
[246] Literally 'sobresale' means "project, protrude; jut, overhang; excel, do very well"
[247] Literally 'personal' means "personal, individual; private; particular"

Extract from
The Rosecross Magazine
Bogota, February 1937

Alchemy [part 2]

This word has given rise to different concepts according to the mental and developmental capacity of whosoever tries to analyze its real significance.

The Rosicrucians of all times have seen in Alchemy the most transcendental science, because for them said science holds[248] the mystery of the generation and regeneration of all that exists.

Symbolically they see in alchemy the scientific system for the realization of the great work of nature, in other words **"The Great Work"**.

This great work consists of realizing the transmutation of lead into gold.

This beautiful symbolism tells us, in the spiritual sense, that the true Rose-cross [adepts] must transmute the lead of their personal vulgar passions, into the highest vibrations of the spirit of their inner nature.

But, scientifically, it [also] indicates something else.

In the whole [of] nature [there] is an alchemical process [which is] constantly verifying itself; through time the luminous radiation of the more evolved stars of a system, intensifies (through its radioactivity) the evolution of the substances modifying them in such a way that evidently[249] (through the ages) turns lead into gold; this is the reason why, as the centuries pass by we proceed to find the majority of the gold in the bosom of our mother earth.

---

[248] Literally 'encierra' means "shut in, imprisoned; close on-; surrounded, jailed; confine, include"

[249] Literally 'evidentemente' means "evidently, obviously, apparently; palpably"

| Editor's Appendix | Apéndice del Editor |

By analogy, through the ages [of] evolution in the interior of man, [there emerges] an irradiation of [a] subtle material which permits him to express with great vigor the spiritual power which [is] in the pulsation[250] [of all that exists].

What is necessary to differentiate is: [that] alchemy is a process wherein the work is [done with] the spiritual force of life, and with chemistry which many [researchers] mistakenly confuse with the first, working only [with] the action of a physical fire in order to liquefy the metals and combine them to produce new compounds, but not [by] evolving substances as was commonly[251] believed.

But the symbolism is often misinterpreted when the aspirations of the study are of [a] purely material order.

Hence there have been false Rose-cross [adepts] who, after [beginning] the mission to make (physical) gold, have spent the best of their life in manipulations of [a] chemical order, believing [themselves] to be acting directly in the [sphere of] True and Sacred Spiritual Alchemy.

And not only in past epochs, but also today, we have some corporations ([in the] U. S. A.) who call themselves Rose-cross [associations and] that offer their students scales[252] in order to weigh atoms, and other things like that, so as to deceive unsuspecting[253] [people].

It is not with this pretending [that] we negate the value of the physical sciences, much less the **transcendence**[254] of **chemistry**.

Por analogia al traves de las edades evoluciona en el interior del hombre una irradiacion de sutil materia que le permite expresar con mayor vigor el poder espiritual que en el late.

Lo que es necesario diferenciar es lo siguiente: la alquimia es un proceso en el cual obra es la fuerza espiritual de vida, y en la quimica que muchos equivocadamente confunden con la primera, obra solamente la accion de un fuego fisico para licuar los metales y combinarlos produciendo nuevos compuestos, pero no evolucionando sustancias como vulgarmente se ha creido.

Pero la simbologia suele ser falsamente interpretada cuando las aspiraciones del que la estudia son de orden puramente material.

Por lo tanto ha habido falsos Rosa-cruz que tras la mision de hacer oro (fisico) han estado lo mejor de su vida en manipulaciones de orden quimico creyendo estar rectamente obrando en la Verdadera y Sagrada Alquimia Espiritual.

Y no solamente en pasadas epocas, sino tambien hoy tenemos algunas corporaciones (U. S. A.) que se dicen Rosa-cruz que ofrecen a sus estudiantes balanzas para pesar atomos, y otras cosas por el estilo, con el fin de enganar a incautos.

No es que con esto pretendamos negar el valor de las ciencias fisicas, ni mucho menos la **trascendencia** de la **quimica.**

---

[250] Literally 'late' means "beat, throb, pulsate"
[251] Literally 'vulgarmente' means "vulgarly, in a manner befitting the masses; coarsely, obscenely"
[252] Literally 'balanzas' means "scales; balance; judgement, assessment"
[253] Literally 'incautos' means "incautious, unwary, unguarded; dupe, fool, sucker, person who is easily deceived"
[254] Literally 'trascendencia' means " implications; momentousness; transcendence"

But it is our duty to indicate where truth and where error [are to be found].

Alchemy is a spiritual process in which the vibrations of life are progressively elevated from the slow state of semi-animal evolution, to the superior state to which man should aspire [by] refining his internal culture, by means of the governing of his own nature, through the mental transmutation of his emotions into goodness[255] and harmony, and also through the **transubstantiation of his creative force** so that the divine flame within the Undefiled[256] garment[257] illuminates his inner senses in order [for him] to be able to progressively become[258] the radiant[259] philosophical stone of the three divine colors which embody[260] POWER, WISDOM and LOVE so that he can be [a] Master and guide his younger brethren in the school of life.

[Huiracocha.]

Pero si es nuestro deber indicar donde esta la verdad y donde el error.

La alquimia es un proceso espiritual en el cual las vibraciones de la vida son elevadas progresivamente desde el estado lenito de la evolucion semi-animal, hasta el estado superior al cual debe aspirar el hombre refinando su cultura interior, por medio del gobierno de su propia naturaleza, por la transmutacion mental de sus emociones en bondad y en armonia, y tambien por la **transustanciacion de su fuerza creativa** para que en el prenda la divina llama de Amianto[261] iluminando sus internos sentidos para que progresivamente se pueda ir convirtiendo en la fulgurante piedra filosofal de los tres divinos colores donde encarna el PODER, la SABIDURIA y el AMOR para que pueda ser Maestro y guía de sus hermanos menores en la escuela de la vida.

[Huiracocha.]

---

[255] Literally 'bondad' means "goodness; graciousness, kindness; benignity; bonhomie"
[256] Literally the Spanish word 'Amianto' means "Asbestos". The origin of this word is Greek, and in both modern and ancient Greek, *amiantos* [αμίαντος] which means "undefiled" or "pure".
[257] Literally 'prenda' means "pledge; favor; forfeit; garment; token; gift; pawn"
[258] Literally 'convirtiendo' means "transform, convert; proselytize"
[259] Literally 'fulgurante' means "aglow, ablaze; radiant with warmth or excitement"
[260] Literally 'encarna' means "incarnadine; incarnate, embody; blood"

[261] El palabra Amianto es del latín *amiantus*, y este del griego αμίαντος [amíantos] que significado 'sin mancha'.

Extract from Lecture #132, on pages 1366-1368 of *El Quinto Evangelio* (2000) by Samael Aun Weor	Extracto de la Conferencia #132, de páginas 1366-1368 de *El Quinto Evangelio* (2000) por Samael Aun Weor
"[THE] GNOSTIC VISION OF SEXUALITY"[262]	"VISIÓN GNÓSTICA DE LA SEXUALIDAD"
...What is missing here, in this talk, is to say how.	...Lo que faltaría aquí, en esta plática, es decir cómo.
I will be glad to explain a very unique trick[263] that the Medieval Alchemists taught their disciples.	Yo tendré mucho gusto en explicarle un artificio muy singular que los Alquimistas Medievales enseñaban a sus discípulos.
The trick that I will teach you was also taught [by] men of science, such as Brown-Sequard, in the United States.	El artificio que voy a enseñarles a ustedes también lo enseñaron los hombres de Ciencia, como Brown-Sequard, en los Estados Unidos.
Dr. Krumm Heller (Medical Colonel of our glorious Mexican army) taught it, Jung also taught it and it is taught [in] the Asian Schools of Oriental Tantrism.	Lo enseñó el Dr. Krumm Heller (Médico Coronel de nuestro ejército glorioso Mexicano), lo enseñó también Jung y lo enseñan las Escuelas Asiáticas del Tantrismo Oriental.
This is not something particular to me, [that] I invented; I have learned from all these Sages and in your turn, they are communicating with you, not as an article of faith or as an unshakable dogma, no.	No es una cosecha mía, particular; yo la he aprendido de todos esos Sabios y a su vez, se las comunico a ustedes, no como un artículo de fe o como un dogma inquebrantable, no.
If you want to accept it, accept it; if you do not want to accept, do not accept it.	Si ustedes quieren aceptarlo, acéptenlo; si no lo quieren aceptar, no lo acepten.
Many schools have accepted it, many schools have rejected it; everyone is free to think as they like, I only give you my modest opinion.	Muchas escuelas lo han aceptado, muchas escuelas lo han rechazado; cada cual es libre de pensar como quiera, yo únicamente les doy mi modesta opinión.
The trick is this: "CONNECTION OF THE LINGAM-YONI (Lingam: You already know what the Lingam is, the Phallus. Yoni: You already know that it is the Uterus, the Eternal Feminine, the sexual organ of the woman) WITHOUT THE EJACULATION OF THE ENTITY OF THE SEMEN..."	El artificio consiste en esto: "CONEXIÓN DEL LINGAM-YONI (Lingam: Ya saben ustedes cual es el Lingam, el Phalo. Yoni: Ya saben ustedes que es el Útero, el Eterno Femenino, el órgano sexual de la mujer) SIN LA EYACULACIÓN DE LA ENTIDAD DEL SEMEN"...

---

[262] This lecture has also been called "TRANSCENDENTAL SEXOLOGY"
[263] Literally 'artificio' means " craft; artifice; contrivance; trick; shift"

Dr. Krumm Heller said [or] gave the formula in latin. He said: "Immissum Membrum Virile In Vaginam Feminae Sine Eiaculatione Seminis..."

Some modern scientists have accepted it; there, in the United States, the ONEIDA SOCIETY experimented with this formula.

In the Oneida Society, you [can] see what was done: They had about 25 couples, men and women who worked with sex.

During [a] certain time they were ordered to copulate, but without the ejaculation of the Entity of the Semen.

Then they were subjected to clinical trials[264].

In the United States, it was possible to observe the complete seminization of the brain, the increased hormones in the blood, the complete improvement of the organism, the fortification of the sexual potency[265], etc., and many illnesses disappeared.

When scientists researched[266] the need to have children, they then also gave (in the Oneida Society) the freedom to copulate with seminal ejaculation; then reproduction was obtained. In this way many experiments were made in the Oneida Society.

In any case, the interesting thing about this nice[267] trick which constitutes the Secret-Secretorum of the Medieval Alchemists, consists in the sexual glands never degenerating.

---

[264] Literally 'estudios' means "study; investigation; research, survey; plan, design; schooling, education; planning; atelier, studio, artist's studio or workroom; room in which reading or studying is done"
[265] Literally 'potencialidad' means "potency, potentiality"
[266] Literally 'resolvían' means "resolve, determine, decide; solve, find a solution; separate into constituent parts"
[267] Literally 'fino' means "fine, choice; nice; refined; slender, delicate; dainty; shrewd, discriminating; subtle"

You know very well that when the sexual glands degenerate, the Hypophysis [or Pituitary gland] also degenerates and all the glands of internal secretion degenerate.

The whole Nervous System goes through processes of degeneration; then decrepitude[268] and death occur[269].

Why does old age exist? Simply because the sexual glands go into decrepitude.

When [they] go into decrepitude, all the endocrine glands enter into decrepitude [as well], and then, this issue of old age and decrepitude manifests[270].

But if there was a system that did not allow the sexual glands to degenerate, to not enter into decrepitude, [then] the whole Nervous System could be preserved, in perfect activity, and then, there would be no old age nor decrepitude; that is obvious.

Well, now, through this nice trick: "Connection of the Lingam-Yoni without the ejaculation of the Ens-Seminis" (as the famous doctors Krumm Heller and Brown-Sequard said), it is then possible to maintain active sexual glands throughout [one's] whole life.

This means that a man (who practices such a system) could reach the age of 90 to 100 years old, yet still with the ability to copulate and to freely enjoy the sexual pleasure (which is a legitimate pleasure of man, which is not a "sin", which is not a taboo, which is not a cause of shame or pretense, etc., but, again, a legitimate right of man).

---

[268] Literally 'decrepitud' means "decrepitude (decrepit condition; dilapidated state; feebleness, especially from old age)"
[269] Literally 'viene' means "come; reach; arrive; result from; happen, occur; infiltrate; settle; land"
[270] Literally 'procesa' means "impeach; indict; process; prosecute"

Well, now, through the Transmutation of the Entity of the Semen into Energy, extraordinary psychological changes are possible[271], [and] the PINEAL GLAND develops.

This Gland was active in other times, in ancient times of History; then the human being possessed that "EYE" of which we speak.

Homer in his "Odyssey" [calls this]: 'The Eye of the Lacertidaes', the Eye he saw on that terrible giant that intended[272], then, to devour him.

This 'Eye of the Lacertidaes' is not a mere legend without any foundation...

Through Sexual Transmutation, this gland develops, entering into new activity; here is that "eye" which allows one to PERCEIVE THE ULTRA of all things.

Our world is not only Three Dimensions, as the "illustrious ignoramuses" believe; our world exists in a Fourth Vertical [as well].

Furthermore, we can say with great emphasis, that there is a Fifth Vertical, a Sixth and a Seventh [Vertical as well].

That is, we have never seen our world as it truly is; and we have not seen it because our five senses are degenerated, our Pineal Gland is atrophied.

There are other Senses in us which are completely degenerated and which are [senses] of perception, but that are [also] degenerated.

Ahora bien, mediante la Transmutación de la Entidad del Semen en Energía, se procesan cambios psicológicos extraordinarios, se desarrolla la GLÁNDULA PINEAL.

Esa Glándula estuvo activa en otros tiempos, en tiempos antiquísimos de la Historia; entonces el ser humano poseía aquél "OJO" del que nos hablara

Homero en su "Odisea": El Ojo de los Lacértidos, el Ojo que viera en aquél terrible gigante que intentara, pues, devorarles.

Ese Ojo de los Lacértidos no es una mera leyenda sin fundamento alguno...

Mediante la Transmutación Sexual, esa glándula se desarrolla, entra en nueva actividad; allí está ese "ojo" que le permite a un PERCIBIR EL ULTRA de todas las cosas.

Nuestro mundo no es solamente de Tres Dimensiones, como creen los "ignorantes ilustrados"; nuestro mundo existe en una Cuarta Vertical.

Aún más, podemos asegurar con gran énfasis, que existe una Quinta Vertical, una Sexta y una Séptima.

Esto es, que nosotros nunca hemos visto nuestro mundo como verdaderamente es; y no lo hemos visto porque nuestros cinco sentidos están degenerados, nuestra Glándula Pineal está atrofiada.

Existen otros Sentidos en nosotros que se hayan completamente degenerados y que son de percepción, pero que están degenerados.

---

[271] Literally 'procesan' means "process; prosecute; indict; impeach; try"
[272] Literally 'intentara' means "intend; try, attempt; bring"

Editor's Appendix	Apéndice del Editor
And if we managed to regenerate them, we could see the world as it is, with its Seven Dimensions.	Y si nos lográramos regenerar, podríamos percibir el mundo como es, con sus Siete Dimensiones.
So the harsh reality of the facts is that through Sexual Transmutation, you can regenerate the Pineal [gland or third eye] and the other Senses that have atrophied.	Así que la cruda realidad de los hechos es que mediante la Transmutación Sexual, se puede regenerar la Pineal y los otros Sentidos que se hayan atrofiados.
Thus we would have access to a world of extraordinary knowledge, and would have access to the Superior Dimensions of Nature and the Cosmos, so we could see, hear, touch and feel the great realities of Life and Death; we could grasp[273], [or] capture all cosmic phenomena in themselves, as they are and not as they appear.	Así tendríamos acceso a un mundo de conocimientos extraordinarios, así tendríamos acceso a las Dimensiones Superiores de la Naturaleza y del Cosmos, así podríamos ver, oír, tocar y palpar las grandes realidades de la Vida y de la Muerte; podríamos aprehender, capturar todos los fenómenos cósmicos en sí, tal cual son y no como aparentemente son.
TRANSMUTATION IS THE KEY: To change the Sperm, to modify it into Energy. Behold what is fundamental.	TRANSMUTACIÓN ES LA CLAVE: Cambiar el Esperma, modificarlo en Energía. He ahí lo fundamental.
The time[274] has come to comprehend this thoroughly, integrally...	Ha llegado pues la hora de comprender todo esto a fondo, integralmente...
If a man proposes[275] to accomplish such a simple formula, with this trick that Brown-Sequard teaches us, that Krumm Heller teaches us and that the Medieval Alchemists teach us, I could say to you with great emphasis and absolute certainty, that this man would, eventually, transform himself into a Superman.	Si un hombre se propusiera cumplir con esa fórmula tan sencilla, con ese artificio que nos enseñara Brown-Sequard, que nos enseñara Krumm Heller y que nos enseñaran los Alquimistas Medievales, podría decirles a ustedes con gran énfasis y absoluta seguridad, que este hombre, a la larga, se transformaría en un Superhombre.
We all need to feel the necessity to change, to become[276] something different; that is, if we are not reactionary, because conservative, retarded [people], do not want to change.	Todos necesitamos, sentimos la necesidad de cambiar, de convertirnos en algo diferente; esto es, si no somos reaccionarios, porque el conservador, el retardatario, no desea cambiar.

---

[273] Literally 'aprehender' means "apprehend"
[274] Literally 'hora' means "hour, unit of time equal to 60 minutes; certain time of day; term; tour"
[275] Literally 'se propusiera' means "propose; purpose; tender"
[276] Literally 'convertirnos' means "transform, convert"

But when one is truly revolutionary, one wants to be different, one wants to fundamentally change, to transform oneself into something different, becoming a Superman, making the doctrine of Nietzsche a reality.	Pero cuando uno es revolucionario de verdad, uno quiere ser distinto, uno quiere cambiar fundamentalmente, transformarse en algo distinto, convertirse en un Superhombre, hacer de la doctrina de Nietzsche una realidad.
It is possible to change through Sexual Transmutation.	Es posible cambiar, mediante la Transmutación Sexual.
The SEXUAL FORCE connects[277] us with the fabric[278] of existence and I can not deny you this [understanding]. We exist, we live, because we had a father, because we had mother.	La FUERZA SEXUAL nos puso sobre el tapete de la existencia y esto no me lo pueden ustedes negar. Nosotros existimos, vivimos, gracias a que tuvimos un padre, gracias a que tuvimos madre.
In final synthesis, the root of our own life is [found] in sexual union[279] of a man and a woman.	En última síntesis, la raíz de nuestra propia vida está en la cópula de un hombre y de una mujer.
Well, now if the Sexual Force, if the Energy of Sex has [the] power to connect us with the fabric of existence, [then] it is obvious that it is the only [thing] that has [the] ability[280], in truth, to radically transform us.	Ahora bien, si la Fuerza Sexual, si la Energía del Sexo tuvo poder para ponernos sobre el tapete de la existencia, es obvio, que es la única que tiene autoridad, de verdad, para transformarnos radicalmente.
In the world there are many ideologies, in the world there are many beliefs, and everyone is free to believe whatever they please, but the only Force that has the ability to transform us, is what created us, what connected us with the fabric of existence.	En el mundo hay muchas ideologías, en el mundo hay muchas creencias y cada cual es libre de creer en lo que le de la gana, pero la única Fuerza que tiene autoridad para transformarnos, es la que nos creó, la que nos puso sobre el tapete de la existencia.
I refer myself, emphatically, to the Sexual Force.	Me refiero, en forma enfática, a la Fuerza Sexual.
Learning how to handle[281] that wonderful Energy of sex, means becoming [a] master[282] of Creation.	Aprender a manejar esa Energía maravillosa del sexo, significa hacerse amo de la Creación.

---

[277] Literally 'puso' means "put, place; lay; insert; impose; mark; adjust; send; contribute; subscribe; perform; translate"
[278] Literally 'tapete' means "rug; billiard cloth; scarf"
[279] Literally 'cópula' means "copulate"
[280] Literally 'autoridad' means "authority, power, control; mastery; weight; pomp"
[281] Literally 'manejar' means "handle, manage; run, operate, work; use; tend; drive; steer"
[282] Literally 'amo' means "owner; householder"

When the Sacred Sperm is transformed into Energy, extraordinary PSYCHOSOMATIC CHANGES occur.

We know well what those Hormonal Vessels of our gonads are: How they work, how they pass hormones from vessel to vessel, how, finally, along the Spermatic Cords, they reach the prostate [and through the Fallopian Tubes they reach the ovaries].

We know well how valuable the prostate [and ovaries] are: Here the biggest transformations of the Entity of the Semen and [of] the hormones ultimately occur, entering into the bloodstream.

The word "HORMONE" comes from a Greek root meaning "LONGING[283] TO BE", "FORCE[284] OF BEING".

Hormones have been studied by our men of science (they are marvelous).

Sexual hormones, for example, enter the bloodstream, [and] accomplish[285] wonders.

When touching the endocrine glands, such as the Thyroid, the Parathyroid, the kidneys or Adrenal[286], or the Thymus, etc., etc., [they] stimulate them, making those little microlaboratories produce more hormones, and these hormones (produced in all the glands in general) enrich the bloodstream in an extraordinary way; [and] then ailments disappear, diseases disappear.

Cuando el Esperma Sagrado se trasforma en Energía, se provocan CAMBIOS PSICOSOMÁTICOS extraordinarios.

Bien sabemos nosotros lo que son esos Vasos Hormonales de nuestras gónadas: Cómo trabajan, cómo pasan las hormonas de vaso en vaso, cómo, por último, a lo largo de los Cordones Espermáticos, llega hasta la próstata.

Bien sabemos lo valiosa que es la próstata: Allí se producen las más grandes transformaciones de la Entidad del Semen y las hormonas por último, entran en el torrente sanguíneo.

La palabra "HORMONA" viene de una raíz Griega que significa "ANSIAS DE SER", "FUERZA DE SER".

Las hormonas han sido estudiadas por nuestros hombres de ciencia (son maravillosas).

Las hormonas sexuales, por ejemplo, entrando en el torrente sanguíneo, realizan prodigios.

Cuando tocan a las glándulas endocrinas, sea la Tiroides, sean las Paratiroides, sean a los riñones, o Suprarrenales, o a la Timo, etc., etc., las estimulan, hacen que esos pequeños microlaboratorios produzcan más hormonas, y esas hormonas, producidas por todas las glándulas en general, enriquecen el torrente sanguíneo en forma extraordinaria; entonces desaparecen las dolencias, desaparecen las enfermedades.

---

[283] Literally 'ANSIAS' means "anxiety, worry; anguish; yearning, longing"
[284] Literally 'FUERZA' means "strength, quality of being strong, might; durability; determination, resolve; power (of electricity, etc.); effectiveness; intensity; compulsion, coercion, use of force; violence, rough unwarranted force"
[285] Literally 'realizan' means "realize, accomplish, actualize; implement; execute; perform; attain; achieve"
[286] Literally 'Suprarrenales' means "suprarenal, situated above the kidney"

Unfortunately, today, the SPERM that is prepared by the gonads and then rises or ascends to the prostate, is, unfortunately, SQUANDERED[287], and the hormones in the famous zoosperms are even left to decompose, when they are kicked[288] out of the organism, when they are rejected[289]…

Desgraciadamente, hoy por hoy, el ESPERMA que es preparado por las gónadas y que luego sube o asciende hasta la próstata, es, desgraciadamente, DESPILFARRADO, y ni siquiera se les deja descomponer, a los famosos zoospermos, en las hormonas, cuando ya se les tira fuera del organismo, cuando se les arroja…

---

[287] Literally 'DESPILFARRADO' means "squandered, wasted"
[288] Literally 'tira' means "pull; throw, toss over; draw; shoot; lay; cast; print; discard; knock off; pitch"
[289] Literally 'arroja' means "throw, cast, toss; emit; shoot; dump; give out; disgorge; release; reject"

Extract from
The Rosecross Magazine
[no date]

THE SECRET OF VOCALIZATION AND ITS ASTROLOGICAL CORRESPONDENCE IN THE HUMAN BODY (THE STARS AND THE ENDOCRINE GLANDS)

It-will-appear [Spanish: Per-sona-re] — to produce edifying, constructive, [and] creative sounds.

Here is the secret of vocalization.

Just as there are atomic forces, [which are] inter- and intra- atomic, there are also inter- and intra- cellular [forces] that translate themselves into two opposite poles.

They are evolutionary and involutionary.

They are what builds and what destroys.

Our vital body is what constantly builds our organism and the astral [body] destroys it in order to give rise to new constructive material for the vital [body to use].

The secret of health consists, in maintaining the right equilibrium between these two disposed[290] forces, [providing] the synthesis between them.

With this we have a totally new pathology and therefore, a superb therapeutic [method].

If the vital force exceeds in its activity and allows the astral [force] to move and to work in its demolishing activity, [then] the results are febrile diseases and, if the contrary [occurs], it destroys more than what is built, [and then] emaciation[291] and debilities [manifest].

---

[290] Literally 'encontradas' means "laid; located; disposed; encountered, found"
[291] Literally 'enflaquecimientos' means "emaciation, loss of weight, weight reducion, wasting"

Extracto del
Revista Rosacruz
[sin dato]

EL SECRETO DE LA VOCALIZACIÓN Y SU CORRESPONDENCIA ASTROLÓGICA EN EL CUERPO HUMANO (LOS ASTROS Y LAS GLÁNDULAS ENDOCRINAS)

Per-sona-re — producir sonidos edificantes, constructores, creadores.

Ahí está el secreto de la vocalización.

Así como hay fuerzas atómicas, inter e intra-atómicas, las hay también inter e intra-celulares que se traducen en dos polos opuestos.

Las hay evolutivas e involutivas.

Las hay que construyen y las hay que destruyen.

Nuestro cuerpo vital es el que constantemente edifica nuestro organismo y el astral lo destruye para dar lugar al vital a que ponga nuevo material constructivo.

El secreto de la salud consiste, en mantener el justo equilibrio entre estas dos fuerzas encontradas, la síntesis entre ellas.

Con esto tenemos toda una patología nueva y de consiguiente, una terapéutica soberbia.

Si se excede en su actividad la fuerza vital y deja mover y trabajar al astral en su actividad demoliente, resultan enfermedades febriles y, si al contrario, se destruye más de lo que se edifica, vienen enflaquecimientos y debilidades.

| Editor's Appendix | Apéndice del Editor |

The constructive part is summarized in the albumenary processes.

Albumen is the great agent who gives the *materia prima* [Latin: "*first matter*" or "primordial matter"], we say it thus, because it is really secondary from the esoteric point of view and the formative part we could call 'antimony'.

Well now. The latter we received from the Cosmos, they come to us from the Stars and each Star vibrates in a sound which is peculiar to it.

The Sun vibrates in "A U", Venus in the "A", Mercury in the "I", the Moon in the "A I", Mars in "E", Jupiter in the "E", and Saturn in the "U".

In the consonants corresponding to Aries [are] the "W" and "V", "R" and "RR" [correspond] to Taurus, "H" to Gemini, "F" to Cancer, "G" to Sagitarius, "L" and "LL" to Capricorn, "M" to Aquarius, "N" and "Ñ" to Pisces, "T" to Leo, "B" to Virgo, "C" to Libra and "Z" to Scorpion.

Only in order to give an example, I refer to the latter, because I am extending myself too much and desire to treat this in a public lecture in America in order to prove everything that we needed to know in order to form mantrams and to what extent we can benefit[292] from the Eurithmic Vocalization.

The liver is already formed, beginning in[293] intrauterine life, by the forces emanated from Jupiter.

The lungs with [the forces of] Mercury and the spleen with [those of] Saturn.

La parte constructiva se resume en procesos albuminicantes.

La albúmina, es el gran agente que da la *materia prima*, digámoslo así, porque realmente es secundaria desde el punto de vista esotérico y la parte formante podríamos llamarla antimonizante.

Ahora bien. Estas últimas, las recibimos del Cosmos, nos vienen de los Astros y cada Astro vibra en un sonido dado que le es peculiar.

El Sol vibra en A U, Venus en la A, Mercurio en la I, la Luna en la A I, Marte en E, Júpiter en la E, y Saturno en la U.

En las consonantes corresponde la W y V a Aries, R y RR a Taurus, la H a Géminis, la F a Cáncer, la G a Sagitario, la L y LL a Capricornio, la M a Acuario, la N y Ñ a Piscis, la T a Leo, la B a Virgo, la C a Libra y la Z a Escorpión.

Sólo para dar un ejemplo, refiero lo anterior, pues me estoy extendiendo demasiado y deseo tratar esto en una conferencia pública en América para probar todo lo que necesitamos saber para formar mantrams y hasta que punto nos podemos valer de la Euritmia Vocalizadora.

El hígado se forma ya, desde la vida intrauterina, de las fuerzas emanadas de Júpiter.

El pulmón con Mercurio y el bazo con Saturno.

---

[292] Literally 'valer' means "aid, help; protect; serve; avail; cause; earn; cost; be useful; be valid; score; amount; hold"

[293] Literally 'desde' means "since; from the; from"

When pronouncing a vowel, the sound opens [a] passage towards the currents of the stars (to which it corresponds) and we can, for example, pronouncing badly, load the lung with [the] forces of Jupiter that [should] correspond to the liver, causing then a sickly state that we know with the denomination of **PULMONARY HEPATIZACION.**

So that, the vowels, bring about emanated forces of the stars, verified by spectrum analysis, and lay the way towards our body.

Consonants correspond to the zodiacal constellations and if we study the origin of a disease and the remedy that we are going to apply to it, [then] from the astrological point of view, there appear mantrams as [a] grandiose curative medium and now we know its mode of operation.

The plants have, [just] like the human organism, their vital and astral body that grows and develops [for] each one, under the influence of certain stars.

During the Spring the vital constructive [force] acts with more persistence[294], whereas in the Fall and Winter the Astral one acts, destroying what was done before[295].

Well, then. We have already said it. There are morbid[296] or diseased states that require a vital increase and [yet, some people] purport[297] to cure them with plants cut in the Fall, [but the] result [will be] counter-productive.

Other times we need for the life to have more place [or space] in order to develop itself and [yet] it cannot reach [this level], because the construction that precedes it is not quite active and then dried plants and roots are precisely what is required.

---

[294] Literally 'empeño' means "pledge, obligation; determination, persistence; pawnshop"
[295] Literally 'lo hecho anteriormente' means "what was done previously"
[296] Literally 'morbosos' means "unhealthy, morbid, sick"
[297] Literally 'pretender' means "purport, pretend; profess, allege, claim"

| Editor's Appendix | Apéndice del Editor |

Now the reader will comprehend that they do harm[298] in Medical Schools by teaching us that this or that plant or its product is used for this or that disease, while nothing is said about the time in which they must be cut.

Additionally, everything is [in a] dual rhythm, [the] feminine and masculine principle, and this rhythm, which seems so similar[299] in the plant as [it does] in man, must also be considered in therapeutic applications.

Finally. Thus the stars (like everything that [gives] us impressions from the exterior [world]) pass through certain[300] magnetic centers that, in their turn, are subject to our endocrine glands.

They are, beginning from above going downwards:

The Epiphysis [or Pineal Gland].
The Hypophysis [or Pituitary Gland].
The Thyroid.
The Epithelial Bodies [or Parathyroid Glands].
The Thymus.
The Adrenal Glands.
The Sexual Glands.

[In] this septenary each [gland] has a [corresponding] star that produces[301] its basic substance and a sound that corresponds to it.

Ahora comprenderá el lector, que mal hacen en las Escuelas Médicas en enseñarnos que tal o cual planta o su producto se use para tal o cual enfermedad, pero nada se diga del tiempo en que deban cortarse.

Además. Todo es ritmo dual, principio femenino y masculino y ese ritmo, que suena tanto en la planta como en el hombre, también debe tomarse en consideración en las aplicaciones terapéuticas.

Por último. Tanto los astros, como todo lo que nos impresione del exterior, pasa por determinados centros magnéticos que, a su vez, están sujetos a nuestras glándulas endocrinas.

Ellas son, empezando de arriba hacia abajo.

La Epífisis.
La Hipófisis.
El Tiroides.
Los Cuerpos Epitelares.
El Timo.
Los Riñones Suplementarios.
Las Glándulas Sexuales.

Este septenario, tiene cada uno un astro del que saca su substancia base y un sonido a que corresponde.

---

[298] Literally 'mal' means "badly, in a bad way; wrong, amiss; poorly, ill; naughtily; evil; inhumanity; trouble; harm, damage; illness, malady; cowardice; infertility"
[299] Literally 'suena tanto' means "sound so much, seems very"
[300] Literally 'determinados' means "certain, particular, specific; determined, decided, resolved"
[301] Literally 'saca' means "take out, remove; bring out; draw out, extract; get; take; bring up; let; produce; educe, deduce; protract; (vulgar) have sexual intercourse"

Editor's Appendix

The occult powers also reside in these centers and whosoever wakes up those powers, will show[302] that within mantrams [is] enclosed the force of the vowels in order to give[303] help[304].

Our organism, as we the seers see it, has a ternary division.

The one corresponds to the senses and nerves; the other to nutrition and material assimilation and, within these two [is the third,] rhythm.

The vowels are syntheses and their forces activate the stars.

The consonants, [as] I already said, correspond to the zodiacal constellations and they act upon the chakras which are, even in their form, connected with the consonants.

Let us look [at] the form of a consonant.

We have the "S". Does it not look like a snake that moves[305] and introduces itself throughout?

And if we look at our intestines, are they not something like a series of **SSSSSSSSSS**?

For here we see this relationship that makes us notice Paracelsus and when we suffer a chronic disease of the intestines we constantly dream of vipers.

This is very interesting for the psycho-analytical [person]…

Apéndice del Editor

Los poderes ocultos residen también en estos centros y el que despierta esos poderes, se tendrá que valer de los mantrams, encerrando en ellos, la fuerza de las vocales para actuar.

Nuestro organismo, como lo vemos los videntes, tiene una division ternaria.

La una corresponde a los sentidos y nervios; la otra a la nutrición y asimilación material y, dentro de estas dos, el ritmo.

Las vocales son síntesis y sus fuerzas actuantes los astros.

Las consonantes, ya dije, corresponden a las constelaciones zodiacales y actúan sobre las chacras que están, hasta en su forma, conectadas con las consonantes.

Veamos la forma de una consonante.

Tenemos la S. ¿No se parece a una culebra que se mete y se introduce por todas partes?.

Y si miramos nuestros intestinos, ¿No son algo así como una serie de **SSSSSSSSSS**?.

Pues ahí se ve esa relación que nos hace notar Paracelso y cuando sufrimos una enfermedad crónica de los intestinos soñamos constantemente con víboras.

Esto es muy interesante para el psicoanalítico…

---

[302] Literally 'tendrá' means "have, possess; hold; bear; carry; wear; experience; practice; meet with; travel; show"
[303] Literally 'actuar' means "act, perform; play; appear; operate; proceed; sit"
[304] Literally 'valer' means "value, worth; aid, help; protect; serve; avail; cause; earn; cost; be useful; be valid; score; amount; hold"
[305] Literally 'mete' means "put, place; insert; shove; introduce; enclose; intrude; involve; engage"

Illness lies in the subconsciousness and it sometimes sends us a dream, a nightmare.

[Which] is an effort made by the subconsciousness to bring this dream into the consciousness.

We wake up and we are frightened [and] many times [even] thinking that the viper is still in the bed, but the remarkable thing is that the day after having had that heavy sleep, we wake up always better and, many times, radically healed.

We, the Rose Cross [adepts] intentionally provoke dreams in order to be able to cure to a person and for this[306] we have perfumes, vowels and consonants.

La enfermedad reside en el subconsciente y él nos manda a veces un sueño, una pesadilla.

Es un esfuerzo que hace el subconsciente mismo por llevar este sueño a la conciencia.

Despertamos y nos quedamos asustados pensando muchas veces que la víbora aún está en la cama, pero lo notable es, que al día siguiente de haber tenido ese sueño pesado, despertamos siempre mejor y, muchas veces, radicalmente curados.

Los Rosa Cruz provocamos, intencionalmente, sueños para poder curar a una persona y para ello tenemos perfumes, vocales y consonantes.

---

[306] Literally 'ello' means "it"

Extract from
The Rosecross Magazine
[no date]

EURYTHMOSOPHIA

There is a new science, Eurythmia, or it would be better to say **EURYTHMOSOPHIA.**

With it we learn to do our gymnastic movements imitating the consonants and pronouncing vowels.

With this system, I have been able to return lunatics [back] into rational [people] who had spent[307] [many] years in the mental hospital, because they had lost the rhythm and [when] having rhythmically put them back [in alignment], [they were] instantly healed.

You see dear readers, all this that I am giving in broad strokes, What does [this] field of investigation offer to us?

Ignorant humanity is generally scared of death and forgets that we are born and we died at each moment.

Every seven years, all our cells have been replaced by others.

While one is born, another one dies and in this rhythm of being born and dying is **LIFE.**

Immortality or we [could] say it in another manner, longevity is [achieved] by dying in the same way[308] that we are born.

One whosoever is born in themselves more than [they] die, becomes ill.

---

[307] Literally 'estar' means "be; stay, remain; hold; be found; be present"
[308] Literally 'medida' means "measurement, calculation of size or extent; assessment of capacity or dimension; system of measures; measure; size, fitting; action, something that is being done"

Extracto del
Revista Rosacruz
[sin dato]

LA EURITMOSOFÍA

Hay una ciencia nueva, La Euritmia, o sería mejor decir **LA EURITMOSOFIA.**

Con ella aprendemos a hacer nuestros movimientos gimnásticos imitando a las consonantes y pronunciando vocales.

Yo he podido con este sistema, poder volver la razón a locos que tenían años de estar en el manicomio, porque habían perdido el ritmo y mandándoles poner rítmicamente de nuevo, instantáneamente sanaron.

Vean ustedes queridos lectores, todo esto que doy a grandes rasgos, ¿Qué campo de investigación nos ofrece?.

La humanidad ignorante tiene generalmente miedo a la muerte y olvida que nacemos y morimos a cada momento.

Cada siete años, todas nuestras celdillas han sido reemplazadas por otras.

Mientras una nace, otra muere y en este ritmo de nacer y morir está la **VIDA.**

La inmortalidad o digámoslo de otro modo, la longevidad está en morir en la misma medida que nacemos.

El que en sí nace más de lo que muere, se enferma.

The same thing happens to whosoever dies more than they are born.

This powerful dualism of our vital and mortal body, gives us the explanation us of many biological phenomena.

Wanting to sustain[309], modify or intercept this rhythm with one or another substance taken at random, is the result of a blind empiricism, it is ignorance, which we are taught in Medical Schools.

For the majority of doctors, man is a corpse in movement and they do not know that we are a trio of body, soul and spirit and that [the human being] cannot be operated or provoked with impunity[310], either on one or on the other, without injuring[311] to the others.

With the vowels and consonants, we give life and we act upon the intimate cause of the being.

The stars, musical notes and the colors, correspond as follows:

Mars	Red	do
Sun	Orange	re
Mercury	Yellow	mi
Saturn	Green	fa
Jupiter	Blue	sol
Venus	Indigo	la
Moon	Violet	si

The creative word (sound) exists in the very root of all manifestation.

The "Vach" of the Indians, the Greek "Logos", the Latin "verb".

In the gospel of Saint John, it is the **WORD** without which "nothing that has been created would exist".

---

[309] Literally 'sostener' means "sustain, uphold, support; maintain; bear; live"
[310] Literally 'impunemente' means "with impunity (exemption from punishment)"
[311] Literally 'lesionar' means "injure, hurt; wound"

Igual le pasa al que muere más que nace.

Este poderoso dualismo de nuestro cuerpo vital y mortal, nos da la explicación de muchos fenómenos biológicos.

Querer sostener, modificar o interceptar ese ritmo con tal o cual substancia tomada al azar, es el resultado de un empirismo ciego, son ignorancias, que nos enseñan en las Escuelas Médicas.

Para la mayoría de los médicos, el hombre es un cadáver en movimiento y no saben que somos un trío de cuerpo, alma y espíritu y que no se puede impunemente operar o provocar, ya al uno ya al otro, sin lesionar a los demás.

Con las vocales y consonantes, damos vida y actuamos sobre la causa íntima del ser.

Los astros, notas musicales y los colores, se corresponden así:

Marte	Rojo	do
Sol	Anaranjado	re
Mercurio	Amarillo	mi
Saturno	Verde	fa
Júpiter	Azul	sol
Venus	Añil	la
Luna	Violado	si

La palabra creadora (sonido) que existe en la raíz misma de toda manifestación.

El Vach de los indios, el Logos griego, el verbo latino.

En el evangelio de San Juan, es la **PALABRA** sin la cual "nada de lo que ha sido creado existiría".

In Genesis, [it is] the **"FIAT"** [or in Hebrew "Bereshith" בראשית].

What did Pythagoras mean when he said, that "he heard the rhythmic music of the stars in movement"?

That vibratory electrical energy is what beats throughout the solar Universe, dragging[312] planets towards a Central Sun, as such they are chained electron to electron, atom to atom, molecule to molecule, cell to cell in each of its combinations and of the forms of this vast system that works under the same Law of **RHYTHM**.

Harmony and music are produced, when the vibratory values of the notes of the scale are encountered in relation to the others.

Every musician knows that the chords formed by a note and with third or fifth its **OCTAVE**, are harmonic[313]. Contrarily [they are] discordant[314].

There is only one reality in the Universe, **ENERGY**.

Matter is nothing else but the **GEOMETRIC** or **GEOCENTRIC** place of the singular points of [an] energy field.

For that [reason] neither the thinker, nor the sage, nor the artist **CREATE**.

The materiality of their objectification is to make[315] visible (in [a] state of vibration) what before only existed (already in the nature) in [an] invisible state (also vibratory).

---

[312] Literally 'arrastrando' means "drag, haul; be pulled; creep; grovel; trail; blow away; wash down"
[313] Literally 'armónicos' means "harmonic, melodious, compatible; of or relating to musical harmony"
[314] Literally 'discordantes' means "inconsonant; discordant, disharmonious"
[315] Literally 'tornar' means "turn down; dial; transform, to make"

What is it that completely **ANIMATES EVERYTHING**?

THE VOICE, THE SPIRIT AND THE WORD, THE GREAT BREATH, THE HOLY SPIRIT.

The Universe has to be a wonderful concert of vibratory movements.

This great divine concert is musical, through [the] Law of harmony (although it is not perceived) and music is only its manifestation or expression in the world[316] of sounds.

Rhythm, [just] as in music, must be the condition that prevails for all [of] this great accumulation of vibrations.

In the human organism itself, everything also obeys [a] rhythm.

The heart itself keeps the beat.

IN THE BEGINNING WAS THE RHYTHM, says Genesis: And as [the] first manifested law had to be the [law of] vibratory movement or that primitive **GENESIS-IZING**[317] light or [the] vital electricity that generated **LIGHT, HEAT, SOUND**, etc., etc.

You remember the chromatic prelude of the **RHINE-GOLD** which fecundates the symbolic waters of the River?

That must have been the biblical genesis-izing principle.

That of Pan's Flute, of Papageno or the Lire of Apollo, is not fiction. It is an eternal truth.

Music is **NUMBER** and sound, the **VIBRATION** had to construct everything that exists with its word, verb or **LOGOS**.

---

[316] Literally 'modo' means "way, mode; manner; line; wise; digit; mood"
[317] Literally 'GENÉSICA' means "genetic, of or pertaining to genetics; reproductive"

Editor's Appendix / Apéndice del Editor

Astral, Celestial and Other Hebrew Alphabets

Numeric Value	Kabalistic Value	Square Hebrew:	Hebrew Letter Name:	"Astral" Hebrew Alphabet:	"Celestial" or Angelic Hebrew Alphabet:	Ancient Chaldean Alphabet:	Ancient Hebrew Alphabet:	Modern Hebrew Alphabet:
1	1	א	Aleph					
2	2	ב	Beth					
3	3	ג	Gimel					
4	4	ד	Dalet					
5	5	ה	Heh					
6	6	ו	Vau					
7	7	ז	Zayin					
8	8	ח	Cheth					
9	9	ט	Teth					
10	10	י	Yod/Jod					
11	20	כ	Kaf/Kaph					
12	30	ל	Lamed					
13	40	מ	Mem/Men					
14	50	נ	Nun					
15	60	ס	Samech					
16	70	ע	Ayin					
17	80	פ	Peh/Pei					
18	90	צ	Tzadik					
19	100	ק	Kuf/Qoph					
20	200	ר	Resh/Reish					
21	300	ש	Shin					
22	400	ת	Tav					

"The ancients, in comparing the calm and peaceful immensity of heaven (completely populated with immovable lights) to the agitation and darkness of this world, believed themselves to have discovered (in that beautiful book of golden letters) the final word of the enigma of destinies; **they traced, through the imagination, lines of correspondence between these shining points of divine writing,** and it is said that the first constellations marked out by the shepherds of Chaldea were also the first characters of kabalistic writing."
- Eliphas Levi from Ch. 17 of *Ritual of High Magic*

*Sources: "The astral origin of the emblems, the zodiacal signs, and the astral Hebrew alphabet" (1881) by John Henry Broome, "Book of the Words" (1878) by Albert Pike, "Manuel Typographique" (1766) by Pierre Simon Fournier & Nicolas Gando, and "Curiositez Inouyes" (1629) by Jacques Gaffarel

Daath Gnosis: Bilingual Translations

"The Book of the Virgin of Carmel" by Samael Aun Weor

"Universal Charity" by Samael Aun Weor

"Gnostic Christification" by Samael Aun Weor

"Logos Mantram Magic" by Krumm-Heller (Huiracocha)

"The Reconciliation of Science and Religion" by Eliphas Levi

"The Bible of Liberty" by Eliphas Levi

"The Initiatic Path in the Arcanum of the Tarot & Kabalah" by Samael Aun Weor

"Esoteric Course of Kabalah" by Samael Aun Weor

"Magic, Alchemy and the Great Work" by Samael Aun Weor

"Dogma of High Magic" by Eliphas Levi

"The Awakening of Man" by Samael Aun Weor

"Gnostic Rosicrucian Astrology" by Krumm-Heller (Huiracocha)

"The Kabalistic and Occult Philosophy of Eliphas Levi" Vol.1 by Eliphas Levi

"Gnostic Rosicrucian Kabalah" by Krumm-Heller (Huiracocha)

"The Kabalistic and Occult Philosophy of Eliphas Levi" Vol.2 by Eliphas Levi *

"Ritual of High Magic" by Eliphas Levi *

* Current projects for future publication from Daath Gnostic Publishing

Daath Gnosis: Reprints[1]

"The Psychology of Man's Possible Evolution" by P.D. Ouspensky *(English-Español)*

"In Search of the Miraculous" Vol. 1 & 2 by P.D. Ouspensky *(English-Español)*

"Mystical Kabalah" by Dion Fortune *(English - Español)*

"Rito Memphis y Misraim Guias del Aprendiz, Compañero, y Maestro" by Memphis y Misraim Argentina *(Español)*

"The Theosophical ZOHAR" by Nurho de Manahar *(English)*

"The Oragean Version" by C. Daly King *(English)*

"La Science Cabalistique" by Lazare Lenain *(Français)*

"The Antiquities of the Christian Church" by Joseph Bingham *(English)*

"The Secret Discipline, Mentioned in Ancient Ecclesiastical History" by Samuel Lorenzo Knapp *aka* Theodore Temple *(English)*

"The Veil of the Temple Torn (Unpublished Writings of Eliphas Levi – Part 1)" by Eliphas Levi *(English)*

"Unpublished Writings of Eliphas Levi – Part 2" by Eliphas Levi *(English)* *

"The Fourth Way" by P.D. Ouspensky *(English - Español)* *

* Current projects for future publication from Daath Gnostic Publishing

---

[1] These are books which were 1) either originally in English and have been republished by Daath Gnosis in order to either make them bilingual or 2) to provide access to difficult to find documents in their original language.

Daath Gnosis: Study Guides

"Gnostic Egyptian Tarot Coloring Book" *(English - Español)*

"The Gnostic Kabalistic Verb" *(English - Español)*

"The Gnostic and Esoteric Mysteries of Freemasonry, Lucifer and the Great Work" *(English - Español)*

"The Kabalistic and Occult Tarot of Eliphas Levi" *(English)*

"Esoteric Studies in Masonry" Vol. 1 *(English - Français)*

"Esoteric Studies in Masonry" Vol. 2 *(English - Français)* *

* Current projects for future publication from Daath Gnostic Publishing

A word about "**Daath Gnostic Publishing – Art, Science, Philosophy and Mysticism (A.S.P.M)**" and our motivation:

> In an attempt to integrate the large amount of enlightening material on the subject of GNOSIS into the English language and to provide a way:
> - for non-English speakers to give lectures & assignments to English speaking students (and vice versa) and be able to reference specific topics or quotes, and
> - for English speakers to access materials previously unavailable in English (or not critically translated into English)
>
> we have decided to translate and publish these materials for the serious Gnostic Students.

Almost all our publications are bilingual, giving access to the original source material and the translation so that the reader can decide for themselves what the meaning of each sentence is.

We are also working on Study Guides that are a combination of Gnostic Materials from multiple sources which provide further insight when taken together.

Because of the need for a practical GNOSIS in these revolutionary times, we have focused on, and continue to benefit from, the writing and teachings of Samael Aun Weor. We encourage you to study his materials, they are wonderful.

In *Endocrinology and Criminology* (1959), at the end of Ch. 15, he says:

"Before delivering ourselves to the development of occult powers, we need to study ourselves and make a personalogical and psycho-pathological diagnosis of our own personality.	"Antes de entregarnos al desarrollo de los poderes ocultos necesitamos estudiarnos a sí mismos, y hacer un diagnóstico persona-lógico y psico-patológico de nuestra propia personalidad.
After discovering our own particular Psycho-bio-typo-logical "I", it is necessary for us to reform ourselves with intellectual culture.	Después de haber descubierto nuestro propio yo Psico-Biotipológico, necesitamos reformarnos con la cultura intelectual.
A Pedagogic[2] Psychotherapy is necessary in order to reform ourselves.	Necesitamos una Psicoterapia Pedagógica para reformarnos.

---

[2] Pedagogy: 1) the function or work of a teacher; teaching. 2) the art or science of teaching; education; instructional methods.

The four gospels of Jesus Christ are the best Pedagogic Psychotherapy. It is necessary to totally study and practice all the teachings contained in the four gospels of Jesus Christ. Only after reforming ourselves morally can we deliver ourselves to the development of the chakras, discs or magnetic wheels, of the astral body. It is also urgent to study the best authors of Theosophy, Rosicrucianism, Psychology, Yoga, etc., etc."	Los cuatro evangelios del Cristo Jesús, son realmente la mejor Psicoterapia Pedagógica. Es necesario estudiar y practicar totalmente todas las enseñanzas contenidas en los cuatro evangelios del Cristo-Jesús. Sólo después de habernos reformado moralmente podemos entregarnos al desarrollo de los chacras, discos o ruedas magnéticas del cuerpo astral. Es también urgente estudiar a todos los mejores autores de Teosofía, Rosacrucismo, Sicología, Yoguismo, etc., etc."

In *The Seven Words* (1953), about a third of the way through, he says:

"I dare to affirm that all the books which have been written in the world on Theosophism, Rosicrucianism, Spiritualism, etc., are completely antiquated for the new AQUARIAN Era, and therefore they should be revised in order to extract from them only what is essential. Here I, AUN WEOR, deliver to humanity, the authentic message that the WHITE LODGE sends to humanity for the new AQUARIAN Era. God has delivered to men the wisdom of the Serpent. What more do they want? This science is not mine; this science is from God; my person is not worth anything; the work is everything, I am nothing but an emissary."	"Yo me atrevo a afirmar que todos los libros que se han escrito en el mundo sobre teosofismo, Rosacrucismo, espiritismo, etc., están ya completamente anticuados para la nueva Era ACUARIA, y por consiguiente deben ser revisados para extraer de ellos únicamente lo esencial. Yo, AUN WEOR, aquí le entrego a la humanidad el auténtico mensaje que la LOGIA BLANCA envía a la humanidad para la nueva Era ACUARIA. Dios le ha entregado a los hombres la sabiduría de la Serpiente. ¿Qué más quieren? Esta ciencia no es mía; esta ciencia es de Dios; mi persona no vale nada, la obra lo es todo, yo no soy sino un emisario."

So let us practice the Science of the Serpent, *la magia amorosa*, while we study and extract only what is essential from the Esoteric texts of the past, in order to synthesize the truth within ourselves.

If you are interested:
- in receiving a list of our currently available materials,
- or would like to suggest a better translation for anything we publish,
- or if you would like to take the responsibility and time to translate or proofread a chapter or a book (in English, French or Spanish),
- or would like to suggest or submit materials for publication,
- or would like to inquire about purchasing Gnostic Tarot Deck(s)

please send us an email at:
DaathGnosis@gmail.com

Or join our group for the latest updates:
http://groups.yahoo.com/group/DaathGnosis/